Selected Books by Dave DeWitt

The Complete Chile Pepper Book (with Paul W. Bosland)

The Spicy Food Lover's Bible (with Nancy Gerlach)

Da Vinci's Kitchen: A Secret History of Italian Cuisine

The Chile Pepper Encyclopedia

Barbecue Inferno (with Nancy Gerlach)

A World of Curries

And about thirty other books on chile peppers and fiery foods.

THE
FOUNDING
FOODIES

How Washington, Jefferson, and Franklin Revolutionized American Cuisine

By Dave DeWitt

This publication is designed to provide accurate and authoritative information in regard to the subject matter covered. It is sold with the understanding that the publisher is not engaged in rendering legal, accounting, or other professional service. If legal advice or other expert assistance is required, the services of a competent professional person should be sought.—*From a Declaration of Principles Jointly Adopted by a Committee of the American Bar Association and a Committee of Publishers and Associations.*

All brand names and product names used in this book are trademarks, registered trademarks, or trade names of their respective holders. Sourcebooks, Inc., is not associated with any product or vendor in this book.

Published by Sourcebooks, Inc.
P.O. Box 4410, Naperville, Illinois 60567-4410
(630) 961-3900
Fax: (630) 961-2168

Printed in the United States of America.

Book Club Edition

This book is dedicated to all my professors at the University of Virginia, 1962–1966, without whom I could never have completed this project.

Acknowledgments

Hillel Black, my first editor at Sourcebooks, now retired, who taught me a few things about writing more interesting nonfiction. Joseph Lee Boyle, former historian for the National Park Service at Valley Forge National Historical Park, who compiled quotes from primary sources documenting the food situation there during 1777 and 1778, mostly from the National Archives.

Nancy Carter of North Wind Picture Archives, who has helped me illustrate various book projects for nearly two decades.

Emily DeWitt-Cisneros, my niece, who proved to be an excellent research assistant while working on her first book project.

Google Books, the single greatest history research tool of the last decade.

Gwyneth Doland, who made excellent suggestions about the development of this project.

Barbara Kerr, of the Medford (Massachusetts) Historical Society, who uncovered some obscure details about the history of rum and Paul Revere for me and who urged me to consult the research miracle of Google Books.

Peter Lynch, my second editor at Sourcebooks.

Dona McDermott, archivist at Valley Forge National Historical Park.

Scott Mendel, my agent with the Mendel Media Group, who has managed to find a home for all of my book projects that have made it into proposal form.

Wayne Scheiner, my closest friend for thirty-five years, who first suggested that I examine the culinary legacy of Thomas Jefferson.

Mary Scott-Fleming of Monticello and the Thomas Jefferson Foundation.

Mary Jane Wilan, my wife, who knows that each manuscript that I turn in to a publisher results in a nice trip overseas to celebrate.

Contents

FOODIES AND POLYMATHS

Few scholars are cooks—and fewer cooks scholars. Perhaps this accounts for the fact that no other aspect of human endeavor has been so neglected by historians as home cooking.

—FOOD HISTORIAN KAREN HESS IN *MARTHA WASHINGTON'S BOOKE OF COOKERY*, 1981

In April 1962, two months before I graduated from James Madison High School in Vienna, Virginia, President John F. Kennedy, at a dinner honoring Nobel Prize winners of the Western Hemisphere, paid homage to Thomas Jefferson's wide-ranging interests and talents when he remarked, "I think this is the most extraordinary collection of talent, of human knowledge, that has ever been gathered together at the White House, with the possible exception of when Thomas Jefferson dined alone." Five months later, I was enrolled at Mr. Jefferson's Academical Village, the University of Virginia, and was living in Echol's Hall as an Echol's Scholar.

To say that Jefferson was—and still is—worshipped at the university is an understatement. His legacy lingers everywhere, from the serpentine walls he designed for the gardens to the buildings he modeled after Greco-Roman structures and the statues of him and of George Washington opposite each other on the lawn. The story went that, if a virginal woman passed between the two statues, Mr. Washington would bow to Mr. Jefferson.

It was a tradition that we wore coats and ties to class. We were not required to do this, of course, but everyone dressed up because we were Virginia gentlemen (we even drank that brand of bourbon!). Our "uniform" was a blue blazer, khaki slacks, a light-blue button-down shirt (Gant, of course), a rep tie in the university's colors of orange and navy blue, and Weejun penny loafers with no socks in warm weather. One morning during my first year, on the way to take an exam that I had studied most of the night for, I was crossing the lawn when I passed Dr. Edgar F. Shannon, the president of the university. I was mortified because that morning I had skipped the tie, but Dr. Shannon made no mention of it. He merely said, "Good morning, David." Unbelievable—he had remembered my name after a single meeting months earlier at an Echol's Scholar orientation party.

My education at the university—I majored in English and took creative writing courses—ultimately led to my writing career, but not before a radical change in focus. No longer would I specialize in animal symbolism in the novels of James Joyce, my masters' thesis title; I would study and write about my first loves, food history and cooking.

Jefferson became my most significant hero. After I graduated from the university in 1966, I knew from the history I had absorbed that Thomas Jefferson was the ultimate multitalented and multidimensional historical figure. But I didn't know about his love of food and wine until many years later, when I began to read more history, especially more food history. Jefferson's name appeared time and time again in the history of wine, horticulture, and food importation. While working on *Da Vinci's Kitchen*, I consulted Silvano Serventi and Françoise Sabban's *Pasta: The Story of a Universal Food* and discovered that Jefferson was widely credited with being the first American to import pasta into the new United States. It wasn't precisely true, but that did it—I was hooked.

During my subsequent research, I realized that the story of early American food and wine was not just about Jefferson but also included Benjamin Franklin, George Washington, and many obscure but brilliant individuals who became my "founding foodies." I decided that this was a food history that had to be written, but there were obstacles. The first and most important challenge was the lingering reputation of colonial-era food—it was not good at all, according to most accounts.

But in 1977, food historians John Hess and Karen Hess wrote this in *The Taste of America*: "Thus, in this bicentennial period, such quasi-official historians as Daniel J. Boorstin and James Beard assure us that we have never had it so good—that Colonial Americans were primitives and ignoramuses in matters gastronomic. The truth is almost precisely to the contrary. The Founding Fathers were as far superior to our present political leaders in the quality of their food as they were in the quality of their prose and of their intelligence." My research proves that the Hess theory is true, and what I've learned has opened a window into the past culinary triumphs of those founding foodies.

After I developed the concept for this book, I returned to the University of Virginia in 2007 to participate in a tour of Virginia vineyards conducted by the School of Continuing and Professional Studies. The program was excellent, with a private tour of Monticello and the location of Jefferson's failed vineyards. There were lectures on Jefferson's influence on wine and wine making in the United States, and we saw a very nicely produced PBS video documentary titled *The Cultivated Life: Thomas Jefferson and Wine*.

While I was in Virginia, I also took a tour of George Washington's Mount Vernon and the restored gristmill and distillery, and I was impressed by the detailed exhibits that revealed Washington's importance in colonial whiskey making, farming, and ranching. The return to Virginia gave me a renewed sense of both place and history. My journey to write *Founding Foodies* has been long, but that now seems fitting, because I knew I had finally learned enough to attempt such a challenging project.

The term *foodie* encompasses a devotion to food in its many contexts. I've decided to use the word *foodie* in this book because I have been unable to find a better, more inclusive term that describes food devotion. *Gourmet* applies in only some cases of food devotion, not, for example, to people who devoted their lives to agricultural experimentation to find better crops. Likewise, *epicure, gastronome,* and *gourmand* do not work in the broad contexts that this book explores.

So what is a foodie? The restaurant critic Gael Greene coined the term *foodie* in the early 1980s, and it moved into common usage when foodies became the targets—and the heroes—of Ann Barr and Paul Levy's 1984 book *The Official Foodie Handbook.* In that prescient and hilarious work, the authors defined a foodie as "a person who is very, very, very interested in food. Foodies are the ones talking about food in any gathering—salivating over restaurants, recipes, radicchio. They don't think they are being trivial—foodies consider food to be an art, on a level with painting or drama…The purpose of life is eating well."

In the popular culture of the United States, foodies differ from gourmets, although the two terms are sometimes used interchangeably. Gourmets are epicures of refined taste who are often food professionals—chefs, restaurant and winery owners, and gourmet food manufacturers. Gourmets simply desire to eat the finest food, but foodies, who are mostly amateurs, want to learn everything there is to know about their favorite subject—the history, the science, the industry, and the personalities surrounding food. They love to create with their own hands in the kitchen and then consume their passion or to experiment with a new exotic flavor or ingredient when they dine out. For purposes of this book, I have broadened the definition of foodie to include a consuming interest in any and all aspects of food, from agriculture to fine dining, and especially wine. There are also what I like to call the inadvertent foodies, those unsung heroes who assisted in the development of American food not through their passion for food and drink but through their inventions: the solar salt maker, cod fishing, and the automated wheat mill. Now that we know what a foodie is, what is a founding foodie?

In their never-ending attempts to fully understand American history, historians began using the phrase "Founding Fathers" to designate the men and women, mostly early politicians, who founded the United States or were influential in its founding. At first, the phrase referred to three super-star fathers, George Washington, Thomas Jefferson, and John Adams. That list was later expanded to include James Madison, Alexander Hamilton, Benjamin Franklin, and John Jay. Eventually, the list of the Founding Fathers was expanded further to include many of the lesser-known signers of the Declaration of Independence, members of the Constitutional Convention, and others.

Given the number of Founding Fathers, it should not come as any surprise that some of them had a very profound interest in food and drink. Some might think that by calling these people, some of the most famous and talented people in American history, foodies I am trivializing them. I don't think so. To the contrary, I am elevating them into a new dimension of humanity, one that transcends politics. Today, the Founding Fathers would be superstars of sustainable farming and ranching, exotic imported foods, brewing, distilling, and wine appreciation. In other words, they would be foodies.

All of the founding foodies lived during times of constant crisis, which makes their accomplishments in both politics and food even more remarkable. From 1775 through 1783, they experienced the grueling Revolutionary

War with England, then the world's greatest military power. They helped their fledgling country form a new government that was torn between the liberal Republicans and the conservative Federalists. Then came the embargo depression of 1807; the War of 1812; and, for Jefferson, scandals and enormous debt.

Yet despite the perilous times in which they lived, Thomas Jefferson, George Washington, and Benjamin Franklin, along with the unsung and mostly inadvertent foodies I document here, profoundly influenced the course of American food.

Note: In the historical recipes that follow, the original spellings and punctuations have been retained.

Chapter One

THE FIRST FOODIES

CAPTAIN JOHN SMITH FEEDS THE COLONISTS

Captain John Smith

When the flagship of the Virginia Company's James-town colonists, the *Susan Constant*, arrived in Chesapeake Bay on April 26, 1607, Captain John Smith, in chains below decks, was extremely irritated. He called himself Captain, although he held no command on this particular voyage. Weeks before, in the Canary Islands, the high-ranking Edward Wingfield had accused Smith of plotting mutiny. Smith narrowly escaped summary execution thanks to the intervention of Captain Christopher Newport, the one-armed admiral of the voyage. Even so, Smith was "restrained as a prisoner" and probably knew that he faced possible death when he arrived on land in the New World. He had but a single hope for survival: the iron strongbox in Newport's cabin that held the names of the seven members of the governing council of the new colony. The names had been placed in the strongbox and locked by the top officials of the Virginia Company, who were hoping to make a profit from New World goods and crops. No one on board knew who had been selected.

Smith's predicament was only one of the dangers faced by the first colonists of what would eventually become the United States of America. In the early seventeenth century, the newly established colonists were in a world of trouble. They didn't know how to farm, fish, or hunt, and they knew next to nothing about cooking. Their future looked bleak. According to William Bradford, a governor of Plymouth Plantation, the Pilgrims faced "a hideous and desolate wilderness, full of wild beasts and wild men." When the colonist Thomas Dudley arrived in Massachusetts nearly twenty-five years later, he found the colony in a "sad and unexpected condition, above eighty of them being dead in the winter before, and many of those alive weak and sick, all the corn and bread among them hardly sufficient to feed them for a fortnight."

Back at the first arrival in Chesapeake Bay, Smith probably was feeling confident, if not invulnerable. In his mere twenty-six years, he had survived

being thrown overboard during a storm; had won three jousts against Turkish opponents determined to kill him; had been wounded on the battlefield and left for dead; and had escaped from slavery and survived, wandering 2,500 miles in leg chains through Eastern Europe. When the strongbox was opened, Smith's name was on the list of the governing council along with that of Wingfield, who would be named president. Initially, Smith was not allowed to take the oath of office, but soon that would not matter, as the colonists fought for their survival.

Algonquian man   Despite nearly daily attacks by the native Algonquian Indians, the Jamestown colonists managed to build a fortified stockade and survived on food provided by the ships of Captain Newport—mostly ship biscuit that would later be called hardtack. But on June 22, Newport set sail back to England, the ship loaded with oak clapboard, slats of wood for barrel making, and two tons of wild sassafras. This meager cargo was not nearly enough to turn a profit for the Virginia Company, but Wingfield and Smith joined forces to send a positive letter back to the investors, promising that gold and silver would soon be found.

For the 104 colonists left in Jamestown, who had enough food for only thirteen to fourteen weeks, disaster struck in the form of an epidemic that was probably typhoid fever. The Reverend Robert Hunt had been previously infected by typhoid, and the extremely unsanitary conditions at the Jamestown settlement exacerbated the rapid spread of the disease. Smith wrote that only ten people could even stand up, and he blamed the illness on lack of proper food. Without the biscuit supply from Newport's ships, all that was left for a daily ration was, as Smith wrote, "halfe a pint of wheat and as much barley boyled with water." And as Smith wrote, the wheat and barley, "having fryed for some 26 weekes in the ships hold, contained as many wormes as graines." From late June through September, nearly half the colonists died of what then was a mysterious disease. The dead were buried inside the fort, which further compounded the unsanitary conditions.

Smith additionally blamed the epidemic on Wingfield and accused him of hoarding beef, eggs, cooking oil, and strong drink for his circle of friends. But more likely, the causes were the lack of sanitation and the fact that, in the humid heat of the summer, the colonists had only their heavy woolen clothing to wear. They also knew very little about hunting or fishing. Smith wrote, "Though there be fish in the Sea, foules in the Ayre, and Beasts in the woods, their bounds are so large, they so wilde, and we so weake, and ignorant, we cannot much trouble them." The colonists at Jamestown were soon so desperate that they finally taught themselves minimal hunting skills, but they could kill only gulls, herons, raccoons, and turtles.

After a rebellion, fueled by rumors that he planned to take the remaining ship and desert the colony, Wingfield was imprisoned, leaving the colony without a leader. Smith decided to take over the leadership role and was aided by the Algonquians, who unexpectedly appeared in September bearing food, corn. History reveals the reason for this peace gesture (the Algonquians wanted access to English weapons), but Smith credited it to God, who had "changed the heart of the Savages." He also noted that "the [Indian] women be verie painefull [hardworking] and the men often idle."

Despite the generosity of the Algonquian people, the English colonists were skeptical. In England and Europe, hunting and fishing were recreational activities for the leisured classes, and agriculture was mostly the job of male farmers. It appeared to the colonists that Indian men were lazy for indulging in hunting and fishing while women toiled at gathering, gardening, and cooking. The colonists also had a low opinion of Native American agricultural practices, which combined slash-and-burn methods with crude clamshell hoes and haphazard planting of many crops in the same fields. The Native American fields lacked the neat rows of crops, the fences, and the plowed furrows that were so familiar to the colonists. Yet despite their skepticism, the food provided by the Algonquians proved to be an essential part of the settlers' diet.

As the winter approached, Smith warned the colonists that their flimsy tents would not protect them from cold weather and storms, and he oversaw the construction of crude houses. Jamestown soon began to look more like a fortified settlement. Smith's title was now "cape merchant," and he was in charge of trading with the Algonquians. He led a series of expeditions from Jamestown to various Algonquian settlements, and after several skirmishes, he convinced them that trade was a better option than warfare.

It was on one of these trading expeditions in the late fall of 1607 that Smith was captured by Algonquian forces of Chief Powhatan and his brother Opechancanough. This led to the formation of one of the principal legends of early America: Smith's supposed rescue from death by Powhatan's daughter, eleven-year-old Pocahontas. Regardless of the circumstances surrounding this tale, Smith did survive and returned to Jamestown after making peace with Powhatan. Pocahontas later married John Rolfe, Virginia's first tobacco baron.

Seemingly, all was well in Jamestown. The colonists had food from the Algonquians and had learned from them how to fish and hunt for game. Smith wrote, "The rivers became so covered with swans, geese, duckes, and cranes, that we daily feasted with good bread, Virginia pease, pumpions [pumpkins], and putchamins [persimmons], fish, fowle, and diverse sorts of wild beasts as

Pocahontas saves Smith, 1607—as legend has it.

fat as we could eat them." But there was bad news, too. Although there was ample food, the supply ship from England captained by Newport had not yet returned, and in Smith's absence, the political situation had changed yet again. The settlers believed that the natives had killed Smith, and they decided to abandon Jamestown and return to England. Smith's sudden reappearance threatened to spoil their plans. They blamed Smith for the deaths of two of his men at the hands of Powhatan's forces and demanded the proverbial "eye for an eye."

Smith was put on trial when he returned from Powhatan's settlement, found guilty, and sentenced to be hanged the next day. But again Smith was saved, this time on the day of his hanging, when a ship was spotted in Chesapeake Bay. It was Newport's long-awaited ship, with eighty new colonists, and the captain's first act was to void the judgment against Smith and take temporary charge of Jamestown. "It pleased God to send Captayn Newport unto us," Wingfield wrote ruefully, "whose arrival saved Master Smyth's life."

In the years that followed, Powhatan remained friendly with the colonists until he felt that they were threatening his lands. Trouble brewed when Smith left Jamestown to explore the Chesapeake Bay and search for more food but neglected to search for the gold that Captain Newport demanded on behalf of the Virginia Company. Powhatan declared war on the Jamestown settlement in 1708, but Smith ended the conflict by taking Powhatan's younger brother captive. Smith wrote that he did "take this murdering Opechancanough… by the long lock of his head; and with my pistol at his breast, I led him [out of his house] amongst his greatest forces, and before we parted made him [agree to] fill our bark with twenty tons of corn." War again broke out a year later, and a gunpowder burn seriously injured Smith, forcing him to return to England in October 1609. He never returned to Virginia, but he did come back to explore New England—he inadvertently founded its cod industry by discovering the huge schools of cod in New England waters.

In 1614, he persuaded four London businessmen to fund a voyage back to the New World to search for another kind of wealth—whales and their valuable oil. In his proposal, he also mentioned that he would "make trials of a mine of gold and copper," because he knew that might loosen their purses. He didn't search for those minerals, of course, and soon discovered that the whales in the area of what is now Penobscot Bay in Maine were "jubartes," a Brazilian name for humpback whales, which were hunted for their meat but didn't yield much oil.

Determined to bring a profitable cargo back to England, Smith ordered his crew to start fishing for cod, which was in abundance in the area. Smith, who disliked fishing, left the ship in an open boat to chart the coastline of North Virginia, from Penobscot Bay in Maine to Cape Cod in Massachusetts, and drew a map of all the "excellent good harbors." Smith then returned to England ahead of his ship, which soon crossed the Atlantic under the command of Officer Thomas Hunt, with seven thousand green cod (salted but not dried), which he sold in England, and forty thousand stockfish (unsalted, dried fish, probably cod or pollack), which he sold in Málaga, Spain.

He might not have liked fishing, but Smith understood that rich stocks of fish in nearby waters would attract settlers. In his *Description of New England*, published in London in 1616, he wrote, "Herring, Cod, and Ling, is that triplicitie that makes their wealth & shippings multiplicities, such as it is, and from which (few would thinke it) they yearly draw at least one million & a halfe of pounds starling…" Such a description of the possible wealth to be earned from fishing apparently gained the attention of the Pilgrims, who were very interested in all the fish in the region. The only problem was that the Pilgrims knew nothing about fishing and lacked the foresight to bring fishing tackle with them when they sailed to Plymouth in 1620. The historian Mark Kurlansky observed, "The year after the Plymouth land-ing, 1621, while the Pilgrims were nearly starving, ten British ships were profitably fishing in New England waters." Smith was also interested in salt production, which was essential to a cod industry. He had established saltworks (where seawater was boiled to obtain salt) during his first year in Jamestown in 1607 and later scouted possible saltworks locations in New England. Cod fishing will return later in this chapter, but another legacy of John Smith's food-finding efforts was the discovery, through the Native Americans, that lowly corn could indeed nourish the colonists.

Fish were not the only cargo destined for sale in Spain. Officer Hunt took it upon himself to lure about twenty Native Americans onto his ship at Pawtuxet and sailed off with them. His goal was to sell the men and women as exotic slaves to rich Spaniards. One of these Native Americans, named Tisquantum, wound up playing a role in the evolving story of American food. In Málaga, Hunt attempted to sell Tisquantum into slav-ery for £20, but some local friars thwarted that effort when they rescued Tisquantum and others in an attempt to convert them to Christianity. Details on this are sketchy, but the bare bones of the story are found in Sir Ferdinando Gorges's *A Brief Relation of the Discovery and Plantation of New England* (London, 1622). Tisquantum's subsequent journeys led him to London, Newfoundland, and back to London again, where in 1619 he joined an exploratory expedition destined for the New England coast. After discovering that a plague, probably smallpox, had wiped out his tribe, the Wampanoag—as well as most of the coastal New England tribes, including the Massachusett—Tisquantum finally settled with the Pilgrims at the site of his original kidnapping, his former village of Patuxet, now renamed Plymouth. Tisquantum had experience trading in corn and an aptitude for languages, so in Plymouth, as had the Native Americans further south, in

Jamestown, he helped the Pilgrims survive by teaching them how to grow and harvest North American foods.

JOHN WINTHROP THE YOUNGER, BENJAMIN FRANKLIN, AND THE LIBERATION OF CORN

In 1614, John Smith observed, much as Samuel de Champlain had in 1605, that most of the coast between Massachusetts and Plymouth Bay was under cultivation, with the Native Americans growing the triumvirate of corn, beans, and squash. There was ample food available for the colonists, but they needed to learn how to grow those strange New World crops in an unfamiliar environment.

Squanto Greets the Pilgrims

Tisquantum, of course, was Squanto, the mythic Native American who inspired the idealized first Thanksgiving and the union between the settlers and the disappearing Wampanoag. After the disastrous winter of 1621, when half of the Plymouth colonists died, including their leader, John Carver, it was Squanto who came to the rescue. In the spring, the herring began their run up Town Brook, and Squanto showed the colonists

Squanto at the first Thanksgiving—as legend has it.

how to catch them, not only for food but for fertilizer as well. He placed a dead herring in each mound of earth with a corn kernel, then added beans and squash seeds. The beans would grow up the corn stalks and the squash plants would fit neatly between the mounds.

Or so the story goes. Is this tale historically true or just a legend? It has created a classic battle between historians and scientists, which has lasted for decades and still has not been settled. In 1957, Erhard Rostlund published an article in *Journal of Geography* titled "The Evidence for the Use of Fish as Fertilizer in Aboriginal North America." In it, he questioned the historical evidence and found it lacking. And in 1975, Lynn Ceci added more fuel to the fire when she presented even evidence against the theory in "Fish Fertilizer, A Native American Practice?" published in the scholarly journal *Science*. As Ceci noted, no reliable ethno-historic source has documented anyone who actually observed a Native American using fish as fertilizer.

The negative response to Ceci's assertions came mostly from critics who, instead of following her argument, accused her of "trying to remove American Indians from our folklore." Another critic argued speciously that Ceci "did not prove conclusively that the Indians of New England were ignorant or incapable of using fish for fertilizer." Ceci, who had proposed that Indians used fallowing instead of fertilizer, in a classic early agrarian slash-and-burn process, replied: "My conclusion that fallowing was the more adaptive cultivation practice…implies no value judgment on my part regarding the capabilities of Indians, nor should any scholar interpret it as such." Historian Thomas Woods concluded: "For such critics, history involved not an impartial search for the truth wherever it led but the vigilant custodianship of entrenched myths—and hostility toward contrary evidence."

And as another historian, William Cronin, pointed out: "Having no easy way to transport large quantities of fish from river to field, and preferring quite sensibly to avoid such back-breaking labor, Indians simply abandoned their fields when the soil lost its fertility." He also cited William Woods, who wrote in *New England Prospect* in 1633, "The Indians who are too lazy to catch fish plant corn eight or ten years without it, having very good crops."

And even experts who do not doubt that Squanto showed the Pilgrims the rotting-fish technique suggest that he was actually demonstrating a technique he had learned from observing Europeans using the same method in Newfoundland. But this was far from the last word on the subject. In fact, some scientists supported the rotting-fish scenario that others had claimed was myth. Anthropologist Stephen Mrozowski excavated fish bones in a precolonial cornfield on Cape Cod in 1991 and published his findings in the journal *Archaeology of Eastern North America*. And then language scholars got into the act by pointing out that *munniahatteaûg*, the Algonquian word meaning "herring" or "menhaden," translated as "that which manures" or "he enriches the land." And further, among the Abenaki Indians of coastal Maine, the word *punhagen*, for "menhaden," also translated as "fertilizer." It is likely that the legend is true, but that the only Native Americans who used the fish as fertilizer had fields that were very close to the sea or the rivers that herring or shad visited on their spring spawning runs. The inhabitants of the more inland villages simply used fallowing.

After Squanto and other Native Americans gave some of the first agricultural lessons to the early colonists, the settlers soon learned that corn produced a crop greater and more reliable than the English grains wheat, barley, and oats. Eventually, the colonists overcame their prejudices against corn as a food fit only for animals as it was used in England; grew it regularly; and avidly consumed it in puddings, breads, beer, and even on the cob. By the eighteenth century, farmers in tiny Hingham, Massachusetts, were harvesting

11,000 bushels of corn a year, and some farmers had yields of 150 bushels from six acres of farmland. Food historian James E. McWilliams observes, "Right after settlement, New England depended on Native Americans and Virginians for much of its Indian corn." Back in England, scientists were becoming curious about the cultivation of corn in the colonies.

Remember Boyle's law from high school chemistry and physics classes? The law holds that the pressure and volume of a gas at a fixed temperature are inversely proportional—when one goes up, the other goes down. Robert Boyle, of the Royal Society of London for the Improvement of Natural Knowledge, devised the law in 1662, the same year he gave corn its first hearing in England as a people food as well as a pig food. That happened because of the collaboration of two polymaths. Boyle, a natural philosopher, chemist, physicist, inventor, theologian, and gentleman scientist, met the governor of Connecticut, John Winthrop Jr., who was a politician, scientist, alchemical "pyrotechnist," medical practitioner, passionate book collector, and food expert.

Winthrop was the son of John Winthrop, Sr., the Puritan governor of Massachusetts Bay Colony, and he was inducted into the membership of the Royal Society in January 1662. He wrote to Boyle and told him of his interest in agriculture in the colonies, especially maize, or corn. Boyle was interested for two reasons. First, he was on the Georgical Committee of the Society, which was charged with the advancement of English farmers; second, there was a long-standing debate in England about the value of maize. People fed it to pigs and considered it unfit for human consumption.

Winthrop presented his 4,500-word essay, "Indian Corne," to the Royal Society in late 1662, but it wasn't published in the Society's *Philosophical Transactions* until 1678. His story of corn is well organized and almost modern in its complete coverage of the various aspects of this "animal food," detailing everything about the grain, from its physical appearance to its use in making "beere."

"Nature hath delighted it selfe to beautify this Corne with great Variety of Colours, the White, and the Yellow being most common, being such a yellow as is betwene Straw Colour, and a pale yellow; there are also of very many other Colours, as Red, Yellow, Blew, Olive Colour, and Greenish, and some very black and some of Intermediate degrees," Winthrop wrote, also noting that "Crowes" and "Sterlings" ate the tender "eares." Indian corn grew tall, "to the Height of 6 or 8 foot and more or less according to the Condition of the Ground," and produced a "sweete Juice like the Sugar Cane" that could be made into a "Syrrop as sweete as Sugar Syrrop."

Then Winthrop gave details about the methods of planting the corn, fertilization with "the Dung of their Cattle well Rotted," and intercropping: "[At] every hill of Corne [they] will plant a kind of Beans with the Corne (they are like those here called French Beans or turky Beans) and in the Vacant places and betweene the Hills, they will plant Squashes and pumpions [pumpkins], loading the Ground with as much as it will beare; The Stalkes of the Corne serveing in stead of poles for the Beans to Climb up, which otherwise must have poles to hang upon." His description closely matches the techniques used today by growers on small, organic farms.

Winthrop described the techniques for weeding; the methods of harvesting and preserving; and finally how the grain was boiled whole and eaten with fish and venison, made into bread and pancakes, and used to make a pudding. He also noted that the Indians invented popcorn. Winthrop concluded with a lengthy section on the brewing of corn beer—"very wholesome without any windy Quality." It was certainly an impressive presentation from our hindsight-inspired point of view. But were the Royal Society members buying it?

At least one modern historian doesn't think so. "Winthrop's novel plea amused many and convinced none," wrote James E. McWilliams. "It would have been like someone today saying that we should eat dog food." He also observed, "Their [the settlers] acceptance and incorporation of Indian corn into the English diet—indeed, their unabashed celebration of it—was but a small brushstroke on the larger canvas of New England cooking."

This is the first recipe for corn bread published in any cookbook. It demonstrates the early New England technique of sweetening the batter with molasses. Other sources replaced molasses with maple syrup.

Johny Cake, or Hoe Cake, by Amelia Simmons, 1796

Scald 1 pint of milk and put to 3 pints of Indian meal, and half pint of flower—bake before the fire. Or, scald with milk two thirds of indian meal, or wet two thirds with boiling water, add salt, molasses and shortening, work up with cold water pretty stiff, and bake as above.

Franklin on Corn

The colonists learned how to grow many crops in New England, and by the end of the seventeenth century, the food supply was abundant. Supplies of beef and pork had increased dramatically, and because colonists began importing English clover and meadow grasses and the growing of hay, dairying could be done year-round, providing adequate supplies of milk and cheese. Kitchen gardens were common by the 1730s and became a key to survival, as beets, carrots, and onions could be stored in root cellars over the winter. Those vegetables were quite an improvement over the dried peas colonists were forced to consume before the advent of kitchen gardens.

New England families, without slaves, bred livestock; grew their own vegetables; made butter and cheese; raised cows and pigs for slaughter; and grew corn, wheat, and rye. The situation was different in the middle colonies. The Chesapeake Bay settlers, for example, lacked the religiously inspired drive to build farms and imitate English agriculture; instead, profit motivated them, and they eventually adopted a standard crop like tobacco. But corn did not diminish in importance in the early colonies or after the Revolution, because it had another polymath champion: Benjamin Franklin.

Because of Franklin's enormous popularity as a writer, he was able to influence the personality and character of the American nation more than any of the other Founding Fathers (though he did fail in trying to convince the new American public that the turkey, not the bald eagle, should have been the national bird). Franklin was a corn aficionado and one of the crop's biggest public supporters. In January 1766, while living in London as an agent for the colonies of Pennsylvania, Georgia, New Jersey, and Massachusetts to protest the Stamp Act, he could not resist writing a succinct rebuttal to "Vindex Patriae," a correspondent to the *Gazetteer and New Daily Advertiser* who had disparaged corn. Franklin wrote:

A writer in your paper comforts himself, and the India Company, with the fancy, that the Americans, should they resolve to drink no more tea, can by no means keep that resolution, their Indian corn not affording "an agreeable, or easy digestible breakfast." Pray let me, an American, inform the gentleman, who seems quite ignorant of the matter, that Indian corn, take it for all in all, is one of the most agreeable and wholesome grains in the world; that

*its green ears roasted are a delicacy beyond expression; that samp, hominy,
succatash, and nokehock, made of it, are so many pleasing varieties; and that
a johny, or hoe-cake, hot from the fire, is better than a Yorkshire muffin.*

A Receipt for Making Sweet Corn, and Suckahtash By Benjamin Franklin, 1757

Take the Ears of Indian Corn when in the Milk, and boil them almost
enough to eat, then shell it, and spread it on a Cloth very thin, and dry
it in the Sun till it shrinks to half its Bigness, and becomes very hard,
then put it into any dry Cask, and it will keep the Year round. When
you use it, you must put it into a Pot, and let it warm moderately over
a Fire for three or four Hours, but which Means it swells considerably,
then boil it till you find 'tis fit to eat. In order to make Suckahtash,
'tis only putting about a third Part of Beans with the Corn when you
boil it.

Franklin wrote most extensively about corn around 1785, while living in Paris and dining often with Thomas Jefferson, who was growing
it in his Paris garden at the same time. Because of his advancing years
(Franklin died in 1790) and the fact that he no longer was actively seeking
publishers for his writing, his comments on corn, titled "Observations on
Mayz, or Indian Corn," remained unpublished until 1836, when Jared
Sparks included the essay in *The Works of Benjamin Franklin*. The essay was
reprinted again in 1931, when Nathan Goodman included it in his book
The Ingenious Dr. Franklin:

Franklin discusses Parched corn, later called popcorn, in a manner that recalls the method described by John Winthrop the Younger 123 years earlier, except that a pot is used Franklin's method, rather than just pitching the kernels into the embers. Popcorn is then reduced to a powder (for making a smooth corn bread or a pudding) rather than being eaten as a snack as is common today. "An iron pot is fill'd with sand, and set on the fire till the sand is very hot. Two or three pounds of the grain are then thrown in, and well mix'd with the sand by stirring. Each grain bursts and throws out a white substance of twice its bigness. The sand is separated by a wire sieve, and return'd into the pot, to be again heated and repeat the operation with fresh grain. That which is parch'd is pounded to a powder in mortars. This, being sifted, will keep long for use." The sand was used to provide a consistent heating of the kernels.

In his corn essay, Franklin gives one of the first descriptions of the origin of what later, in the South, became known as grits. Franklin wrote, "The dry grain is also sometimes ground loosely, so as to be broke into pieces of the size of rice, and being winnow'd to separate the bran, it is then boil'd and eaten with turkies or other fowls, as rice. Ground into a finer meal, they make of it by boiling a hasty-pudding, or bouilli, to be eaten with milk, or with butter and sugar; this resembles what the Italians call polenta."

This recipe by Mary Randolph, whose brother Tom was married to Thomas Jefferson's daughter Martha, was published in her cookbook The Virginia Housewife *in 1824. It is one of the earliest American recipes published for polenta, which is closely related to grits.*

To Make Polenta

Put a large spoonful of butter in a quart of water, wet your corn meal with cold water in a bowl, add some salt, and make it quite smooth, then put it in the buttered water when it is hot, let it boil, stirring it continually till done; as soon as you can handle it, make it into a ball, and let it stand till quite cold—then cut it in thin slices, lay them in the bottom of a deep dish so as to cover it, put on it slices of cheese, and on that a few bits of butter; then mush, cheese and butter, until the dish is full; put on the top thin slices of cheese and butter, put the dish in a quick oven; twenty or thirty minutes will bake it.

There is one slightly confusing corn reference in the essay. Franklin writes, "The stalks, press'd like sugar-cane, yield a sweet juice, which, being fermented and distill'd, yields an excellent spirit." Because Franklin undoubtedly knew that rum was distilled from fermented sugar by-products originally extracted from sugarcane, by "spirit" was he referring to a liquor, moonshine made from corn stalks, or a beer? In Franklin's day, *spirit* meant any alcoholic beverage, not just distilled beverages as it does now. A family recipe for green-corn-stalk beer by Landon Carter, published in the *Virginia Gazette* in 1775, hints that Franklin was most likely referring to a beer. Landon's recipe reads:

The [corn] stalks, green as they were, as soon as pulled up, were carried to a convenient trough, then chopped and pounded so much, that, by boiling, all the juice could be extracted out of them; which juice every planter almost knows is of saccharine a quality almost as any thing can be, and that any thing of a luxuriant corn stalk is very full of it… After this pounding, the stalks and all were put into a large copper, there lowered down it its sweetness with water, to an equality with common observations in malt wort, and then boiled, till the liquor in a glass is seen to break, as the breweres term it; after that it is strained, and boiled again with hops. The beer I drank had been made above twenty days, and bottled off about four days.

THE SWINISH CONQUISTADORS: HERNANDO DE SOTO, PEDRO MENÉNDEZ DE AVILÉS, AND AN INFESTATION OF HOGS

Many people think that things were always orderly and peaceful during the Columbus Exchange of foodstuffs between the Old World and the New, with corn saving starving tribes in Africa and pastoral herds of sheep providing meat, fleece, and cheese all over the New World. But in one instance, things got dangerous.

The result today is 3 million to 4 million descendants of "pioneer pigs"—feral hogs—that weigh up to six hundred pounds, run loose, and breed prolifically in the United States. Once a sow reaches breeding age at seven or eight months, she can produce up to a thousand feral swine in a five-year period! Of course,

Berkshire pig

another result of the importation of swine into the colonies was the ham eaten at Easter.

The first pigs to arrive in the New World were eight Iberian hogs that Christopher Columbus brought to Hispaniola (now Haiti and Dominican Republic) on his second voyage in 1493. The pigs were turned loose in the marshes, where they started breeding prolifically. By 1497, they were also running wild in Jamaica and Cuba. Pig expert Lyall Watson noted in his 2004 study *The Whole Hog*, "Soldiers hunting escaped slaves found their jungle missions greatly complicated by belligerent boars."

The Caribbean pigs produced a lot of lard, which was the primary fat used in the islands because of the lack of olive oil, and the pigs helped sustain the fleets that constantly moved between Spain and the Caribbean. "Fed with maize stored on board," wrote historian John Super, "pigs provided fresh meat for the return voyage." In Mexico, after Hernán Cortés introduced pigs in 1519, they multiplied so rapidly that between 1524 and 1526 the cost of pork dropped by 75 percent. Europeans loved New World pork. According to one explorer, Francesco Carletti, the meat was "very sweet and savory, and so wholesome that they give it to sick folks instead of hens and capons."

In 1539, Hernando de Soto introduced swine to what is now the United States. His three-year expedition to explore Florida and what is now the American South consisted of six hundred soldiers, twenty-four priests, their horses, thirteen Iberian sows, and two boars. By the end of the first stage of his exploration, most of the horses and many of the soldiers had died. The pigs saved those who remained. The drove had grown to three hundred boars and sows, and by the end of the expedition, it had increased to seven hundred, despite a loss of four hundred to Native Americans who had captured them during a raid.

De Soto continued to explore and fought with Native Americans along the way. When he finally reached the Mississippi River in 1542, he died of a fever and most of his swine were slaughtered by his men for food. Historian Theodore Irving described it this way in 1868: "De Soto's effects, consisting in all of two slaves, three horses, and seven hundred swine, were disposed of at public sale. The swine were sold…at two hundred crowns apiece. Henceforth, the greater number of the soldiers possessed this desirable article of food, which they ate of on all days save Fridays, Saturdays, and the eves of festivals, which they rigidly observed, according to the customs of the Roman Catholics." Today, the descendants of de Soto's herd still run wild in the South, where they are avidly hunted as "razorbacks."

More pigs were brought to Florida in 1565, when Admiral Pedro Menéndez de Avilés imported a herd of four hundred. "A resource that resulted a century later," writes Lyall Watson, "in eight large towns, seventy-two missions, and two royal haciendas, all depending more or less on pigs."

Further north, Walter Raleigh brought three sows with him on the colonizing expedition that set up the Virginia Company at Jamestown in 1607, and that herd multiplied to sixty during the first year. By 1627, settlers could count the number of cattle, but pigs were "innumerable." Thus, pigs greatly eased the colonists' reliance on supply ships from England during the two decades after the founding of Jamestown.

Pigs, along with corn, went a long way toward saving the colony from starvation, though they also managed to wreak plenty of havoc on both Native American and British crops. Pigs were smart, powerful, and constantly hungry, devouring nuts, fruits, shellfish, and corn, and turning up the soil with their shovel-like noses when looking for edible roots. Natives and settlers alike found themselves competing for food with nuisance herds of feral pigs.

Eventually, settlers rounded up many of the pigs and moved them to a barrier island near the mouth of the James River, which became known as Hog Island. The isolated pigs could no longer ravage crops, and colonists instead harvested them at their leisure. It is commonly believed that the Native Americans taught the settlers how to smoke the pig meat to preserve it, as they had been smoking venison for an untold number of years. It is also possible that some of the settlers had learned how to smoke meat in England. However it happened, the early smoking of pork at Jamestown was the beginning of the tradition of Virginia hams.

Hog Island Sheep

Sheep from England were imported and released around 1800 on Hog Island, one of Virginia's barrier islands, near the mouth of the James River. Hog Island sheep were one of the few populations of feral sheep in the United States. Feral sheep are rare worldwide, because sheep do not adapt easily to unmanaged habitats. The feral sheep usually lived on islands in the colonies, which lacked predators.

The entire sheep population was removed from Hog Island during the 1970s, when the Nature Conservancy purchased the island. Remnant flocks of the breed are at Gunston Hall in Mason Neck, Virginia, and at Mount Vernon to demonstrate early sheep-raising methods and to save the remainder of this rare breed.

The Virginia Department of Game and Inland Fisheries now manages Hog Island Wildlife Management Area primarily for the benefit of migratory waterfowl.

Curing and exporting hams was another of the colonies' early forms of trade. In 1779, the first Virginia Smithfield hams, made from peanut-fattened pigs, were exported to Bermuda and the West Indies, where they were called tropical-cured hams. Because they could be stored without refrigeration (which, of course, had not yet been invented), the hams were very popular with the islanders, where the climate was too warm and moist to cure meat.

Further north still, at the colony of Massachusetts Bay, pigs were released into the surrounding forests to forage on acorns and roots, and they decimated shellfish beds on the tidal flats. At Concord, before the pigs were released, their ears were snipped, much like a brand, so that when they were rounded up for sale, they could be identified as belonging to specific colonists. If a Native American brought a pig to market, he or she was allowed to sell it only if the ears were not marked. In 1633, the colony government decreed that colonists feed pigs only corn that was unfit for human consumption so that the pigs would not deplete the settlers' food supply; however, they could not stop the pigs from rooting up newly planted gardens and fields.

The excess pork in the northern colonies was salted and became barreled pork, a product that was popular in Europe and as a provision aboard all kinds of ships. Herds of corn-fattened pigs were driven to market to be slaughtered, salted, and packed tightly in barrels for shipment all over the world and to other colonies. Barreled pork soon became one of the largest exports of the northern colonies.

Though not the favorite meat, pork became essential to the New England diet because beef supplies ran low by the end of each spring, whereas pork was plentiful. Pork consumption increased greatly over the years, and the average household use went from 120 pounds a year in 1710 to more than

200 pounds about a century later. "Pork, in short, was never central to the New England diet, but it became a necessary supplement to the more highly valued beef," noted James E. McWilliams.

This recipe is from Emerson's cookbook, The New-England Cookery, 1808.

To Roast a Whole Pig, by Lucy Emerson, 1808

Spit your pig, and lay it down to a clear fire kept good at both ends: put into the belly a few sage leaves, a little pepper and salt, a small crust of bread, and a piece of butter, then sew up the belly. Flour it all over very well [with Indian corn]... When you find the skin is tight and crisp, and the eyes are dropped, put two plates into the dripping pan, to save what gravy comes from it: put a quarter of a pound of butter into a clean, coarse cloth, and rub all over it until the flour is quite taken off; then take it up into your dish, take the sage, etc. out of the belly, and chop it small; cut off the head, open it and take out the brains, chop, and put the sage and brains into a half pint of good gravy, with a piece of butter rolled in flour; then cut your pig down the back...cut off the two ears...take off the underjaw, cut it in two, and lay one upon each side; put the head between the shoulders, pour the gravy out of the plates and into your sauce, and then into the dish.

In New Amsterdam, serviced by the Dutch West Indies Company, the pigs brought across the Atlantic on Dutch ships were allowed to roam free in northern Manhattan. The pigs were kept out of lower Manhattan and the trading posts by a palisade, a structure that later gave Wall Street its name.

The further legacy of the introduction of corn and pigs in the colonies has to do with slavery and an important nonfood crop, tobacco. In the West Indies, the sugarcane growers gave their slaves a day and a half off each week to grow their own crops, hunt, fish, and barter in markets. But because tobacco was such a demanding crop, such "freedom" was impossible in Virginia, and the growers worked their slaves at least six and a half days a week. Because the slaves had no time to grow their own crops, slave owners had to feed them and keep them healthy—their profits depended on it. Once again, corn was the solution, as it was relatively nutritious and easy to grow.

Interestingly, the slaves preferred corn to the wheat that had been introduced in the early 1700s to diversify the crops and lessen the dependence on tobacco. George Washington attempted to feed his slaves wheat but discovered that "the Negroes, while the novelty lasted, seemed to prefer Wheat bread as being the food of their masters…but they soon grew tired of it." Washington also noted that, if the slaves were given wheat rather than corn, "they would, in order to be fit for the same labor, be obliged to have a considerable addition to their allowance of meat." That, of course, would be more expensive. Undoubtedly, the slaves preferred corn because their ancestors and relatives had been

Flowering tobacco

eating it since it had been introduced into West Africa in the early 1500s. Ironically, corn was the typical food of slaves during their transport to the New World.

Of course, some protein was necessary to keep the slaves fit for the tobacco fields, and for this sustenance, once again, the pigs, both feral and domesticated, were the primary source of it, and the slave owners provided pork in very modest amounts. Thomas Jefferson told his overseer that he would need "about 900 pounds more [pork] for the people [slaves] so as to give them one half a pound a-piece once a week."

Slaves, corn, and swine were part of a system that produced increasingly huge amounts of tobacco for export. As the tobacco colonies' populations increased, so did their production of tobacco. Exports to England rose drastically from 60,000 pounds in 1622 to 500,000 pounds in 1628, and to 1.5 million pounds in 1639. By the end of the seventeenth century, England was importing more than 20 million pounds of colonial tobacco per year.

The negative aspects of tobacco growing on such a scale—displacement of Native Americans, slavery, and a monocultural crop that was not food— were irrelevant to the colonists because of the incredible economic growth that tobacco production provided. Slaves, corn, and pigs had combined to make tobacco king—at least in the South. But in the New England colonies, another kind of harvest was happening, and this one was from the stormy seas.

THE FATHER OF THE SCHOONER AND KING COD

Captain Andrew Robinson was not overly passionate about food. In fact, when out fishing on Newfoundland's Grand Banks with his schooner, he wouldn't leave his command even to eat; instead, a crew member would

bring him the noto-
rious ship biscuit to fill
his mouth while he kept
his hands busy with the
hook and lines, pulling
in cod.

Cod fishing off Newfoundland in a schooner

Robinson's place as a
founding foodie results
from his invention that
revolutionized the cod-
fishing industry in New
England. In 1713, he
built and launched the
first schooner in Gloucester, Massachusetts. The invention was a matter
of necessity, for previous ships were not efficient for fishing in the ocean
conditions off the coasts of New England and Newfoundland. Square-
rigged vessels, those classic ships with sails draped from horizontal spars
perpendicular to the masts, were fine for transporting settlers and goods
across the Atlantic, but they were clumsy and not maneuverable enough
for fishing. The alternate choice, small fishing ketches, had holds that
could not contain enough fish to make a profit for the captains. Also, the
ketch rigs, though popular in the seventeenth century, were not suited for
the highly variable winds on the New England coast and could not change
their course quickly because that required raising and lowering the sails.

Captain Robinson abandoned square-rigged shipbuilding and, instead
of rigid spars, used movable booms to attach the sails to the masts, which
eliminated the need to raise and lower the sails and made the ship highly
maneuverable in the prevailing wind conditions. According to many

sources, when he launched his new fishing ship before a crowd of skeptical onlookers, someone in the crowd shouted: "Oh look how she scoons,"
using the Scottish word that referred to a flat stone skipping over the
water. When told of this, Robinson said, "A schooner let her be." Thus
was born, in the words of maritime historian Raymond McFarland, "The
most efficient vessel of its size for the practical mastery of the seas." Other
advantages of the schooner were that the same number of men could
handle a hull of twice the capacity of an ordinary sloop, and the cost to
build the schooner was less than that of any other for a hull of similar size.
"In short," wrote another maritime historian, John Spears, "a schooner
gave her owner more ton-miles of work than any other kind of vessel for
each dollar of expense."

More schooners were built in the colonies than in any other country,
and they were used in sea applications that required speed and wind-
ward ability. Schooners were used not only in offshore fishing but also in
privateering (a private, government-licensed vessel used to seize enemy
ships), slaving, and blockade running. Most of the schooners were based
in the ports of Marblehead and Gloucester, and they also carried on
trade between the colonies during a time when inland transportation
was very difficult because of poor roads. Shortly before the onset of the
Revolutionary War, Massachusetts alone had 542 schooners engaged in
fishing and trade, with many of the schooners sailing to Spain with salted
cod and returning with wine and salt. After the war began, thousands
of schooner-trained seamen manned the privateers and the ships of the
Continental Navy, along with the whalers of Nantucket. Widows and
orphans eventually filled Gloucester and Marblehead, as half of the sailors
were dead or missing when the war concluded.

But what became of Captain Robinson? Ten years after he launched his first schooner, he was fighting Native Americans along the coast for the colonial government, using a small sloop with a crew of two. In 1723, he and his crew were captured while at anchor and carried off to the natives' village. His crew members were killed, but Robinson managed to escape and run back to his sloop. He quickly set sail, but calm winds foiled him, and the natives overtook him in their canoes.

The cod industry needed more than just fish to thrive. Salt had been a necessity for preserving the catch since the Pilgrims established the original colonial cod industry. At first, the Pilgrims not only did not know how to fish but also were repulsed by the other sea creatures that the Native Americans were consuming—clams, mussels, and lobsters—and refused to eat them. However, they would eat cod, and gradually they learned how to fish after they received advice and equipment from England. In 1623, they established a fishing station in Gloucester, and more stations soon followed in Salem, Marblehead, and Penobscot Bay. They obtained salt for preserving the cod from tidal pools and by trading with the Spanish Basque port of Bilbao and various colonies in the West Indies. By 1640, the Pilgrims were catching three hundred thousand cod a year.

The salt demand was driven not only by fishing but also by the increasing population of the colonies, who salted their beef in the fall as well as the herring and shad they caught during the spring runs in the rivers and streams. As early as 1688, the colonist Daniel Cox, of New Jersey, was complaining that the fish were abundant but that the colony could not establish a successful fishery because of a "want of salt." Adding to the demand for salt was the fact that pelts of otter, bear, moose, and beaver, shipped overseas on the same ships as the cod to England, Spain, and the Caribbean Islands, also needed to be salted.

After Captain Robinson's invention of the schooner in 1713 made cod fishing more efficient and greatly increased the catches, the need for salt increased exponentially. By the time of the Revolutionary War, the salt situation had reached crisis proportions (see chapter 2 for the continuation of the saga of salt).

This recipe, from The Virginia Housewife, *by Mary Randolph (1824), describes the traditional Southern preparation of salt cod from New England.*

To Dress Any Kind of Salted Fish

Take the quantity necessary for the dish, wash them, and lay them in fresh water for a night; then put them on the tin plate with the holes, and place it in the fish kettle—sprinkle over it pounded cloves and pepper, with four cloves of garlic; put in a bundle of sweet herbs and parsley, a large spoonful of tarragon, and two of common vinegar, with a pint of wine; roll one quarter of a pound of butter in two spoonful of flour, cut in small pieces, and put it over the fish—cover it closely, and simmer it over a slow fire half and hour; take the fish out carefully, and lay it in the dish, set it over hot water, and cover it till the gravy has boiled a little longer—take out the garlic and herbs, pour it over the fish, and serve it up. It is very good when eaten cold with salad, garnished with parsley.

Salt cod proved to be the perfect trade item, and thus evolved into the first product of the triangle trade. In the triangle trade, ships left New England with salted cod of varying quality and arrived in Bilbao, where they traded the best fish for wine, iron, coal, and fruit. Then the ships sailed to the West Indies and traded the lower-quality cod, plus some of the Spanish goods, for molasses, sugar, tobacco, and salt. The ships then returned to New England with both European and Caribbean products. In some instances, the ships sailed to Africa to buy slaves that were then taken to the Caribbean. In Africa, slaves were paid for in one of three currencies—Spanish coins, rum, or salt cod.

That was the idea behind the triangle trade, but in reality, it was more of a piecemeal operation. No New England traders are known to have completed a full sequential circuit of the triangle. Historian Clifford Shipton spent years studying New England shipping records and failed to find a single instance of a ship completing the full triangle. Later, slaves and rum were added to the trade mix, and the trading system of the colonies further diversified.

The success of the colonies' trading caused the politicians in Britain to sit up and take notice. Eager to grab a piece of this trade, England passed the Navigation Act of 1663 (also called the Act for the Encouragement of Trade), which required all European goods bound for America (or other colonies) to be shipped through England first. In England, the goods were unloaded, inspected, taxed, and reloaded. The trade had to be carried in English vessels or those of the colonies. Furthermore, "enumerated commodities" from the colonies, such as sugar, rice, and tobacco, had to travel to England first to be taxed before going on to other countries. This increased the cost to the colonies and the shipping time.

Because cod had literally saved the New England colonies, the fish was soon worshipped as a symbol of prosperity, with its image appearing on official crests, the first American coins, the 1776 New Hampshire state seal, and tax stamps.

New Hampshire state seal

The colonists, of course, mostly ignored the Navigation Act. In 1667, about a hundred years before the Declaration of Independence, New Englanders dispatched to the British Crown ten barrels of cranberries, two barrels of corn mush, a thousand codfish, and a note that read: "We humbly conceive that the laws of England are bounded within four seas, and do not reach America. The subjects of his majesty here being not represented in Parliament, so we have not looked at ourselves to be impeded in trade by them."

The point was moot, though, because New England produced too much cod for the markets of England and its colonies, and England lacked a large-enough merchant fleet to reexport the cod. So colonial traders and merchants went about their business and traded freely with all countries and their colonies. This resistance to the power of England led to repressive taxes such as the Molasses Act of 1733; the Sugar Act of 1760; the Stamp Act of 1765; the Townsend Act of 1767 (taxes on lead, paper, paint, glass, and tea); and finally the Restraining Act of 1775, which restricted all New England trade to the ports of England and barred New England fishermen from the Grand Banks of Newfoundland. But by 1775, another tax act was simply too little and too late. The Revolution had already begun.

The Halls of Medford and the Republic of Rum

All it took was one taste of the water from the spring and Andrew Hall knew for certain it would make excellent rum. Then and there, he decided that he would build his distillery at that spot in Medford on the Mystic River, where ships built in that Massachusetts town unloaded molasses from the Caribbean Islands. The year was 1735, and Hall, visiting from Boston, began an industry that would make the town famous for its Old Medford Rum, which would last until 1905.

Or maybe not. Another account, published in 1855 by Charles Brooks, proves that printed histories are not always accurate. A hundred twenty-five years later, Carl and Alan Seaburg,

Demons in the distillery, Salem, Massachusetts

with the help of the Medford Historical Society, discovered that the origins of rum in Medford were even older than Brooks had thought. Sometime between 1715 and 1720, John Hall built a still over that spring, bought some hogsheads of molasses from a ship at the Medford docks, and began to make Medford rum. He sold the operation to his brother Andrew in 1735, and there the story of Andrew starts.

Andrew and those who followed, including Massachusetts merchants, businessmen, and sea captains, had to survive the Sugar Act of 1764, the Revolutionary War that seemed to stretch forever past 1776, and the persuasive arguments of the fervent antiliquor crusaders like Dr. Benjamin Rush, a friend of Benjamin Franklin's.

After Andrew Hall died, his eldest son, Benjamin, took over the distillery and soon ran into trouble. After having invested all his savings in the molasses that filled his vats, into the Mystic River "came a tide so high that it overflowed his premises and gave him a stock of salt water and molasses, that proved to be utterly useless." That "tidal wave" nearly ruined him, but two sea captains who were his molasses suppliers backed him in building a second distillery, and the rum continued to flow from Medford.

As the rum flowed, its fame spread all over the eastern seaboard and soon other towns were stenciling the name *Medford* on their barrels. This was an early example of brand recognition by word of mouth. "The Ballad of Medford Rum" was sung as far south as Kill Devil Hills in North Carolina, but the lyrics have long since disappeared. *Kill-devil* was another name for rum, which had early origins in the Caribbean. Rum promoters eager to counter the demons-in-the-distillery imagery of the early prohibitionists probably adopted it. Medford rum was exported all over the world, but particularly to Africa and the West Indies.

This recipe appeared in an early bartenders' manual, dated 1888.

Medford Rum Punch

(Use a large bar glass.) 3/4 table-spoonful of Sugar; 2 or 3 dashes of Lemon juice, dissolve well with a little water; fill the glass with fine shaved ice; 1 1/2 wine glass of Medford rum; flavor with a few drops of Jamaica rum, stir up well and dress the top with fruit in season, and serve with a straw.

Medford Rum logo

Why did an American rum like Medford gain such popularity? Earlier, American drinkers had depended on homemade alcoholic beverages like hard cider, applejack, and beer, but those were all trumped when "Barbadoes Water" was imported from that island colony to New England in 1647. The early rum imports were ominously called kill-devil because of the warnings of teetotalers that rum was a poison that could lead to death. The colonists couldn't have cared less about that term, although the name of the liquor was changed to *rum*, short for *rumbullion*, possibly a term meaning an "orgy of cider-drinking," in the words of rum historian Hugh Barty-King. Alice Morse Earle tracked down the earliest use of the word *rum* in 1922. "The name is doubtless American," she wrote. "A manuscript description of Barbadoes, written twenty-five years after the English settlement of the island in 1651, is thus quoted in The Academy: 'The chief fudling [befuddling drink] they make in the island is Rumbullion, alias Kill-Devil, and this is made of sugar canes distilled, a hot, hellish, and terrible liquor.'"

During the following forty years, Barty-King noted, "West Indian Rum became the universal hard drink of Colonial America and before whisky had been heard of, except as a curiosity, these colonists of rough territory with a ferocious winter began to hanker for a sugar cane spirit of greater potency than the kill-devil which satisfied those who lived and worked in the tropical islands of the Caribbean Sea." The desire for a stronger rum led to the importation of molasses and the beginning of the American rum industry.

THE LARGEST RUM PUNCH BOWL IN THE WORLD

Alexis Lichine, in his definitive *Encyclopedia of Wines and Spirits*, records a description of rum excesses in Barbados in the eighteenth century: "A marble basin, built in the middle of the garden especially for the occasion, served as the bowl. Into it were poured 1,200 bottles of rum, 1,200 bottles of Malaga wine, and 400 quarts of boiling water. Then 600 pounds of the best cane sugar and 200 powdered nutmegs were added. Then the juice of 2,600 lemons was squeezed into the liquor. Onto the surface was launched a handsome mahogany boat piloted by a boy of twelve, who rowed about a few moments, then coasted to the side and began to serve the assembled company of six hundred, which gradually drank up the ocean upon which he floated."

After some unknown sugarcane processor invented a method to concentrate molasses so that it would not ferment during the long voyage from the Caribbean, New Englanders were able to import it for distillation in small pot stills from about 1687. During the first decade of the eighteenth century, distilleries sprang up in Massachusetts, Rhode Island, and Connecticut. By 1725, distilling was becoming big business in New York, Salem, Boston, Philadelphia, and Newport. Barty-King has claimed, "The distilling of rum became the largest manufacturing industry in the pre-revolutionary American colonies," and he's undoubtedly right. In 1774, there were 141 distilleries in the colonies, with 92 percent of them located in the northern colonies, driving Barbadian rum out of every colonial market except for Charleston.

New England distilleries were making so much rum that they were exporting six hundred thousand gallons a year to England, Ireland, Europe, the West Indies, and especially Africa—after New England rum entered the triangle trade and was used in Africa to buy slaves. This flood of rum lead to the inevitable oversupply and price drops. Between 1722 and 1738, the price of rum in taverns dropped nearly 40 percent to a low two shillings a serving, and all classes could afford to drink it. "When it came to rum, life became a perpetual happy hour for the colonial consumer," noted McWilliams. But low prices for rum meant additional burdens for the Hall family in Medford. Although the distillery employed a number of local people, "It was never a profitable branch of trade," observed historian Charles Brooks, writing in his history of Medford in 1855.

LET THEM DRINK RUM!

The colonists hated to drink water. Historian Dale Taylor noted that "most colonists avoided water, which could be fatal…as a result, most drinks were alcoholic, because no bacteria known to be harmful to man can survive in them." Bacteria was discovered in 1676, but it wasn't until the nineteenth century that it was associated with disease. Experience and common sense prevailed. Governor William Bradford of Plymouth Colony wrote that the enemies of health and the causes of disease were "unholesome food, much drinking of water." Because of pollution from sewage, "travelers to New York City [in the late seventeenth century] remarked that even horses balked at the quality of water offered them."

Drink historian Sharon Salinger noted, "Colonists regarded water as 'lowly and common,' a drink better suited to barnyard animals than humans. As a result, colonists avoided water as much as possible and quenched their thirst with a variety of alcoholic beverages." And Benjamin Franklin commented that, if God had intended man to drink water, "He would not have made him with an elbow capable of raising a wine glass."

It was fortunate for the rum producers that England was unable to enforce the Molasses Act of 1733, which levied an onerous duty of nine pence a gallon on rum and sixpence a gallon on molasses from all countries and colonies except British ones, and they couldn't supply all of New England's needs. When the Molasses Act began to be enforced three decades later, it further drove a wedge between the colonists and the mother country.

Rum was unique and important to American food history in several ways. It was the first "colonial" product, one that colonists from the north and south incorporated into their daily routines and culinary life. It was a unifying drink that had nothing to do with England and so was embraced heartily, despite the fact that taverns still served beer, wine, hard cider, and brandy in great quantity. Also, unlike those beverages, rum required trade both internal and external, which was good for the colonial economy. Take the trade with the West Indies, for example. Between 1768 and 1772, the northern colonies shipped £95,000 worth of fish in return for £120,200 worth of sugar and molasses. Internally, between those same dates, New England distilleries sold tens of thousands of gallons of both rum and molasses to the other states. Many historians believe that rum spearheaded inter-colony trade in such foods as corn, rice, flour, bread, salt cod, oats, rye, loaf sugar, salt, and dozens of other foodstuffs.

Back in Medford, the Hall distillery was again passed down the family line, this time to Isaac Hall. The date this happened is uncertain, but it must have been prior to the Declaration of Independence, because we know that Hall was a captain in Medford Minutemen, and that he played a small but interesting role in the beginning of the American Revolution.

Chapter Two

HERE'S TO FOOD, DRINK, AND WAR!

THE MIDNIGHT REVELRY OF PAUL REVERE

Not only was Isaac Hall one of the most successful rum distillers in the colonies and a captain of the Minutemen of Medford, located just a few miles from Boston, he also acted as the commissary for the Revolutionary troops of the area, supplying his fellow Minutemen with medical and military supplies—and rum. It is not commonly known, but at the time of the Revolution, the Minutemen had already been a well-trained volunteer militia for six generations in the Massachusetts Bay Colony.

As a Minuteman, Hall was part of a small, elite force that was highly mobile and able to assemble its armed men quickly. His corps of men, called the Eight Months' Men because of the length of their enlistment, were chosen for their enthusiasm, reliability, and physical strength. Hall's men, in addition to their pay, received a coat at the end of their eight months' service. They were part of a colony-wide force of "training bands" that were assembled to counter the emergencies that the colonial towns regularly faced: Native American uprisings; war with France; and the very real potential for local insurrections, social unrest, and rioting. In Hall's case, the adversary was the British Army, the Regulars or Redcoats.

On the evening of April 18, 1775, according to Charles Coulombe, author of *Rum* (2004), Captain Hall was entertaining his sixty Minutemen at his house in Medford (now the Gaffey Funeral Home), and the militiamen were "liberally imbibing" his rum. Paul Revere arrived and "fortified himself with his host's family beverage." Coulombe continued: "After he told them of the advance by British regulars, they set off for Lexington; alas, they were too befuddled to find the place and never did make the battle."

It's a great story, but is it true? Coulombe's book has no citations for such a claim, and a reading of his brief bibliography does not reveal a primary source. The Medford Historical Society Papers reveal a different version of the story. On the 150th anniversary of Paul Revere's famous ride, April 19, 1925, the mayor of Medford, Richard Coolidge, gave a dramatic reading at the Medford Theatre. Of course, his account isn't footnoted either, but at least it's based on oral history passed down in Medford.

Quite the storyteller, the mayor set the scene:

Up the road to Menotomy, the moonlight fell upon the steeple of the third meeting house, silent in its mid-week desertions. Beyond the square, about an equal distance down the road to Charlestown, it greeted the last flickering candle-light in the Admiral Vernon. There, too, the vague rumors of the day, discussed at the tavern bar over many a round of "flip" were lulled in the quiet of the surrounding night. Medford slept. But it was a restless sleep, both within and without, where the chill wind of an early spring, coming over the hills, rustled the tree tops as if in apprehension.

The downing of flip at the Admiral Vernon bar is the only mention of drinking in Coolidge's story.

The flip was a popular way to prepare a mixed drink of all brands of rum, including Medford. In the early days, a red-hot fireplace poker was thrust into the mug with the rum to warm it up further. This recipe is from 1878.

Rum Flip

Prepare grated ginger and nutmeg with a little fine dried lemon peel rubbed together in a mortar; to make a quart of flip, heat rather more than a pint and a half of ale; beat up three or four eggs with four ounces of moist sugar; a tea-spoonful of grated nutmeg or ginger; and a gill of good old rum or brandy; and when it is nearly boiling, put it into a pitcher and the rum and eggs, &c., into another. Mix and pour it from one pitcher to the other till it is as smooth as cream.

Coolidge's account of Revere's meeting with Captain Hall is brief and makes no mention of rum. He met with Hall, left his house in a hurry, and "gave the alarm at almost every house on the way to Lexington." The mayor goes on to relate how the Minutemen of Medford assisted in the rout of the British forces through numerous towns, including Concord and Lexington, until the Redcoats retreated to Charlestown, causing the citizens there to flee to Medford.

But oral history couldn't leave the Paul Revere rum story alone. In 2002, an anonymous message was posted and reposted, and eventually ended up on Snopes.com, the website debunking urban legends. The legend goes that Revere was on a mission to Lexington to warn Sam Adams and John Hancock that the British were coming. His route took him through Medford, where he stopped at the house of Minuteman and rum maker Hall and got so drunk that when he finally made it to Lexington, his "drunken caterwauling" roused Adams and Hancock at about 4:30 in the morning, only half an hour before fighting broke out on Lexington Green. This story originated in Charles William Taussig's *Rum, Romance, and Rebellion*, published in 1928.

Many other sources give alternative versions of Revere's midnight ride, so it is next to impossible to determine what is really true. Barbara Kerr, of the Medford Historical Society, went on record about the society's official opinion of what happened that night:

> *At the Medford Historical Society, the general consensus is that Paul Revere probably had a rum when he stopped at the Isaac Hall house. Besides the fact that it makes a better story, there are a lot of historical reasons to support the "drinking and riding" theory. To begin with, the water quality in Medford in 1775 was probably not great. Although Medford Rum had a reputation for a good flavor because of the local water, water quality was certainly not up to modern standards. Medford water came from the river and a variety of ponds and creeks, so as in many 18th century places, people drank rum instead of water.*

> *In addition to this, Paul stopped at the Isaac Hall house and the Hall family were the biggest distillers in Medford. Given that Revere arrived after everyone had gone to bed and he was in a hurry, it doesn't seem likely that anyone had the time to brew him a cup of tea (also there was that whole tea tax thing). It's much more likely that the Halls gave him a drink of the rum that they themselves would have been drinking instead of water. So I think it very likely that Paul Revere had a reasonable amount of Medford rum.*

BOOZING PATRIOTS AND TAVERNS OF THE REVOLUTION

Paul Revere's possibly wobbly jaunt through Medford was actually just one of his many Revolutionary rides, and two others also involved a place of drinking—the famous City Tavern in Philadelphia. In December 1773, Revere brought news of the Boston Tea Party to tavern patrons, though he might have mentioned that the affair was more of a Boston Rum Party. Before dumping the tea into Boston Harbor, the tea party leaders had braced

City Tavern, Philadelphia, c. 1790

themselves at the Green Dragon Inn with rounds of beer and rum supplied by the smuggler and patriot John Hancock.

On May 19, 1774, about a year after City Tavern had opened for business, Revere arrived again to announce Parliament's closing of the port of Boston. He had ridden from Boston carrying a letter asking the people of Philadelphia for support and proposing a "solid League and Covenant" among the colonies. Consequently, after city leaders received the letter on May 20, they called a town meeting at the convenient and spacious City Tavern, where resolutions were passed to form a committee to answer the letter from Boston and to assure the people there that the people of Philadelphia felt sorry for the Bostonians and their "unhappy situation." Revere dutifully carried the rather lukewarm response back to Boston.

Later that year, on September 4, General George Washington arrived in

Philadelphia and dined at City Tavern. The next day, members of Congress met at the tavern and passed a resolution declaring it the place of their deliberations. What was it about City Tavern that placed it in the center of Revolutionary history?

Early descriptions note that City Tavern was finished in 1773. It not only had rooms for overnight lodging but also large meeting rooms and a dining hall that was "elegantly lighted." The picky John Adams praised the tavern as "the most genteel one in America."

Walter Staib, the current executive chef at the reconstructed City Tavern, observed:

When the Tavern was completed in 1773, it was one of the most elegant buildings in the city. Situated on Second Street, a main thoroughfare, City Tavern was constructed in the latest architectural style and stood three stories high. Inside, it "boasted" of several large club rooms, two of which thrown into one make a spacious room of nearly fifty feet in length, for public entertainment. There were "several commodious lodging rooms, for the accommodation of strangers, two large kitchens, and every other convenience for the purpose." In addition, there was a Bar and also a Coffee Room, which was supplied with British and American newspapers and magazines.

THE DIVERSITY OF FARE IN THE PORT OF PHILADELPHIA

Philadelphia at the time was the second largest city in the British Empire, after London, and was by far the largest port in the colonies, dwarfing New York and Boston. "About three times a week ships came into the city with fresh West Indian products," wrote Mary Hines and her coauthors in *The Larder Invaded*, "limes, coconuts, bananas, plantain fruit, and guavas… Auctioned at shipside, they were snapped up by taverns and caterers whose turtle stews and soups flowed in unending streams until winter set in." Add to that oranges from Seville, dried plums and cherries from Germany, spices from the Spice Islands, and you have an idea of the incredible diversity of food in Philadelphia. Thus, it is not surprising that spicy dishes such as curries were quite popular.

Mary Randolph's Curry, 1824

Curry powder is used as a fine flavored seasoning for fish, fowls, steaks, chops, veal cutlets, hashes, minces, a la modes, turtle soup, and in all rich dishes, gravies, sauce, &c. &c.

To Make a Dish of Curry after the East Indian Manner

Cut two chickens as for fricassee, wash them clean, and put them in a stew pan with as much water as will cover them; sprinkle them with a large spoonful of salt, and let them boil till tender, covered close all the time, and skim them well; when boiled enough, take up the chickens, and put the liquor of them into a pan, then put half a pound of fresh butter in the pan, and brown it a little; put into it two cloves of garlic, and a large onion sliced, and let these all fry till brown, often shaking the pan; then put in the chickens, and sprinkle over them two or three spoonsful of curry powder; then cover the pan close, and let the chickens do till brown, often shaking the pan; then put in the liquor the chickens were boiled in, and let all stew till tender; if acid is agreeable, squeeze the juice of a lemon or orange in it.

The ships arriving from the Atlantic were often loaded with sea turtles, as the sailors would net them and haul them aboard throughout their journey. If kept fairly damp, the turtles could survive the sea journey to Philadelphia, where they became part of the cuisine, served in soups and stews. The taverns often had turtle-soup banquets, and one advertisement in the Philadelphia Gazette *in 1815 promoted a nine-hour banquet featuring a seventy-pound sea turtle. The demand was so great for sea turtles that Philadelphia cooks scoured the rivers and swamps for local terrapins as a substitute.*

Terrapin Soup

Select three large, live diamond-back terrapins; plunge them in boiling water to take the horny skin off; cook them in slightly salted water; drain and open them; take out every thing from the shells; remove the head, tail, nails, intestines, lights, and gall-bladder carefully and cut the rest in [small] pieces; put in a saucepan two quarts of espagnole sauce, a quart of veal-broth, half a pint of sherry wine, a glass of port wine, two tablespoonfuls of "Harvey's sauce"; and a pinch of red pepper; add the terrapin, boil half an hour, skim well, and serve with slices of lemon on a plate. From *The Franco-American Cookery Book*, 1884.

Ironically, Daniel Smith, a Loyalist to the British Crown, owned City Tavern. Later, in 1779, when the British fled Philadelphia, he left with them, abandoning the tavern, which was worth £1,800.

Before that, City Tavern had played a significant role in the Revolution as the meeting place for the Continental Congress. During those crucial meetings, it served meals combining the elements of both British and French cuisine. The large menu included rib roast and various roasted fowl, with plum pudding, candies, and little cakes for dessert. The drinks were beer, ale, wine, rum, and brandy. In a holdover from British cooking techniques, the meats were roasted in the basement using spits turned by dogs in circular cages.

Turnspit dog

The turnspit dog had short legs, a long body, and was bred and trained specifically to run in a turnspit or dog wheel to turn meat roasting over a fire. It is mentioned as early as 1576 in the book *Of English Dogs*, where it is called a "Turnespete." It was also known as the kitchen dog, the cooking dog, and the underdog, and in Linnaeus's eighteenth-century classification of dogs, it is listed as *Canis vertigus*, or "dizzy dog," which makes a lot of sense. The turnspit dog is now extinct, though some dog breeders believe that it is related to the Glen of Imaal terrier.

Thomas Jefferson, as a delegate to the Continental Congress, was a frequent customer of City Tavern in 1775 while he was writing the first draft of the Declaration of Independence. Many sources even claim that he wrote the draft in the tavern's bar. Other dubious sources claim the location was Indian Queen Tavern, also in Philadelphia, or even nearby Independence Hall. However, Jefferson himself explained where he wrote the document in a letter to Dr. John Mease on September 26, 1825: "At the time of writing that instrument, I lodged in the house of a Mr. Graaf [Graff], a new brick house, three stories high, of which I rented the second floor, consisting of a parlor and bed-room, ready furnished. In that parlor I wrote habitually, and in it wrote this paper, particularly. So far I state from written proofs in my possession. The proprietor, Graaf [Graff], was a young man, son of a German, and then newly married." An early Jefferson biographer, Henry Randall, noted: "Entries of the payment of the weekly rent of his rooms (thirty-five shillings sterling) continued throughout the session. He appears to have taken most of his meals at 'Smith's'—the keeper, we suppose, of the City Tavern."

Hannah Glasse's Pretty Side of Roasted Beef, 1774

What do you do with beef after it is roasted over an open flame? The influential English cookbook author Hannah Glasse instructs with a recipe that was similar to those used in American taverns.

A Pretty Side Dish of Beef

Roast a tender piece of beef. Lay fat bacon all over it and roll it in paper, baste it, and when it is roasted, cut about two pounds in thin slices, lay them in a stew pan and take six large cucumbers, peel them, and chop them small, lay over them a little pepper and salt, stew them in butter for about ten minutes, then drain out the butter and shake some flour over them, toss them up, pour in half a pint of gravy, let them stew till they are thick and dish them up.

Of course, City Tavern was not the only tavern that influenced the Revolution. Men, women, children, servants, and even free blacks frequented taverns. Taverns were everywhere in the colonies, from the backcountry to the big cities, and they were very influential in shaping public opinion. In addition to camaraderie and drinking, they fostered a sense of community, complete with social interactions and business transactions. They were a welcome retreat from rustic colonial homes, transforming eating and drinking into public activities and fostering political action. Colonial patriots viewed taverns as the nurseries of freedom, the places where the British were denounced and where militiamen were recruited. "Taverns ... were seed beds of the Revolution, the places where British tyranny was condemned, militiamen organized, and independence plotted," writes historian W. J. Rorabaugh. In 1930, another historian, Frederick Bernays Wiener, chimed in: "Commerce and politics were so inextricably mingled that rum and liberty were but different liquors from the same still."

All of this socializing began with drinking, and surprisingly, the colonial taste for alcohol actually had a medicinal beginning. The common belief was that strong drink made for a strong body and soul; alcohol was believed to be nutritious and healthful, and it was used in medications that could supposedly cure snakebite, frostbite, fever, cold, melancholy, and even a broken leg. Insurance companies raised their rates for nondrinkers, and hard liquor was even more popular in the colonies than in England. One heavy-drinking Georgia gentleman proclaimed, "If I take a settler after my coffee, a cooler at nine, a bracer at ten, a whetter at eleven, and two or three stiffeners during the forenoon, who has a right to complain?" Benjamin Franklin said that there was no good living where there was not good drinking, and for colonial Americans, this proved true. Colonists drank twice as much as Americans do now.

Regular drinking was normal for all ages, and young students were given ale or hard cider for breakfast. Harvard College even had its own brewery. In courtrooms, all parties, judge and defendant included, passed around and shared bottles of liquor. Stagecoaches stopped every five miles to "water the horses and brandy the gentlemen." Whiskey was served at house-raisings, huskings, reaping, land clearings, or whenever women gathered to quilt, sew, or perform other communal labor.

In 1770, just before the Revolution, the colonies distilled 5 million gallons of rum and imported 4 million more. But during the war, England blockaded most of the molasses and rum imports. Distillers switched to making whiskey, but they couldn't meet the wartime demand. For drinkers, times were so bad that they were forced to drink spruce and pumpkin beers. Even the wartime governor of Virginia, Patrick Henry, served home-brewed beer, much to the chagrin of his friends.

Drunkenness was vehemently denounced, of course, and each colony had its own methods of dealing with it. In Massachusetts, names of sloshed offenders were posted on handbills over the tavern doors as public humili-ation, whereas Pennsylvania Quakers sternly warned problem drinkers against entering taverns. Maryland had fines for drunken tavern customers, and Virginia put repeat offenders in stocks.

Typically, there was an antibooze backlash, led by the Quakers and Methodists, who had completely banned all alcoholic beverages by the 1780s. The leader of the antiliquor crusaders was a Philadelphia doctor, Founding Father, friend of Franklin's, and signer of the Declaration of Independence, Benjamin Rush. His essay "An Inquiry into the Effects of Spirituous Liquors," published in 1784, claimed that hard liquor caused stomach sickness, vomiting, hand tremors, dropsy, liver disorders, epilepsy, palsy, and madness. He recommended replacing hard liquor with beer or light wine, which he called "those invaluable federal liquors!"

But Rush's antiliquor campaign fell mostly on deaf ears. During his later term as governor of New York, George Clinton (who became Jefferson's vice president in 1804) hosted the French ambassador and 120 guests, who in one evening went through 135 bottles of Madeira, 36 bottles of port, 60 bottles of English beer, and topped the festivities off with 30 cups of rum punch! By 1850, more than 170,000 copies of Rush's essay had been cir-culated, and although he changed the minds of many people, the drinking went on and on.

During the years of Jefferson's retirement, in the early 1800s, the annual per capita consumption of distilled spirits exceeded five gallons. The quaffing of hard cider, which was 10 percent alcohol, was fifteen gallons a year per person. In 1829, the secretary of war estimated that three-quarters of the nation's workers drank at least four ounces of hard liquor daily. "During the first third of the nineteenth century," booze historian W. J. Rorabaugh commented, "the typical American annually drank more distilled liquor than at any other time in our history." If the average person consumed five gallons of hard liquor a year, that amounted to 1.75 ounces per day, the equivalent of one strong martini. However, if nondrinkers and young children were factored in, that amount would probably be higher.

Today, Rush is most famous not for his antiliquor campaign but as the negotiator who, in 1812, helped reconcile the friendship of two of the greatest men of the early Republic, Thomas Jefferson and John Adams.

Sleepy John Sears Supplies the White Gold of Cape Cod

Salt was as important to the American Revolution as gunpowder and just as hard to find. Gunpowder was necessary for powering rifles and cannons to annihilate the hated British Army and Navy, but without salt, the fighting patriots would have starved to death. In an age without refrigeration, salt was essential for preserving fish, beef, pork, and poultry.

Salting fish in a schooner's hold

Mary Randolph's Directions for Salting and Aging Beef (Abridged), 1824

The importance of salt for preservation of meats in the days before refrigeration cannot be exaggerated. Here, Mary Randolph, a relative of Thomas Jefferson by marriage, describes the technique that helped feed the Revolutionary Army.

To Dry Beef for Summer Use

The best pieces for this purpose are the thin briskets, or that part of the plate which is farthest from the shoulder of the animal. Salt the pieces as directed, let them lie one fortnight, then put them in brine, where they must remain three weeks; take them out at the end of the time, wipe them quite dry, rub them over with bran, and hang them in a cool, dry, and, if possible, dark place, that the flies may not get to them: they must be suspended, and not allowed to touch any thing. It will be necessary, in the course of the summer, to look them over occasionally, and after a long wet season, to lay them in the sun a few hours. These dried meats must be put in a good quantity of water, to soak, the night before they are to be used. In boiling, it is absolutely necessary to have a large quantity of water to put the beef in while the water is cold, to boil steadily, skimming the pot, until the bones are ready to fall out. The housekeeper who will buy good ox beef, and follow these directions exactly, may be assured of always having delicious beef on her table.

Early in the war, England cut off American trade with Turks Island, southeast of the Bahamas, which was the premier supplier of salt to the colonies. The colonists were forced to depend on greatly reduced supplies of salt smuggled in from Bermuda and certain Bahamian islands in trade for grain and flour. Then, in 1776, General William Howe captured Long Island and New York City, effectively cutting off Washington's army from its supply of coastal salt and seizing its salt reserves. Profiteers began hoarding salt, and prices were soon exorbitant. The salt situation reached a crisis.

Congress responded by permitting the salt-smuggling trade with British colonies, encouraging the formation of new saltworks, and offering a bounty for salt production of one-third of a dollar for each fifty-pound bushel. Colonists scrambled to make salt, boiling saltwater for weeks on end, but because four hundred gallons of water and two cords of wood yielded just a bushel of salt, the effort was mostly futile. Salt makers drove stakes into saltier tidal water and collected the crystals deposited on the wood at low tide, but again the yields were small. Unlike Europe, the colonies had no rock-salt mines, so they desperately needed a new salt-extraction technique. Enter Sleepy John Sears and his solar salt maker, which produced the white gold of Cape Cod.

Born in 1744 in Yarmouth, Massachusetts, Sears earned his nickname from his propensity to nod off during the day. His family described this affliction as "fits of abstraction." Sears was something of a genius and a foodie in a very oblique way. His family history, first published in 1887, tells the story of how, in 1776, he constructed a wooden salt evaporator at Sesuit Harbor that was one hundred feet long and ten feet wide, with movable rafters above it. The rafters could be closed when it rained and opened to the sun to enhance evaporation. Sears lugged thousands of barrels of seawater by hand to the vat, but it was leaky, and the first year provided only eight bushels of salt. His neighbors called the invention Sears's folly, but Sears persevered, plugged the leaks with tar, and the second year's production was thirty bushels. In the fourth year, he salvaged a water pump from the wreck of the

British man-of-war *Somerset*, which required tedious hand operation but still managed to increase production.

By 1783, the price of salt had skyrocketed from fifty cents to eight dollars a bushel, increasing Sears's profit. By then, John Sears had earned a new nickname, Salty John Sears. Salty John

The legacy of John Sears: saltworks, South Yarmouth, c. 1870

did not, of course, solve the problem of the salt supply for the colonists, not to mention the army. His invention, however, launched a salt-making industry around Cape Cod that, in 1832, fifteen years after his death, had 1,425,000 feet of wooden vats that produced 358,250 bushels of salt.

The industry was great for the citizens but, along with shipbuilding, devastated the old-growth forests along the New England coast. The opening of the Erie Canal in 1825 and the development of New York's salt springs at Onondaga led to the decline of Cape Cod's saltworks industry, and by 1888, the last operation had shut its vats. The thrifty Cape Codders dismantled the vats and used them to build houses.

WHAT SAVED THE VALLEY FORGE TROOPS: A SHAD RUN OR THE BAKER-GENERAL OF THE CONTINENTAL ARMY?

As with John Smith and Pocahontas, Squanto and the first Thanksgiving, and Paul Revere's ride, the story of the winter of 1777–1778 at General Washington's encampment at Valley Forge has transcended history and become enshrined in mythology. How bad was the weather? We imagine blizzards and men freezing to death, but in reality, the weather was mostly cold and rainy with very little snow. How many men and women died? Two thousand? Four thousand? We don't know exactly, because no one was buried at Valley Forge—most died in local hospitals. How many died of starvation? Probably none, because disease was the major cause of death.

This is not to say that the men (and the women camp followers) didn't suffer enormously from hunger. Numerous accounts document the shortage of meat and bread and starving horses. And the troops did not have a merry Christmas. "Can assure you, that I never saw a Christmas when I had no other Covering than Towels before," wrote Jonathan Todd, a surgeon's mate, to his father on Christmas Day.

General Washington's own officers criticized him in letters but not to his face. General Johann de Kalb, a German officer and Lafayette's friend, called him "the weakest General" and noted his inability to find competent quartermasters. General George Weedon took Washington to task for allowing the troops to plunder the locals.

Washington's political enemies warned of the doom of the troops at Valley Forge. James Lovell, a congressman from Massachusetts, wrote to John Adams on December 30, 1777: "As a secret I tell you that there is the greatest risqué that the army will be disbanded in a short season, for the Commissary's & Qr. Master's departments are ruined...Buchannan is as incapable as a child and knows not how he can feed the army 3 Weeks from any parts, or how to feed them from day to day with what he has on hand. Mutiny is at present suppressed."

Lovell, as with others, correctly assessed the problem with the commissary, so what happened to save the troops from starvation? In 1938, Harry

Emerson Wildes told the world that shad had saved the soldiers! In *Valley Forge*, he described how the shad swam up the Schuylkill River that ran next to the Valley Forge camp: "Then, dramatically, the famine completely ended. Countless thousands of fat shad, swimming up the Schuylkill to spawn, filled the river…Soldiers thronged the river bank…the cavalry was ordered into the river bed…The horsemen rode up stream, noisily shouting and beating the water, driving the shad before them into nets spread across the Schuylkill…The netting was continued day after day…until the army was thoroughly stuffed with fish and in addition hundreds of barrels of shad were salted down for later use."

After Wildes's book, the shad story was retold again and again. It is true that shad were an important fish in colonial times (see chapter 3 for the story of George Washington's fishing operation on the Potomac River). Salted down and barreled, they were a significant part of the rations for the Continental Army. In one week in May 1778, twenty-two thousand pounds of shad were issued to the army. The spring of that year was an excellent one for the anadromous fish, meaning that they return from the sea to spawn in freshwater, like salmon. But those fish never made it to Valley Forge.

Joseph Lee Boyle, the former National Park Service historian, did a thorough study of the Valley Forge fish story and concluded that no primary sources substantiate the story of shad at Valley Forge. The scarcity of salt to preserve the shad, the lack of cavalrymen to ride horses "driving the shad before them" into nets (an unlikely scenario anyway), and the fact that shad were in short supply around Valley Forge pretty much doom Wildes's fanciful story. In 2002, archaeological excavations of the food remains at the cabin sites at Valley Forge revealed the bones of cattle and pigs but not fish. John McPhee, in his book *The Founding Fish*, studied the shad situation on the Schuylkill River and wrote, "The emotive account of the nation-saving shad is a tale recommended by everything but sources."

On Cooking Fresh Shad

When I was growing up in Virginia, I often caught shad on jigs in the James River during their spring runs. Shad is a great game fish, requiring a lot of skill to land because of their soft mouths—the hook would tear out if you tried to horse them to shore. But shad are so bony that a joke often went around claiming that to cook shad by planking, you nailed a fillet to a plank and placed it before a campfire. When done, you discarded the fillet and ate the plank. As a result of the joke, my fishing friends and I only ever kept female shad. We would cut them open for their roe, fry the whole roes in bacon grease, and serve them for breakfast with scrambled eggs. Delicious! Back in those days, I wasn't familiar with Mary Randolph's recipe.

To Bake a Shad by Mary Randolph (1824)

The shad is a very indifferent fish unless it be large and fat; when you get a good one, prepare it nicely, put some forcemeat inside, and lay it at full length in a pan with a pint of water, a gill of red wine, one of mushroom catsup, a little pepper, vinegar, salt, a few cloves of garlic, and six cloves: stew it gently till the gravy is sufficiently reduced; there should always be a fish-slice with holes to lay the fish on, for the convenience of dishing without breaking it; when the fish is taken up, slip it carefully into the dish; thicken the gravy with butter and brown flour, and pour over it.

Why didn't the shad swim all the way up to Valley Forge? There is some evidence to indicate that the British Army may have blocked the shad migration. In a letter written in April 1778 by a British Army physician, Sir Charles Blagden, to his friend Sir Joseph Banks, one of England's greatest botanists and naturalists, Blagden describes their plan: "During this month a pretty large species of Clupea, called a shad, runs up the Rivers Delaware & Schuylkill in prodigious numbers. It has already proved a very seasonable relief to the inhabitants of this town [Philadelphia]. However, lest our enemies should receive as much if not more advantage from this benefit of nature, we have passed a seine across the Schuylkill, to prevent the fish from getting up that river, upon the banks of which Mr. Washington's army is encamped. I will take some pains to learn how far this precaution is found effectual."

Historian Boyle speculated: "As the British had a floating bridge from Philadelphia across to the west bank of the Schuylkill…nets may have been hung from the bridge to block the shad."

NOT YOUR MOST DELICIOUS FISH DINNER

During the summer of 1780, Joseph Plumb Martin, stationed in West Point, New York, described eating salted shad: "Our rations, when we got any, consisted of bread and salt shad. This fish, as salt as fire, and dry bread, without any kind of vegetables, was hard fare in such extreme hot weather as it was then. We were compelled to eat it as it was. If we attempted to soak it in a brook…we were quite sure to lose it, there being a great abundance of otter and minks in and about the water, four-legged and two-legged…so that they would be quite sure to carry off the fish, let us do what we would to prevent it."

If it wasn't shad that saved the soldiers, maybe it was bread baked by the first (and probably the only) baker-general of the army.

Christopher Ludwick arrived in Philadelphia in 1754; married a young widow, Catharine England; and set himself up in business, specializing in confectionery and gingerbread. He was a highly successful baker, and by 1775, he owned nine houses, a farm in Germantown, and had £3,500 invested in bonds—a huge sum in those days. He strongly supported the colonies against the British and donated hundreds of pounds to the Pennsylvania militia.

As an army volunteer, Ludwick pulled off a spectacular espionage assignment. A congressional committee, with Thomas Jefferson and Benjamin Franklin as members, designed a plan, as described by Congress on August 9, 1776, to encourage the "Hessians and other foreigners" to desert from the British Army. A major component of the plan was to offer free land to German deserters. George Washington approved the plan, and Ludwick was rowed across the Hudson. He infiltrated the British Army at Staten Island and, dressed like a deserter from the Americans and speaking in German, convinced many Hessian mercenaries to desert and join the German farmers living in Pennsylvania. Hundreds of German farmers did so, and Ludwick was then put in charge of the Hessian deserters. He soon came up with yet another plan. As he told Washington, "Let us take them to Philadelphia and let them see how our tradesmen eat good beef, drink out of silver cups every day; and then let us send them back to their countrymen, and soon they all run away and come and settle in our city." Washington agreed.

Christopher Ludwick's many accomplishments did not escape the notice of the congressmen, who soon decided to employ his finest talent. Congress, on May 30, 1777, commissioned him as superintendent of bakers and director of baking in the army. He was to receive as pay $75 a month and "two rations a day."

The new baker-general of the army went to Morristown, began setting up ovens (many of which he paid for himself), and recruited bakers
from the militia. General Washington, on the march to Philadelphia to
protect the city from Howe and his army, wrote to Ludwick on July
25: "I imagine you must by this time have a considerable parcel of hard
bread baked. I am moving towards Philadelphia with the Army, and
should be glad to have it sent forward…You will continue baking as fast
as you can because two other Divisions will pass thro' Pitts Town and
will want bread."

Washington, however, could not protect Philadelphia. Howe's forces
seized it on September 25, and they destroyed four thousand barrels of
flour. Ludwick moved his baking operation to Skipjack, where, with newly
recruited bakers, he set up rudimentary ovens and continued to supply the
army, again defeated at Germantown, with bread. He was then ordered to
move his ovens to Valley Forge.

Exactly what ovens did Ludwick set up at Valley Forge? They must have
been significant and elaborate, because Treasury records in the National
Archives show that on March 26, 1778, Ludwick was paid the huge sum
of $5,315.43 "for the amount of his account, for building ovens at differ-
ent posts, Bakers wages, Travelling Expences, his own Pay from the 3rd
of May last to the 3rd inst. at 75 dollrs. Pr. Month." Historian William
Condit revealed that Ludwick set up most of the ovens in the house of
Colonel William Dewees, Jr., (who owned the original forge the valley
is named for) and scattered smaller ovens around the encampment. Flour
was scarce as usual, so Ludwick cajoled the German farmers of Bucks and
Montgomery counties and even sold one of his own houses to pay for
flour, which he stored mostly in a depot in Reading. He was very well
liked at camp, despite the trying times, and George Washington, drinking

from his china punch bowl, would often toast him: "Health and long life to Christopher Ludwick and wife."

However, Condit's story conflicts with some other historical and archeological evidence of Valley Forge. In 1946, George Edwin Brumbaugh was appointed architect for the "improvements to Valley Forge Park." During his renovation of the Washington Inn (an old mansion near Washington's headquarters that had been remodeled and turned into a nice hotel) for weeks he looked for evidence of the ovens. He never found any, and the historian Lorett Treese reported:

> He found nothing in the cellar except a "curious curved wall, one brick in thickness, surrounding a depressed, brick-paved pit, 27 inches below the earth floor of the basement"... There was no evidence that it had ever been subjected to heat... Brumbaugh recommended that no oven replicas be constructed in the cellar until more evidence was uncovered. Instead, Brumbaugh suggested that a more typical oven be built outside the house. But Brumbaugh was not consulted in 1963 when the park commission decided to go ahead and build oven replicas in the cellar anyway, even moving the cellar entrance to a new location to accommodate their construction.

If Ludwick didn't build standing brick ovens, what did he build? In a letter to General Washington written on New Year's Day, 1778, General Jedediah Huntington wrote, "Each Brigade should be attended with a traveling Oven." The term *traveling oven* in this context means "portable oven." It wasn't until after the mid-1800s that it came to mean a mechanized oven whereby the items baked traveled through the oven on conveyor belts. On January 9, a general order from headquarters commanded each brigade's quartermaster to pick up traveling iron ovens. The iron ovens were placed in mounds of dirt that were built to insulate the ovens and facilitate bread making. The use of earthen mounds for baking bread in army camps lasted for at least 120 years after their appearance at Valley Forge.

During the mapping phase of a 2000 archeological dig at Valley Forge National Park, the archeology team identified two fairly large, circular earth features that appeared to be camp kitchens or bake ovens. The theory of the archeologists is that bread was baked for the brigade in ovens placed in the central earthen mound, and food was prepared in pots arrayed around the mound's perim- eter. "The Valley Forge experts assumed that the cooking area would be a focus of activity in the camp," reported the National Park Service.

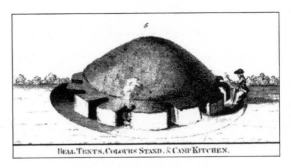

Camp kitchen, c. 1777

Although the order for brigade masters instructed them to pick up an iron oven for each unit, the reconstructed demonstration bake oven at Valley Forge National Historical Park has a brick oven buried in a large mound of earth. When the replications were first made to the historic park, the park directors did not know about the existence of the iron ovens. In reality, either type of oven, brick or iron, could be used in an earthen mound. The cast-iron ovens used were probably large versions of Dutch ovens, with legs and a handle, so that they could be used as ovens when buried in the mounds, or as stewpots when removed and set on their legs over the flames or coals of an open fire. Although they were heavy, iron ovens were far more portable than brick ones.

Baking for all those trips with such equipment must have been a challenge for Ludwick and his bakers, but although it was not easy to bake bread in an iron oven, it was not impossible. Thomas Webster and William Parkes observed in 1855 in their *Encyclopaedia of Domestic Economy*, "Iron ovens are, therefore, frequently more convenient, and even more economical. There are many persons who imagine that it is quite impossible to bake bread and pastry well in an oven of iron; but this opinion arises from want of experience. It must be observed that much more skill is required in fitting up and managing an iron oven than a brick one; but when the former are fitted up in a proper manner, and persons understand the method of using them, they answer the purpose very well, and have, at the same time, many advantages in baking."

Ludwick got to work with his staff, and on Christmas Day, 1777, Colonel Henry Lutterloh of the New York regiment wrote, "The Bakery is now almost upon a footing to deliver Bread for the whole Army, which may be done regularly every three days." By February 9, Thomas Jones, the deputy commissary general of issues, reported that the bake house had 123 barrels of flour and 45,600 pounds of bread, and as a result, the critical food situation seemed to be easing at Valley Forge.

But Ludwick's bread did not reach everyone. Lieutenant Colonel Alexander Hamilton, who was not present at the camp but rather stationed in New Jersey, wrote to Governor George Clinton of New York on February 13: "We are reduced to a more terrible situation than you can conceive...By injudicious changes and arrangements in the Commissary's department, in the middle of a campaign, they have exposed the army frequently to temporary want, and to the danger of dissolution, from absolute famine. At this very day there are complaints from the whole line, of having been three or four days without provisions; desertions have been immense, and strong features of mutiny begin to show themselves." Thankfully, on that same day, Jones reported the delivery of 2,250 pounds of pork.

The main supply problems, besides letters crossing in the sporadic continental mail system, stemmed from the bad roads in the winter, the falling value of colonial currency, "the avarice of farmers," and the general scarcity of food in the Valley Forge area.

Of course, as spring arrived in 1778, the weather improved, as did the condition of the roads, and droves of cattle began to arrive at Valley Forge. By April 16, things were pretty much back to normal, and General Washington assigned sutlers—liquor sellers—to each brigade. In his words, they were permitted to sell "Whiskey, Peach brandy, Apple brandy, Cordials of all kinds, and any other home-made Spirits, West India Spirits, full proof," and "a bowl of Toddy, containing half a pint of Spirits."

Christopher Ludwick remained at Valley Forge until camp was struck on June 18, 1778, and after that, he set up army ovens in New Jersey, New York, Connecticut, and Massachusetts, and he did some private baking for General Washington. He submitted a bill to the general for £13 10s and was paid in full ten months later. So it was the baker-general who saved the troops at Valley Forge, not a shad migration.

Another of Ludwick's assumed culinary legacies was "the Soup That Won the War," or Philadelphia pepper pot. Because good beef was initially scarce at Valley Forge, Ludwick supposedly combined tripe (cows' stomach lining) and other scraps with onions, black peppercorns, and cayenne to make something warm and filling for the troops. Of course, even if he did serve pepper pot to the soldiers, Ludwick certainly didn't invent the dish. Pepper pot came to the colonies from the West Indies and was a part of the Philadelphia cooking culture before the Revolution began. It was one of many hot and spicy dishes served in the colonies, along with curries. Chef Walter Staib commented, in *The City Tavern Cookbook*, "It is assumed that George Washington was familiar with pepperpot soup long before he camped at Valley Forge. During his only trip abroad in 1751, Washington visited Barbados with his brother, where he enjoyed Cohobbloplot, a version of pepperpot soup made with okra."

PHILADELPHIA'S PEPPER-POT HERITAGE

In the colonies, especially Philadelphia, pepper-pot soup became a staple of African Americans and later of people of all heritages, and street vendors often sold it. John Lewis Krimmel was the first Philadelphia artist to depict street scenes in fine art.

Pepper-Pot: A Scene in the Philadelphia Market (1811), by John Lewis Krimmel (Courtesy: Sunbelt Archives)

Philadelphia Pepper Pot

Put two pounds of tripe and four calves' feet into the soup-pot and cover them with cold water; add a red pepper, and boil closely until the calves' feet are boiled very tender; take out the meat, skim the liquid, stir it, cut the tripe into small pieces, and put it back into the liquid; if there is not enough liquid, add boiling water; add half a teaspoonful of sweet marjoram, sweet basil, and thyme, two sliced onions, sliced potatoes, salt. When the vegetables have boiled until almost tender, add a piece of butter rolled in flour, drop in some egg balls, and boil fifteen minutes more. Take up and serve hot.

Pepper pot was hardly unique to Philadelphia.. Along with gumbo and oxtail soup, it was prepared all over the colonies, and particularly in the South, where the African American population was greater. Mary Randolph has an abbreviated recipe for it in her 1824 cookbook *The Virginia Housewife*: "Boil two or three pounds of tripe, cut it in pieces, and put it on the fire with a knuckle of veal, and a sufficient quantity of water; part of a pod of pepper, a little spice, sweet herbs according to your taste, salt, and some dumplins; stew it till tender, and thicken the gravy with butter and flour."

Another version of pepper pot, but made with spinach and crabs or lobsters in the manner of callaloo, a West Indies spicy soup native to Trinidad but also made in Barbados, appeared in *The Carolina Rice Cookbook* (1901) by Mrs. Samuel G. (Louisa) Stoney. She calls for "long red peppers" (cayenne) to spice it up. Food historian Karen Hess has called pepper pot "an infinitely varied festival dish" and has observed, "The authenticity is not surprising, given the strong South Carolina connections with Barbados and the Bahamas."

After danger of starvation was over, two soldiers, both recovering from war wounds, arrived at Valley Forge. They would play significant roles in the story of the founding foodies. One was a twenty-one-year-old French soldier, whom Benjamin Franklin had recommended as Washington's aide-de-camp in the hope that France would send more aid to support the American cause. Washington agreed and told the soldier that he would act as a "father and friend" to him. The soldier was Gilbert du Motier, also known as the Marquis de Lafayette.

The other soldier was a thirty-seven-year-old hero of the Battle of Saratoga, which had left him with his left leg two inches shorter than his right. When he arrived at camp at Valley Forge in May, the men applauded him for his bravery at Saratoga. He then participated in the first recorded Oath of Allegiance with many other soldiers as a sign of loyalty to the United States. A month later, the British withdrew from Philadelphia, and Washington broke camp at Valley Forge and appointed the soldier military commander of Philadelphia. He was Benedict Arnold.

Chapter Three

FARMER WASHINGTON, ENTREPRENEUR EXTRAORDINAIRE

D espite the threat of the British Army, City Tavern was the entertainment capital of the former colonies on the first anniversary of Independence Day. On July 5, 1777, John Adams, a member of the Continental Congress,

Life of George Washington the farmer

wrote to his twelve-year-old daughter Abigail and described what had happened the previous day.

I went on board the Delaware *with the President and several gentlemen of the Marine Committee, soon after which we were saluted with a discharge of thirteen guns, which was followed by thirteen others, from each other armed vessel in the river...At three we went to dinner, and were very agreeably entertained with excellent company, good cheer, fine music from the band of Hessians taken at Trenton, and continual vollies between every toast, from a company of soldiers drawn up in Second-street before the City Tavern, where*

we dined. The toasts were in honour of our country, and the heroes who have
fallen in their pious efforts to defend her.

The partying was short lived for Washington, who still had a war to deal
with. After Cornwallis surrendered four years later at Yorktown, Virginia, in
1781, the commander in chief then had to deal with the starving British pris-
oners of war. Again, it was the baker-general to the rescue. "On Cornwallis's
surrender, Washington asked for six thousand loaves of bread to feed the
British," Stewart Holbrook wrote in 1948 in his book, *Lost Men of American
History*. "It was a stupendous order for the equipment Ludwick had in the
field, but he met it within twelve hours."

In 1985, Dr. David Kimball, the lead historian at Independence Hall
in Philadelphia, turned over his vast collection of transcriptions of original
records to Gordon Lloyd so that Lloyd could research them for the bicentennial of the Constitution of 1787. Eventually, Lloyd discovered the bill
for the farewell dinner of George Washington on September 14, 1787.
The bill was to the event's sponsor, the Light Troop of Horse. The bill for
the farewell dinner was £89 for fifty-five "Gentlemen" (women could not
dine in public for another century). According to the bill, the gentlemen
consumed fifty-four bottles of Madeira, sixty bottles of claret, twenty-two
bottles of porter, eight bottles of hard cider, twelve bottles of beer, and
seven large "bowels" of punch.

The bill only mentions "Rellishes, Olives etc." as food items, but because
the charge for that was £20, there was probably a lot more food involved. The
usual City Tavern fare was probably served alongside all the drinks. As detailed
by Carl G. Karsch in his article "City Tavern: A Feast of Elegance," "Typically,
dinner included two tureens of soup—one at each end of the table—at least
two fish dishes, a shoulder of mutton, a ham, a roast of pork or beef, wild

game, chicken or turkey. In addition were salads, sauces and relishes. For dessert: cakes, tarts and puddings followed by fruits, nuts and the inevitable decanters of Madeira wine. For large parties, depending on the host's budget, perhaps as many as 20 dishes were served."

City Tavern today—rebuilt according to the original plans

As stupendous as that party was, it did not break the City Tavern record for excessive partying. That went to the gala event celebrating the election and installation of Philadelphia's president of the Supreme Executive Council in 1778, attended by 270 aristocrats, including the ministers of France and Spain. Chef Walter Staib reported in 2009: "There was a stupefying amount of alcohol, including 522 bottles of Madeira, 116 large bowls of punch, nine bottles of toddy, six bowls of sangria, twenty-four bottles of port, and two tubs of grog for artillery soldiers. Understandably, the party grew boisterous—the bill also covered 96 broken plates and glasses, as well as five decanters."

THE FOUNDING FARMER

After his presidency and farewell party, Washington retired to his beloved plantation, Mount Vernon. "No estate in United America is more pleasantly situated than this," he wrote in 1793. "It lies in a high, dry and healthy Country 300 miles by water from the Sea…on one of the finest

Rivers in the world…It is situated in a latitude between the extremes of hot and cold, and is the same distance by land and water, with good roads and the best navigation [to and] from the Federal City, Alexandria and Georgetown."

Washington at Mount Vernon, Currier, 1852

Most of the hundreds of books written about George Washington focus nearly exclusively on his involvement with politics and war, and it is rare to see his more human side as a family man devoted to his wife; stepchildren; and his home and plantation, Mount Vernon. In fact, Washington was extremely devoted to his home environment, as historian Bruce Chadwick has noted: "He was an obsessive micromanager who felt it necessary to be completely involved in every aspect of the work at Mount Vernon and its vast farms." It was this dedication to work that made him not only an excellent farmer but also a successful entrepreneur in other endeavors.

Shortly after the presidential inauguration of John Adams in early 1797, Washington gathered his personal effects and his dog and the effects of Martha, including her pet cockatoo, and headed back to Mount Vernon. He had not spent much time there during the previous eight years, and he was eager, at the age of sixty-five, to return to farming. On the first day after he arrived at his estate, he "donned the clothes of a farmer" and went out to survey the conditions of his lands and his manor house. He was appalled at the disrepair and soon began a remodeling of the mansion.

Washington's life as a farmer had begun forty-five years earlier, when his elder half-brother Lawrence died of suspected tuberculosis in 1752 and Washington inherited Mount Vernon. Two years later, he leased 2,300 acres from his half-brother's widow and bought the property outright after her death in 1760. He continued to purchase other contiguous lands, and by 1787, he had consolidated the estate of some eight thousand acres into five farms, each with support buildings including an overseer's house, slave cabins, various farming structures, and livestock pens and sheds.

At first, Washington had a tobacco dependency, but in those days, the term didn't mean addiction to nicotine; rather, it referred to the monoculture of tobacco and the convoluted system of the tobacco economy. Washington soon realized that he could not make a decent profit off of tobacco because the shipping fees, import and export duties, brokerage charges, insurance, and commissions of his London agents would cost him 80 percent of the final sale. In addition to its costs, tobacco was also very detrimental to the fertility of the soil on his farms and was a terribly labor-intensive crop. He decided that he had to diversify into other crops and even other endeavors—some farm related and some not.

To accomplish this, Washington began to study the principles of the new husbandry practices already in place in England, which included composting and the use of animal waste as fertilizer. From 1756 to 1760, he ordered several British books on agriculture and gardening that had nothing to do with tobacco cultivation, such as *New Principles of Gardening* (1728), by Batty Langley, and *A Compleat Book of Husbandry* (1758), by Thomas Hale. The books inspired him to begin growing different crops, like wheat, which turned out to be very profitable. Eventually, he grew not only wheat but also sixty different crops, including corn, barley, buckwheat, oats, clover, flax, cotton, potatoes, and peas. These were in addition to all of his garden crops.

One of the new husbandry principles that Washington followed religiously was composting. Agricultural historian Dennis Pogue, writing in "Washington, The Revolutionary Farmer," referred to Washington as America's first composter. Washington subscribed to John Spurrier's *The Practical Farmer* and learned the various techniques for adding organic matter to the soil to enrich it. He first mixed compost on April 14, 1760, and after many experiments, he successfully applied manure, river and creek mud, fish heads, and plaster of Paris to his fields. He even ordered his workers to erect a "dung depository" or "stercorary" for the specific purpose of curing manure by composting it.

"When I speak of a knowing farmer," Washington wrote, "I mean... above all, Midas like, one who can convert everything he touches into manure, as the first transmutation towards Gold." He directed his farm-workers to "rake and scrape up all the trash, of every sort and kind around the houses, and in the holes and corners, and throw it (all I mean that will make dung) into the Stercorary." He had conveniently placed his dung depository adjacent to the mansion house stables.

The Farmer's Animals

Washington was one of the finest horsemen of his time and an accomplished horse trainer who entered his Arabian stallion, Magnolia, in horse races. Primarily though, his horses were farm animals who pulled plows and carts; by 1785, he owned 130 of them. One of Washington's principal successes as a stockman used some of these horses and jennets (female donkeys) that he received as a gift from Lafayette. He bred the donkeys with the horses to produce mules, which he said were stronger, had greater endurance, and ate less food than the horses. Alan and Donna Jean Fusonie, writing in *George Washington: Pioneer Farmer*, recalled that another of Washington's honorary titles is "Father of the American Mule," because he was the first farmer in America to breed mules for farm work.

Washington was so enamored with the farming abilities of the mule that, by 1799, his stock of horses had dropped from 130 to 25, but he owned 58 mules. His breeding program and subsequent promotion of the mule as a farm animal led to the early foundation of the Teamster's Union, the famous American mule teams that were used for the transport of commercial freight.

Washington the farmer was also ahead of his time with other livestock, especially sheep, which he raised for both wool and meat. By 1758, his flock numbered about a hundred, making him years ahead of most Virginia planters, and he used selective breeding to improve the flock, which eventually numbered six hundred. He had some particularly horny rams, and he noted in 1766, "Put my English Ram Lamb to 65 Ewes," which is more than double what a typical ram can service today.

Washington's cattle were the Devon milk breed, and he appreciated their versatility—providing not only beef and veal but also milk and its derivative products cream, butter, and cheese. The herd, branded with "GW" on their flanks, generally numbered about 150, and an additional 26 or so were draft oxen used to work plows and wagons and thus were not slaughtered for food. He built a small dairy near the mansion house kitchen, but it was not successful, and in 1799, he complained because he actually was "obliged to buy butter for the use of my family."

Much like the swine of the conquistadors, more than two hundred years before his time, Washington's hogs ran wild, foraging for acorns in the forests surrounding Mount Vernon. When they weighed at least 140 pounds, the slaves rounded them up, penned them for fattening, and then slaughtered them. Washington kept precise records of the slaughter; in December 1785, for example, 128 hogs were slaughtered, for a total meat weight of seventeen thousand pounds. After a ton of that meat was distributed to overseers and preferred workers, seven and a half tons were left for the slaves, Washington's family, "and the poor who are distressed for it." The raw meat was converted into ham, bacon, salt pork, sausage, chitterlings, lard, and scrapple. Washington regularly gave meat to his slaves, unlike many plantation owners, who only provided vegetables and grains, forcing their slaves to hunt game for any meat they consumed.

Washington had a smokehouse, and when he was home, he personally supervised the making of hams and bacon to make certain that the quality was good enough to serve to the many guests who came to Mount Vernon. He did not want Martha to be embarrassed because "Virginia Ladies value themselves on the goodness of their bacon," he wrote to Lafayette in 1786.

Occasionally a thief would break into the smokehouse and steal a ham or two, usually at night. The most famous of all the thieves was named Vulcan, and he operated during the day. He ran into the Mount Vernon dining room and stole a ham right off the table. The servants chased him out of the house and onto the lawn, where he dropped the ham. The servants recovered it, but no one would eat it. Martha was quite irritated, but Washington thought the incident was hilarious and loved to tell and retell the story of his ham-loving hound Vulcan.

Poultry for the kitchen and table was another important element of the farmyard at Mount Vernon, but Washington was not content with just chickens. He also raised turkeys, ducks, and geese for their meat and eggs. Because he was the most famous man in America, he was also the recipient of fowl gifts from notable personalities, such as a Chinese goose and gander from the first Episcopal bishop of Virginia, David Griffith, and Chinese pheasants from Lafayette's Royal Aviary.

The Garden Lover

Immediately upon his retirement, Washington wrote to Dr. James Anderson in 1797: "I am once more seated under my own Vine and Fig-tree, and hope to spend the remainder of my days…in peaceful retirement, making political pursuits yield to the more rational amusement of cultivating the earth." For his visual pleasure, Washington built an extensive flower garden that several slaves tended full-time, but the most important gardens and groves were planted to help feed his family. Brick walls enclosed the lower vegetable garden to keep out marauding animals such as deer, which can be particularly destructive to crops.

On the basis of advice from his library of gardening books, Washington had a planned planting cycle that ran from late fall, when the beds were cleared and compost spread over them, to the following early fall, when most of the root crops and vegetables had been harvested. Root vegetables, beans, and peas were sowed first, usually in March, followed by cabbage, cauliflower, and celery. By April, asparagus had sprouted from the ground, followed by fresh strawberries and lettuce in May. Other garden crops, such as onions, eggplants, cucumbers, artichokes, and peppers were harvested as they ripened during the summer months.

As did Jefferson, Washington planted a vineyard of both native and imported grapes, starting in 1771. Despite having planted more than two thousand cuttings, he didn't have much luck with them (because the war interfered with their proper care), and around 1780, he turned the four-acre vineyard into a nursery for trials for new varieties of grains, fodder crops such as milo and sorghum, and peas. He planted a "fruit garden," as he called it, and he used Phillip Miller's *Gardener's Dictionary* (London, 1771) as a guide for growing pears, apples, plums, apricots, peaches, and cherries.

Washington wanted to have fresh fruits and vegetables available in

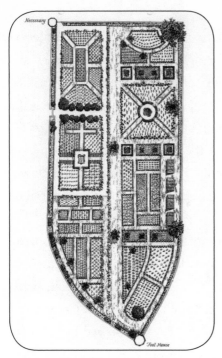

Plan of Lower Garden,
by Morley Jeffers Williams

winter, too, so he drew a sketch for a greenhouse based on one he had seen in Baltimore. He had his workers build it with a rather ingenious system including flues in the floor to provide heat during the winter. The work was finished in 1787, and he started stocking it the next year with tropical plants that were given to him by Mrs. Margaret Carroll, of Mount Clare in Baltimore, who claimed that her own greenhouse was overstocked. To guide him in greenhouse growing techniques, especially of pineapples, Washington had a copy of John Abercrombie's *The Hot-House Gardener* (London, 1789). The first plants were orange and lemon trees and some aloes. Others were added later, such as coffee, lime, and sago palms. During the spring, summer, and early fall, the plants grew in tubs outside in the garden. In the winter, a slave who lived in the adjacent stove room tended the fire to keep the greenhouse warm.

The Modern Miller

Farming was hardly a hobby; it was a business, and Washington was good at it. His financial success was a result not so much of growing a crop and selling the harvest but of turning that crop into a value-added commodity.

To do that, he had to take risks and invest money in his projects, just as entrepreneurs have always done. In Washington's case, his first value-added commodity was flour made from his own wheat. When he inherited Mount Vernon, it came with a gristmill that

The reconstructed greenhouse at Mount Vernon

his father, Augustine, had probably built, but it was in bad shape. In 1771, he built a new gristmill with two state-of-the-art millstones fashioned from imported French buhrstone, which was so hard that the millstones could produce superfine, premium-quality flour.

The new millstones, combined with a new millrace (a water canal combining two nearby streams to power the millstone) and new hoisting gear and sifters enabled the mill to produce three distinct products: superfine flour, shorts (bran, germ, and coarse meal), and bran—the husks of the wheat, rye, and oats being milled that was sifted from the flour. Washington thus could mill his own grain to make flour, buy grain from his neighbors and mill it, and lease the mill to others for a fee of one-eighth of the grain being milled. In June 1771, he sold 128,000 pounds of flour in 426 barrels to Robert Adams & Co. in Alexandria, who then shipped half of the flour to Jamaica via a West Indies trader in Norfolk, Virginia.

Ever the innovator, Washington had his manager William Pearce conduct experiments to determine whether flour was more profitable than unprocessed grain (it was), and he eagerly embraced new technology.

In 1790, a farmer and inventor in Delaware, Oliver Evans, another inadvertent founding foodie, received U.S. Patent No. 3 for an automated mill that greatly reduced the workforce needed in mills by using mechanical conveyors powered by the water wheel.

Patent No. 3 was ingenious. In the old-fashioned mill, the miller had to carry the grain up the stairs on his back, one sack at a time, and dump it into a tub, which he then wrestled to the granary, then to a hopper to be screened, and then to another to be ground and emptied into a trough. By the time it was sifted and resacked, the flour had been mixed with a "great quantity of dirt…from the dirty feet of every one who trampled in it, trailing it over the whole Mill and wasting much," as Evans recalled. A great portion of the flour was spoiled, "for people did not even then like to eat dirt, if they could see it."

Early mill designs made no sense, for the traditional mill used four floors to process flour, and not in a top-to-bottom sequence. Grain was cleaned on the top floor, ground on the second, collected on the first, and then hoisted back up to the third to cool and dry. To solve this problem, Evans radically modified several existing devices: a continuous bucket-and-chain elevator powered by the mill wheel, a gravity-powered belt conveyor running over two pulleys, and a horizontal conveyor that used the ancient Archimedes

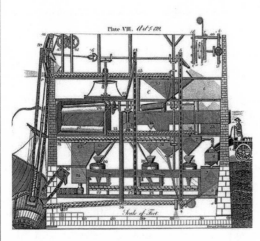

Evans's automated mill, 1790

screw in a close-fitting trough. Evans was the first inventor to use the Archimedes screw to lift dry material, and his automated mill was a continuous manufacturing process.

Evans's design had the grain delivered at a window of the ground floor; then carried to the top floor by waterpower; descended by gravity; and moved by waterpower through all the stages of drying, grinding, spreading, cooling, and sorting. The plan was totally unique in food manufacturing. In the words of Eugene Ferguson, a leading authority on the technology of the early nineteenth century, the combination was a "totally fresh concept of a continuous manufacturing process" and "demonstrated for the first time the fully integrated automatic factory." Bob Shaver, a technology historian, added, "In an Evans mill, the only work the miller had to do was to stop and start the machinery."

After Evans patented his invention, George Washington became one of the first licensees of the mill design, paying a $40 license fee to the inventor. Evans sent his brother and helpers to Mount Vernon in 1791 to install the system in Washington's gristmill, and they were paid for twenty days' work. Patent commissioner and secretary of state, Thomas Jefferson, countersigned the patent and became another early licensee when he switched from growing tobacco to wheat around 1794. Evans went on to write the definitive book on American milling, *The Young Mill-Wright and Miller's Guide*, which went through more than fifteen editions and was revised with the automatic mill design in 1795.

Washington was not finished with his plan to discover more efficient and profitable ways to mill grain into flour. In 1793, Washington designed and built a barn for threshing purposes that was so enormous that it needed sixteen sides. He calculated that 140,000 bricks would be required for the

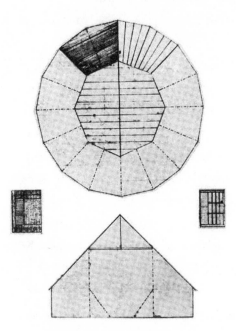

Washington's plan for his sixteen-sided barn

The reconstructed sixteen-sided barn at Mount Vernon

structure, which were made in a kiln at Mount Vernon. The barn was notable for its thirty-square-foot threshing floor, with gaps one and a half inches wide between the floorboards so that the grain, when stepped on by horses, would fall through to the floor below, leaving the straw (or chaff) above. Of course, any farm building is only as good as the workers who use it. Washington complained: "I have one of the most convenient barns in this or perhaps any other country, where thirty hands may with great ease be employed in threshing. Half the wheat of the farm was actually stowed in this barn in the straw by my order, for threshing; notwithstanding, when I came home about the middle of September, I found a treading yard not thirty feet from the barn-door, the wheat again brought out of the barn, and horses treading it out in an open exposure, liable to the vicissitudes of the weather." Historian Paul Haworth summed it up: "I think we may safely conclude that this was one of those rare occasions when George lost his temper and 'went up in the air!'"

The barn, which was so well built that it lasted well into the nineteenth century, was considered a milestone of American farm architecture. Curiously, Washington's records do not reveal how efficient it was for threshing. It was also used to store farm and garden food crops, such as turnips and potatoes.

Paul Haworth summed up Washington as a farmer in 1915:

He was one of the first American experimental agriculturists, always alert for better methods, willing to take any amount of pains to find the best fertilizer, the best way to avoid plant diseases, the best methods of cultivation, and he once declared that he had little patience with those content to tread the ruts their fathers trod. If he were alive today, we may be sure that he would be an active worker in farmers' institutes, an eager visitor to agricultural colleges, a reader of scientific reports and an enthusiastic promoter of anything tending to better American farming and farm life.

Washington strongly believed in the new viability of American farms and wrote to his good friend Lafayette in 1788, "I hope, some day or another we shall become a storehouse and granary for the world."

THE FOUNDING FISHERMAN

Washington was very fond of fish and a sport fisherman who liked to eat his catch. Bill Mares, who wrote *Fishing with the Presidents*, called him the "First

Angler" and documented many of his sport fishing excursions. Historian Paul Haworth, in his book, *George Washington: Farmer* (1915), noted:

> When on his eastern tour of 1789 he went outside the harbor of Portsmouth to fish for cod, but the tide was unfavorable and they caught only two. More fortunate was a trip off Sandy Hook the next year, which was thus described by a newspaper: "Yesterday afternoon the President of the United States returned from Sandy Hook and the fishing banks, where he had been for the benefit of the sea air, and to amuse himself in the delightful recreation of fishing. We are told he has had excellent sport, having himself caught a great number of sea-bass and black fish—the weather proved remarkably fine, which, together with the salubrity of the air and wholesome exercise, rendered this little voyage extremely agreeable."

Washington was also a commercial fisherman, and during his fishing heyday, he owned waterfront property that ran for about ten miles along the Potomac River. During the spring, as herring and shad swam up the Potomac and its tributaries, Washington had his slaves, plus indentured servants and overseers, net tens of thousands of fish with seines that were about twelve feet long. Washington allowed the poor people who lived near Mount Vernon to fish from his shoreline if they first received permission from one of the overseers. It was a very organized enterprise, as Haworth reported: "Herring and shad were the chief fish caught and when the run came the seine was carried well out into the river in a boat and then hauled up on the shelving beach either by hand or with a windlass operated by horse-power. There were warehouses and vats for curing the fish, a cooper shop and buildings for sheltering the men." The fish were cleaned, salted down, and packed into barrels that would feed the slaves at Mount Vernon over the rest of the year.

But Washington had farther-reaching goals than merely feeding his slaves. He purchased larger seine nets made of high-quality material that measured twenty feet long and salt in quantity and lengths of nautical lines to haul in the catches. Many of the nets were strung together to make a seine five hundred feet long. The plan worked, and a visitor to Mount Vernon, Julian Neimcewicz, reported a catch of a hundred thousand herring in a single day. Washington rewarded his hardworking men with a pint of rum a day.

After packing enough food for the slaves, most of the catch was shipped to the West Indies (1.5 million herring in 1772, worth £184). To accomplish this, Washington hired Captain Lawrence Sanford of the brig *Swift* to ship the salted fish to Jamaica starting in 1769. Washington hired other captains as well to ship fish to the West Indies, but collecting money from them sometimes proved to be a challenge. In 1773, he sued Daniel Adams, but instead of money, he received the brigantine *Fairfax* as compensation, which he renamed, appropriately, *Farmer*. It was promptly loaded with salted herring and sent back to the West Indies.

Of all of Washington's entrepreneurial operations, fishing was consistently the most profitable. He enjoyed dining on fish as well. Some sources say that his favorite fish was shad, but whether that preference was the result of the fish's impact on his wallet or his taste buds remains a mystery.

Cooking Shad

Shad is very bony, so it's difficult to imagine that cooks and diners preferred it to the more delectable fish that inhabited the same rivers. In my opinion, the roe is the best part of the fish, so I searched for references to shad roe in books and magazines from 1750 to 1900 and discovered that American cooks didn't think much of shad roe as a food in the early days. The first recipe I could find

was published in 1845, and most citations detailed using shad roe as bait
for the rockfish, or striped bass, which is not nearly as bony.
Frank Forester, writing in Graham's American Monthly Magazine *in*
1850, called the striped bass a "noble fish, a member of a tribe known in
almost every region of the globe, [that] is, as an individual, peculiar to the
waters of North America." He then detailed how to transform shad roe into
bait to catch this fish: "The roe of the female fish—that is the hard roe—
must be taken, cleaned, washed, and washed again, and then potted down
with two ounces of salt to every half pound of roe, pressed close into a stone
pot and hermetically sealed." After three months, the roe was ready to be cut
out of the pot "like cheese," and fashioned to the hook with "light-colored
floss silk, or raveled hemp."
Shad roe graduated from bait to fine-dining status around 1880. Maria Parloa,
who was the founder of the original cooking schools in Boston and New York
and a popular cookbook author, published several excellent shad recipes in her
1887 cookbook Miss Parloa's Kitchen Companion.

Maria Parloa's Shad Roe Baked with Cream Sauce, 1887

For six persons use the roe from two fishes. Wash them, and put them
in a stew-pan with one table-spoonful of salt and enough boiling water
to cover them. Cook for ten minutes, and then put them into a bowl
of cold water for an equal period. On removing them from the water
at the end of that time cut them in slices about half an inch thick. Put
two table-spoonfuls of butter in a frying-pan, and set the pan on the
stove. When the butter becomes hot, add two level table-spoonfuls of
flour. Stir until the flour becomes brown; then draw the pan back to a

cooler place, and gradually pour into it one pint of milk, stirring all the time. Add a teaspoonful of salt and half a teaspoonful of pepper. Boil up once; then pour into a bowl, and set in a warm place.

Butter a tin plate, and place the roe on it. Season well with salt and pepper. Pour four table-spoonfuls of the sauce over the roe, and then bake them in a moderately hot oven for three-quarters of an hour, basting every fifteen minutes with the sauce and dredging lightly with salt and pepper. Five minutes before the roe are done, pour upon the plate any of the sauce that may remain in the bowl at that time. Serve on a warm dish.

THE FOUNDING FOOD HOST AND HIS "WELL-RESORTED TAVERN"

On February 15, 1787, just before he left Virginia to preside over the Constitutional Convention in Philadelphia, George Washington wrote to his mother, Mary, and told her in no uncertain terms that she would not live with him and Martha at Mount Vernon: "I am sure, and candor requires me to say, [living here] will never answer your purposes in any shape whatever," he stated. "For in truth it may be compared to a well-resorted tavern, as scarcely any strangers who are going from north to south, or from south to north do not spend a day or two at it." Even with that description, Washington did not reveal how much more Mount Vernon was like a free hotel with an open bar and a fancy dining room than a tavern. Nearly two-thirds of dinner guests also spent at least one night in the Mount Vernon guest rooms.

It has been estimated that between 1768 and 1775 alone, the Washingtons hosted, fed, entertained, and prepared guest rooms for about two thousand people, or twenty-four guests per month. Later years were even more hectic, with up to 677 people a year descending on Mount Vernon and eating the Washingtons out of house, home, and wine cellar. Of course, it was partially the fault of the Washingtons, because they subscribed to the Southern—and particularly Virginian—tradition of hosting guests lavishly. As historian Bruce Chadwick described, in "hospitality-mad Virginia family reputations were established by the number of signatures in their visitors' books." Some families were so eager for visitors that they assigned slaves to nearby highways to invite strangers to the house for dinner and drinks. One Mount Vernon guest described the food he was served: "Leg of boiled pork, goose, roast beef, mutton chops, hommony, cabbage, potatoes, pickles, fried tripe, and onions," and for dessert, "mince pies, tarts, cheese, nuts, apples, raisins." The Washingtons spared no expense in hosting their guests.

Washington's most famous guest was undoubtedly his good friend Lafayette, who stayed with him in 1784 after Washington invited him to visit in a letter. Lafayette could not resist the invitation and sailed from Le Havre on July 1. Lafayette arrived in New York, then traveled to Mount Vernon, where he stayed from August 17 through August 29 and again from November 24 to 28. During one of the visits, Washington presented Lafayette with a badge of the Order of the Cincinnati. Pierre L'Enfant, who had designed the plan for the city of Washington, D.C., had designed the emblem. In late November, George Washington rode with Lafayette to Annapolis, where there were additional ceremonies before Lafayette departed on his own to New York. Although there are no significant written records of what transpired at Mount Vernon during Lafayette's visit, it is more than likely that Washington brought out the best of his elaborate dining for his friend.

The busy kitchen at Mount Vernon turned out three meals a day despite the number of guests. Breakfast was served at seven in the morning, dinner at three in the afternoon, and tea at six. Sometimes a light supper was prepared for about nine at night. Frank Lee, the mansion

Restored Mount Vernon kitchen, c. 1915

house butler, was married to Lucy, the main cook, and they lived in an apartment over the kitchen. They were assisted by a number of scullions, who lived in various places on the estate, hauled water and wood, washed dishes and cooking utensils, and helped with food preparation. General Washington's step-granddaughter, Nelly Custis Lewis, described his typical breakfast: "He rose before sunrise, always wrote or read until 7 in summer or half past seven in winter. His breakfast was then ready—he ate three small mush cakes (Indian meal) swimming in butter and honey, and drank three cups of tea without cream." Overseeing all food preparation was Martha Washington, who had a handwritten cookbook passed down by her mother as a guide. *The Martha Washington Cookbook,* by Marie Kimball, was first published in 1940 by Coward-McCann and has been in print ever since. The title of the book has led to the misconception that Martha was a cookbook author, and this is not the case. In 1981, Columbia University Press published Karen Hess's *Martha Washington's Booke of Cookery,* and the real story of Martha Washington and food was finally told. Hess wrote an astonishing work of food history and scholarship, working from the original text of "this seventeenth-century English recipe manuscript which was in the possession of Martha Washington for fifty years." She cleared up any notion that Martha wrote it: "By the time the manuscript came into the hands of Martha Custis in 1749, I think that it had long since become a family heirloom."

From the Cookbook Manuscript Used at Mount Vernon

To Bake a Rumpe of Beef

After yr rumpe of beef is salted over night, take time, parsley, winter savory, pot margerum & a little penneroyall; chop ye hearbs wth youlks of hard eggs, & put in a little grated bread, salt & a good piece of butter; stuff yr beefe well wth these, yn put it in a earthen pot with a little water, some pepper & an ounion or 2 slyced & some pickt time, parsley & winter savory. Then make up ye pot very close wth paste & set it in ye oven wth houshould bread, & when it is baked, put yr beef in a dish wth while bread sops & poure ye liquor on it.

Martha, in her late fifties when George retired, was in charge not only of the cooking but also of slave management, production of all clothes and quilts, chopping of wood for the fires, the plantation dairy, soap making, hog killing, the resulting ham smoking and lard making, the garden, treatment of the sick, and (of course) caring for her children and husband. She was a very busy woman who carried a ring with several dozen keys to the buildings on the plantation and the rooms in the Mansion House—she was definitely in charge of things.

By the early 1790s, Washington was grumbling about money. "Those who owe me money cannot or will not pay me without suit," he wrote. He tried to sell off some of his land to raise cash, but he could not find any buyers who would give him a fair price. Washington was not in any danger of bankruptcy from all the guests he hosted, for on paper he was still a very wealthy man. But his wealth was tied up in land, and he, like many other Southern planters, was cash poor. But that would soon change as his true entrepreneurial talents began to shine in his later years.

THE FOUNDING FERMENTER

George Washington was a devoted beer lover. He loved the dark, English-style brew known as porter and always demanded that a good supply of it be kept on hand at Mount Vernon. Immediately after the Revolutionary War, American brewers began to make porter, and Washington made a point of "buying American" when he wrote to Lafayette in 1789: "We have already been too long subject to British prejudices. I use no porter or cheese in my family, but such is made in America: both these articles may now be purchased of good quality." However, it was not porter but rather "small beer," or home brew, for which Washington penned an early recipe that is in a notebook of his in the manuscript collection of the New York Public Library.

To Make Small Beer, by George Washington, 1757

Take a large Siffer [Sifter] full of Bran Hops to your Taste. —Boil these 3 hours then strain out 30 Gall[ons] into a cooler put in 3 Gall[ons] Molasses while the Beer is Scalding hot or rather draw the Melasses into the cooler & St[r]ain the Beer on it while boiling Hot. [L]et this stand till it is little more than Blood warm then put in a quart of Yea[s]t. [I]f the Weather is very Cold cover it over with a Blank[et] & let it Work in the Cooler 24 hours then put it into the Cask—leave the bung open till it is almost don[e] Working—Bottle it that day Week it was Brewed.

In 1796, again seeking to diversify his plantation income, Washington hired James Anderson as his plantation manager. Anderson, a Scottish immigrant, was an experienced distiller and began to persuade his boss to make whiskey at Mount Vernon. It was a good idea, considering the attitude of the general public at the time. People were tired of rum because of its connection with the British production of molasses in the West Indies and more and more were turning to whiskey that was distilled from U.S.-grown grain. Whiskey was easier to transport than bulky grain that tended to spoil, and that fact combined with heavy immigration of Irish and Scottish men familiar with distilling whiskey, proved to be a windfall for a burgeoning new industry. Washington agreed with Anderson's plan and a small cooperage next to the gristmill was converted into a distillery with two stills.

James Anderson was a successful immigrant and another unsung foodie hero who added to the evolution of American food and drink. Washington was clear that the distillery was Anderson's idea: "Mr. Anderson has engaged me in a distillery, on a small scale, and is very desirous of encreasing [*sic*] it: assuring me from his own experience in this country, and in Europe," Washington wrote in 1797. Anderson, when "applying" for the plantation manager job, wrote two letters to Washington that described his experience. He was born in 1745 and grew up on his father's farm, forty miles north of Edinburgh, near the village of Inverkeithing, Scotland. At first, he was a farmer's apprentice, then a farm manager, and finally he farmed grains on his own land and sold them to distillers. But often they failed to pay him, causing him and his family to immigrate to the United States.

They landed in Norfolk, Virginia, in late 1790 or early 1791; moved north; and rented a farm near Mount Vernon. Anderson worked as a manager for a small plantation. Then they moved south near Fredericksburg, Virginia, in 1795 to manage Salvington, the Selden family plantation. Anderson described Salvington as 1,700 acres with twenty-five slaves and a distillery, "which I also conduct." This was his only experience running a distillery before he established Washington's. In Scotland, he only grew and processed grain for large distilleries.

Little is known about Salvington's distillery. At the time in Virginia, distilleries generally had two or three stills and were about one thousand square feet in size. Mount Vernon's distillery had five stills and was more than two thousand square feet, making it considerably larger. In fact, the distillery that Anderson convinced Washington to build was one of the largest distilleries of the time. Anderson may have used the larger distilleries in Scotland as a model for the Mount Vernon operation.

It was a simple process to make the whiskey: crushed corn, rye, and malted barley were poured into tubs of hot water, where fermentation from added yeast converted the starches in the grain to sugar. Soon after, the fermented mash was poured into the bowls of the stills and the bowls were heated. The alcohol in the fermented mash, with a lower boiling point than water, evaporated first and then condensed in tubes as it rose from the bowls—when collected it was a moonshine called whiskey. Just a month after the primitive distillery was installed, Anderson had barreled and stored eighty gallons of whiskey. Over the following year, he produced six hundred gallons—enough to convince him to approach Washington to expand the operation by buying three more stills for $640 and building a new and larger distillery.

Washington consulted with his friend, the rum distiller John Fitzgerald in Alexandria, and Fitzgerald gave his enthusiastic endorsement of the plan. "As I have no doubt but Mr. Anderson understands the Distillation of Sprit from Grain," he wrote to Washington, "I cannot hesitate in my Opinion that it might be carried on to great advantage on your Estate." He went on to estimate that if the quality of the whiskey was good, the proposed distillery could sell ten times as much as was then being produced. Washington took Fitzgerald's advice, and in the latter part of 1797, construction began on a 2,250-square-foot stone building. Soon three copper stills were installed, along with fifty mash tubs and slop coolers so that the spent mash could be converted to feed for the 150 pigs and 30 cattle at Mount Vernon. Washington paid Anderson his highest compliment on June 11, 1798: "I believe you are a man of strict integrity; sobriety; industry & zeal."

The three stills had a capacity of 616 gallons of mash, and the distillery included brick furnaces to heat it and a large storage cellar to store it away from the "undesirable types" that Washington had feared might be very interested in the whiskey business. The result of the expansion was a radical increase in whiskey production. The 600 gallons produced in 1797 became 4,500 gallons in 1798 and 11,000 gallons in 1799—profits zoomed from £83 to £600 in 1799. But the distillery quickly depleted Mount Vernon's supply of grain and the plantation's capacity to produce it, and Washington faced unplanned expenses of purchasing grain from his neighbors or buying it at the Alexandria market price. But he mostly solved the problem through barter—he traded whiskey for grain.

Washington realized the need for varying qualities of his whiskey to satisfy each of his 270 customers. He not only began using cinnamon and persimmon as flavorings but also soon had six other whiskeys: common, rectified, fine rectified, rectified fourth proof, strong proof, and rye whiskey. He also produced small quantities of apple and peach brandies and rum. He sold the varied alcoholic beverages to intermediaries who in turn resold it to their own clients, and he traded them for salt, mustard, butter, molasses, oysters, and other commodities—such as clover seed, candles, tar and "soal [sole] leather," and even the services of his own physician.

Sarah McCarty Chichester's 1799 purchase shows how the barter system worked. Chichester, one of Washington's neighbors, purchased seven thousand herring, thirty-two gallons of whiskey, and one barrel of flour, with a combined value of $32.78. In exchange, she traded 603 barrels of corn and 243 bushels of wheat, valued at $785.38. The difference in the value was credited to her account.

Washington's best whiskey customer was his close friend George Gilpin, who owned a store in nearby Alexandria where he sold the whiskey. Many of the people who worked at Mount Vernon also purchased whiskey, which cost about fifty cents a gallon for the common stuff and a dollar a gallon for the rectified and four-times distilled, finer quality. The whiskey was not aged or bottled, and the colorless spirits were transported and sold in wooden barrels and kegs of varying sizes. Washington, in an early letter to Lafayette, described his retirement at Mount Vernon:

I have not only retired from all public employments, but am retiring within myself, and shall be able to view the solitary walk, and tread the paths of private life, with heart-felt satisfaction. Envious of none, I am determined to be pleased with all; and this, my dear friend, being the order of my march, I will move gently down the stream of life, until I sleep with my fathers.

The distillery was at the height of its production when Washington died on December 14, 1799, and ownership passed on to Lawrence Washington, his nephew. The Andersons—father and son—ran the operation for the next four years until they were dismissed, and Lawrence

Reconstructed distillery at Mount Vernon (Courtesy: Sunbelt Archives)

then leased it out at least until 1808, when it was closed and partially dismantled to provide building materials for local homes. In 1814, what little that remained burned to the ground. It was a sad end to the largest distillery in the Chesapeake Bay area and perhaps the country, and certainly one of the largest producers of its time. However, the partially dismantled and burned distillery would eventually be resurrected.

Mount Vernon officials began considering reconstruction of the distillery in the mid-1990s in conjunction with the plan to reconstruct Washington's gristmill. Archeological work began in 1997, and workers found the remnants of five of the copper pot stills. Reconstruction began soon afterward, and

Vendome Copper and Brassworks of Louisville, Kentucky, fabricated five copper stills that are replicas of eighteenth-century stills now in the collection of the Smithsonian Institution. The Treasury Department had confiscated them in 1940 in Fairfax County, Virginia.

Funded by a $2.1 million grant from the Distilled Spirits Council of the United States, with the support of the Wine and Spirits Wholesalers of America, reconstruction began in 2000, using post-colonial-era tools and techniques. "Mortise-and-tenon joints; hand-hewn and pit-sawn timbers; mortar joint stonework; and, sandstone blocks of the same variety used by George Washington himself are some of colonial-era techniques we're employing in the reconstruction," said John O'Rourke, Mount Vernon's head restoration carpenter, as construction began. "This will not simply be an interpretation of the historic distilling process, but of historic building crafts, too," he added.

The new distillery was dedicated on September 27, 2006, and opened to the public in March 2007. It is the gateway to the American Whiskey Trail, which encompasses historic distilling-related sites in New York, Pennsylvania, Virginia, Kentucky, and Tennessee. Mount Vernon is the only historic site in the country able to show the distilling process from crop to finished product. Mount Vernon's first renewed attempt at distilling was during the summer of 2007; it produced about a dozen gallons, using a recipe of 60 percent rye, 35 percent corn, and 5 percent barley. Unlike Washington's original spirits, however, this production was aged.

Visitors to the distillery can watch costumed distillers operating the copper stills, stirring mash tubs, and managing the boiler as they demonstrate the methods of postcolonial distilling. The reconstructed distillery is a remarkable tribute to the entrepreneurial Founding Fermenter.

Chapter Four

DIPLOMACY, SLAVERY, AND

HAUTE CUISINE IN PARIS

Clearly, Jefferson's years in Paris made a permanent imprint on his food habits.
— FOOD HISTORIAN DAMON LEE FOWLER

Thomas Jefferson was an architect, archaeologist, author, inventor, horticulturist, statesman, politician, violinist, diplomat, wine expert, and founder of the University of Virginia. Some sources describe him as "polymath and president," putting *polymath* first. Jefferson's political achievements included election to the Continental Congress, governor of Virginia, U.S. minister plenipotentiary to France, U.S. secretary of state, U.S. vice president, and U.S. president (two terms). A polymath (from the Greek *polymathes*, or "very learned") is a person of great and varied knowledge, especially one having proficiency and competence in multiple fields of study. Thus, a polymath is the epitome of the Renaissance man or woman.

But being a polymath had some drawbacks for Jefferson. Often, he was more interested in his multiple hobbies than in his dual careers of farming and politics. In the fall of 1777, Jefferson left Philadelphia and returned to Virginia, where he served in the House of Delegates before he was elected governor of Virginia in 1779. As governor, it was not a happy time for Jefferson. He sent Virginia's best troops off on a useless mission against Detroit, leaving Virginia mostly undefended. His Federalist enemies constantly criticized him and threatened to impeach him; his daughter, Lucy Elizabeth, died; and his perilous financial shortfalls constantly troubled him.

Jefferson's situation worsened in June 1781, when the British Army came to Monticello to capture him and the entire Virginia legislature. These troops were part of the British Army under the "execrable traitor" Benedict Arnold, in the words of B. L. Rayner, who wrote *Life of Thomas Jefferson* in 1834. Arnold had just sacked Richmond, burned the armament magazine there, and forced the governor and the legislature to move the state government to the Swan Tavern in Charlottesville. Arnold's success had prompted General Cornwallis to send Lieutenant Colonel Banastre Tarleton and his men on a mission to capture Jefferson, the famous and notorious (to the British) author of the Declaration of Independence, and the entire Virginia legislature, including Patrick Henry. Fortunately, Jack Jouett, the "Paul Revere of Virginia," overheard the plans of the British at the Cuckoo Tavern and rode all night to Monticello to warn Jefferson that, once again, "the British were coming."

According to legend, Jefferson offered Jouett a glass of Madeira for breakfast and then ordered him to ride to the Swan Tavern and warn the rest of the legislators. Jefferson then sent his family away in a carriage, had a "leisurely breakfast," and fled Monticello on a horse ten minutes before the British cavalry arrived. His flight would later result in what the biographer Fawn Brodie described as a "charge of cowardice, like an evil shadow, [which] would follow him through his life." Most people, including General Washington, discounted that charge and thought that Jefferson did the only sensible thing. Although the British captured seven legislators, they did not burn Monticello or kill Jefferson's slaves. However, when Cornwallis reached Jefferson's Elkhill Plantation, in what Jefferson called "that spirit of total extermination," he burned the barns, crops, and fences and seized the slaves, cattle, sheep, Calcutta hogs, and horses.

Considering his financial predicament, his retirement as governor, followed by the death of his wife, Martha, in September 1782, it is not surprising that Jefferson jumped at the chance to escape to Paris. There, with a nice salary for a change, he could immerse himself in society, food, wine, and sightseeing. When he was appointed minister to France, where he would join Benjamin Franklin and John Adams, he did not hesitate to accept the position. As Brodie noted, "France for Thomas Jefferson was in every sense a liberation."

Virginia Tavern Fare

Rural taverns in Virginia were a combination of a bar, an inn, a watering station for horses, and a restaurant of sorts. But the bars did not have bottles, the sleeping accommodations were blankets on the floor in front of the fire (or the front lawn in the summer), and the food was whatever the tavern keeper felt like cooking on a given day.

"In each tavern, there was a room where liquors were sold, which were drawn direct from cask, or jug, as called for…They consisted mainly of whiskeys, rum, apple and peach brandies, and ales," noted James McDonald in his 1907 book *Life in Old Virginia*. The author, who claimed that the mint julep was invented in Virginia, not Kentucky, commented on tavern food: "Side dishes were an unknown quantity in the old time tavern. A whole roast pig, turkey, goose, or ham, a quarter of lamb, or roast of beef, were placed within easy reach of the guest and he was invited, and expected, to help himself."

AMERICA'S FIRST FRENCH CHEF: THE CULINARY EDUCATION OF THE SLAVE JAMES HEMINGS

Four years before Washington's farewell dinner at City Tavern, Jefferson was part of the committee for Washington's formal resignation as commander in chief and helped plan the dinner for two hundred people at Mann's Tavern in Annapolis, Maryland, on Monday, December 21, 1783, just before Washington's resignation ceremony, which was held at the State House on December 23. Jefferson was in Annapolis with James Monroe, working on the articles for peace with England as proposed by Benjamin Franklin, John Adams, and John Jay. Jefferson was also waiting for the British blockade of East Coast harbors to be lifted so that he could join Franklin in Paris as a commissioner. Jefferson and Monroe were staying at a Mr. Dulany's house and taking their meals at Mann's Tavern, where a French chef by the name of Partout served them beef, turkey, duck, veal, and oysters washed down with hard cider and wine.

Annapolis was all abuzz about Washington's visit. The *Maryland Gazette* reported his arrival in their Christmas issue of 1783, noting that he was staying at "Mr. Mann's" and was given a public dinner at Mann's, "where upwards of two hundred persons of distinction were present; everything being provided by Mr. Mann in the most elegant and profuse stile [*sic*]." That "stile" proved to be forty-nine gallons of claret, thirty-five gallons of port, thirty-two gallons of Madeira, and six gallons of "spirits." The total cost for the dinner was 644 colonial dollars. Following the dinner, a formal ball was held for Washington by the General Assembly at the "illuminated" State House.

Shortly after the big party, on January 14, 1784, the articles for peace were ratified, becoming the Treaty of Paris, and officially ending the hostilities with England (for a while, anyway). On May 7, Jefferson was reappointed as a commissioner to France, joining Benjamin Franklin and John Adams.

The future president, then forty-one, did some traveling and sightseeing, finally arriving in Boston on June 18. There his eleven-year-old daughter Martha (called Patsy) and his eighteen-year-old slave James Hemings joined him. Together, the three of them, along with forty-eight bottles of Hock, a German white wine, sailed for Paris aboard the *Ceres* on July 5.

After a brief stop in England, Jefferson arrived in Paris, moved into temporary residence at Hôtel d'Orléans, and enrolled Martha in the fashionable convent school Panthemont. During his first month at the hotel, he bought more than 250 bottles of wine, including dessert wines, Madeira, and eighteen dozen bottles of Bordeaux along with wineglasses, dinner plates, and cutlery in preparation of finding a more permanent residence. Four days after he arrived, he visited Benjamin Franklin in the suburb of Passy, where they enjoyed a typical Franklin dinner: a joint of beef, veal, and mutton; fowl; two vegetables with butter; pickles; relishes; and a great variety of desserts, including fruits, cheeses, bonbons, and ice cream. Wines from Franklin's 1,100-bottle cellar included Bordeaux, Burgundies, sparkling champagnes, and a variety of sherries.

Around the same time, John Adams arrived with his wife, Abigail; daughter Abigail; and son John Quincy, then seventeen. After they were settled, Jefferson and his daughter joined the Adams family for dinner "in the French style" with Thomas Barclay, the American consul general. Wife Abigail described it in a letter: "The men never sat down but walked around the room with their swords on and their small silk hats under their arms. At dinner the ladies and gentlemen are mixed, and you converse with him who sits next to you, rarely speaking to persons across the table…When the food was served, conversations diminished 'til we had finished our ice cream. When the wine began to pass around the table, all their tongues began to be in motion."

After two months in temporary hotel quarters, Jefferson moved to the Cul-de-Sac Taitbout near the Champs-Élysées and began buying furnishings. All his food was catered in, because James Hemings was away learning French cuisine (and the language) as an apprentice to Jefferson's *traiteur,* or "caterer," a man named Combeaux who was also a restaurant keeper in the city. In May 1785, Jefferson was named minister to France, a much more important position than commissioner. He would succeed Benjamin Franklin, and to celebrate his new position, he gave an elaborate dinner that was attended by Franklin, Lafayette, the Adamses, John Paul Jones, and many French notables. Undoubtedly, Combeaux and his assistant, James Hemings, catered the event.

After Hemings's apprenticeship with Combeaux ended in early 1786, he apprenticed under the chefs at the estate of Chantilly a few hours from Paris, which the prince Louis-Joseph de Bourbon owned. Historian and Hemings family expert Annette Gordon-Reed observed, "Chantilly had been known since the days of Louis XIV, who dined, there, for the sumptuous meals the prince's cooks prepared. Hemings was indeed learning with a master, with results that extended beyond his lifetime and live on in recipes that survive at Monticello today."

Jefferson was charged twelve francs a day for the instruction, food, and lodging for Hemings, who was living in extravagant circumstances with a member of the French royal family.

Indeed, Hemings was living a charmed life. Not only was Jefferson paying all his expenses, food, and clothing and giving him an allowance, Hemings had freedom of movement and could do anything he wanted in his spare time. He was also a free man now, because France adhered to the freedom principle, which held that anyone who set foot on French soil, even a slave from another country, was free. Hemings however, knew the limitations of being black anywhere and, as he worked for the kindly Jefferson, decided there was no need to run away. Jefferson was supposed to register his name with local authorities so they could keep track of which blacks were in their country, but he never did.

On July 15, 1787, Hemings's sister Sally arrived with Jefferson's youngest daughter, Mary. Sally was then fourteen and Mary was nine. Sally's arrival further freed Hemings and relieved Jefferson of much of the responsibility for the day-to-day supervision of his daughters, allowing him to travel around Europe finding new wines and foods. However, it would also start rumors about Sally's relationship with Jefferson that last to this day.

After his apprenticeships ended, Hemings was hired as *chef de cuisine* at the Hôtel de Langeac in October 1788, an extraordinary position for a young American. He had, in effect, moved from a position of slave-servant to the supervisor of a kitchen. Jefferson had moved to the hotel, at the corner of the Rue de Berri and Champs-Élysées, in October 1785. He considered this house more worthy of his position and wrote to Abigail Adams just before he moved: "I have at length procured a house in a situation much more pleasing to me than my present. It is at the grille des Champs Elysees, but within the city. It suits me in every circumstance but the price, being dearer than the one I am now in. It has a clever garden to it." In addition to the garden, where Jefferson planted Indian corn and other vegetables, such as sweet potatoes, the hotel had a lovely courtyard—and better still, a large wine cellar.

Despite the opulent food Hemings was preparing for him, Jefferson still missed his familiar Virginia fare, especially the culinary result of de Soto and de Avilés and their hogs: Virginia hams. In November 1787, he wrote to Alexander Donald, his merchant friend in Richmond, "I have taken the liberty of desiring Colo. N. Lewis of Albemarle to send a dozen or two of hams, which the captain who brings them must pretend to be a part of his private stores, or they will be seised [*sic*]." Jefferson never got the hams because his agents in Portsmouth could not find a captain who would risk having his ship seized to satisfy Jefferson's desire for ham. Imported food was considered contraband unless the captain could prove it was part of the ship's provisions for the crew.

This is one of the simpler recipes from Chantilly that James Hemings mastered. It may have been the inspiration for "Bell Fritters" in Mary Randolph's The Virginia Housewife *and was a precursor to the apple fritters served at Monticello.*

Fritters a la Chantilly

Take a pound of flour, three eggs, and a very fresh cream cheese; stir thoroughly together, add a little white wine, an ounce of powdered sugar, and a pinch of salt; plunge a spoonful at a time of the batter into boiling lard, drain, and serve, sprinkled with powdered sugar.

Although it is not known how much influence Jefferson exerted— if any—to help Hemings get the position of *chef de cuisine*, it can be assumed that, because the position was so highly exalted in the realm of Parisian cuisine, Hemings earned it through his education, training, and personality. If Hemings was not the caliber of chef required for the position, the hotel would never have hired him, at the risk of its reputation for fine dining.

Gordon-Reed wrote about the pressure that Hemings was under at the hotel, with his talents on display as Jefferson entertained lavishly, often with thirty or more guests for dinner. And not only did he have to be a star chef in Jefferson's eyes; he also had to dazzle the elite of French society. "The French were as serious about their cuisine as about fashionable attire," she noted. "In fact, the two were closely related, since the presentation of food—the look—took its place alongside taste as a mark of true distinction. Every dish Hemings prepared invited a judgment by a man who was a perfectionist." She also observed that Hemings would "fall prey" to the professional hazard of many chefs under such pressure: heavy drinking.

In addition to Hemings's monthly salary from the hotel, his new position offered him another way to supplement his income. Gordon-Reed wrote, "He also had available to him now one of the traditional perquisites of the chef in great houses, one that could bring him a substantial side income, given the number of people who dined at the Hôtel de Langeac: the right to sell the renderings from the chickens, pork, beef, and any other animals prepared in the kitchen. Nothing was wasted in that era, and there existed a lucrative market in grease and animal skins that might be cast off today."

A few years later, as Jefferson prepared to head back to America, he faced leaving behind Hemings and Sally, who were both free. But Jefferson did not want to lose the cooking services of Hemings, the certified French chef whose training he had paid for. And an additional problem: Sally was pregnant at age sixteen. But by whom?

In turn, Jefferson used his charm and his reputation for honesty with his "servants" to persuade both of the Hemingses to return to America with him. He signed an agreement with Hemings in which he promised him his freedom after he had trained a successor in the techniques of French cooking. For Sally, he promised to free her children (she was pregnant at the time) at the age of twenty-one; she herself would not be freed until Jefferson's death.

We will learn more about Hemings and his culinary accomplishments in America in a subsequent chapter. Meanwhile, Jefferson was on a mission to learn as much about the wines of Europe as he possibly could.

JEFFERSON'S GRAND FOOD AND WINE TOURS

Historians love to speculate about the precise reasons Jefferson left Paris on the last day of February 1787 to visit Burgundy, Bordeaux, and Italy. Was it to find a cure for the sore wrist he broke while flirting with the beautiful but married Maria Cosway? Was it to study classical architecture to model American public buildings after? Was it to tour French ports like Marseilles as possible targets for American exports of tobacco? Was it to learn about European food plants that could be transferred to America? Was it to study the French wine industry as a model for what Jefferson hoped would happen in America?

Perhaps it was all of the above, and as the wine historian John Hailman has observed, "Whatever its motives, the tour changed Jefferson's habits as a wine drinker forever, and was the single greatest factor in his becoming the foremost American wine expert of his age."

Jefferson's European travels were extensive. From 1786 to 1788, he toured England, France, Italy, Holland, and Germany.

England

Jefferson spent six days traveling through London and the rest of England with John Adams. Both men were fond of French wines and had extensive personal collections, and throughout their trip, they managed to spend double on wine what they did on food. The English imposed extremely high duties on French wines, which added to the expense of what Jefferson and Adams drank. The two men bonded over sharing meals and wine, but years later, they would become political enemies.

Jefferson had mixed feelings about England, undoubtedly influenced by the recent war. Regarding English food, Jefferson had defined it for Abigail Adams in a letter sent in 1785, in which he categorized it as uncivilized and suggested that, instead of reforming their churches, they should focus more on reforming their kitchens. He was undoubtedly describing the food he tasted on his brief stop in England before proceeding on to France.

In a letter to John Jay, Jefferson described the eating and wine drinking habits of the Prince of Wales: "He ate half a leg of mutton; did not taste of small dishes; drank Champagne and Burgundy as small beer during dinner, and Bourdeaux after dinner, as the rest of the company. Upon the whole, he ate as much as the other three [put together], and drank two bottles of wine without seeming to feel it."

France

After England, Jefferson's long Continental tour in 1787 was a welcome change of scene. At Aix-en-Provence, the beauty of the countryside entranced Jefferson. He wrote to his secretary in Paris, William Short, "I am now in the land of corn, vine, oil and sunshine. What more can a man ask of heaven? If I should happen to die in Paris, I will beg of you to send me here, and have me exposed to the sun. I am sure it will bring me to life again." According to R. Bowman of the Monticello Research Department, "In 1788, Short followed Jefferson's advice to travel to Italy where he gathered details for making Parmesan cheeses, data on grapes and wine culture, a treatise on silk culture, and a macaroni [spaghetti] mold. According to

Jefferson, Short came back from the trip 'charged like a bee with the honey of wisdom, a blessing to his country and honour to his friends.'"

Along the Riviera and in the Alps, Jefferson found olive trees whose trunks were six feet in diameter, and soon the olive tree topped the list of his most valuable plants, becoming the one that "contributes the most to the happiness of mankind." He wrote to William Drayton, chair of the South Carolina Society for Promoting Agriculture, in 1787:

The olive is a tree the least known in America, and yet the most worthy of being known. Of all the gifts of heaven to man, it is next to the most precious, if it be not the most precious. Perhaps it may claim a preference even to bread, because there is such an infinitude of vegetables, which it renders a proper and comfortable nourishment. In passing the Alps at the Col de Tende, where they are mere masses of rock, wherever there happens to be a little soil, there are a number of olive trees, and a village supported by them.

Take away these trees, and the same ground in corn would not support a single family. A pound of oil which can be bought for three or four pence sterling, is equivalent to many pounds of flesh, by the Quantity of vegetables it will prepare, and render fit and comfortable food. Without this tree, the country of Provence and territory of Genoa would not support one-half, perhaps not one-third, their present inhabitants. The nature of the soil is of little consequence if it be dry. The trees are planted from fifteen to twenty feet apart, and when tolerably good, will yield fifteen or twenty pounds of oil yearly, one with another. There are trees which yield much more. They begin to render good crops at twenty years old, and last till killed by cold, which happens at some time or other, even in their best positions in France. But they put out again from their roots. In Italy, I am told they have trees two hundred years old.

As will be seen in chapter 6, Jefferson became a staunch proponent of olive growing in the United States and shared his ideas with Lafayette.

LAFAYETTE THE AMERICANOPHILE

Lafayette loved all things American. In his house in Paris, Lafayette's children conversed in English, and his servant was a Native American in full native garb, apparently to add an aura of the exotic.

America reciprocated Lafayette's love in odd ways, such as naming a fish after him. Note this definition of Lafayette fish from none other than John Bartlett: "*Leiostomus obliquus*, a delicious sea-fish, which appears in the summer in great abundance at Cape Island on the Jersey coast, and is hence called the Cape May Goody. The name Lafayette Fish, by which it is known in New York and its vicinity, was given it on account of its appearance one summer coinciding with the last visit of General Lafayette to America [1824]." It is also called sea chub, spot, or croaker and is still fished when it swarms in East Coast bays in the United States.

Consuming much more than just olives and vegetables, Jefferson also ate in the French countryside: mutton, poultry, pork, rabbit, and other game, all served with garlic-laden sauces. He washed the food down with inexpensive *vin ordinaire,* which he said was excellent. In Marseilles, he met Henry Bergasse, one of the most important wine merchants in France. Bergasse had Jefferson over for dinner and afterward showed him one of his wine cellars, which was filled with casks holding the equivalent of 1.5 million bottles of wine.

Italy

Near Turin, in the town of Rozzano, Jefferson stayed up all night to observe the making of Parmesan cheese and described the process in his notes. He also studied the icehouses there, which probably gave him suggestions for constructing the one at Monticello. Nearby, in Vercelli, Jefferson wrote, "In the neighborhood of Vercelli begin the rice fields. Poggio, a muletier, who passes every week between Vercelli and Genoa will smuggle a sack of rice for me to Genoa; it being death to export it in that form." The Italians, who had developed a strain of rice that could be grown on dry land rather than flooded paddies, were extremely protective of that strain and declared a penalty of death for anyone caught smuggling it out of the country.

Jefferson succeeded in smuggling the rice out of Italy and sent it to the South Carolina Society for Promoting Agriculture. However, society member Ralph Izard found the rice inferior to what was already being grown there, and fearing an undesirable hybrid, he asked Jefferson not to send any more. Karen Hess discussed this subject in more detail in her book *The Carolina Rice Kitchen*.

JEFFERSON AND THE WAFFLE MYSTERY

In Amsterdam, Jefferson ate oysters and drank chocolate. One night, he and a companion, probably General Frederick Riedsel, ate fifty oysters and drank a bottle and a half of wine. According to his Memorandum Book, Jefferson bought four waffle irons in Amsterdam in 1788, but contemporary claims that

Jefferson's fireplace waffle iron

Jefferson introduced waffles to America are unproven. Food historian Andrew F. Smith has suggested that early Dutch settlers introduced the first waffles to America. They were often served for breakfast topped with creamed chicken or chipped beef. However, the first patent for a waffle maker was not issued until August 24, 1869, so Jefferson may have been the first to bring waffle irons over to America.

THE TOAST OF PARIS SOCIETY: BENJAMIN FRANKLIN AT COURT

Benjamin Franklin wrote about food sporadically; inserted occasional recipes into *Poor Richard's Almanack*; and was particularly fond of beer and wine, despite some of his well-quoted aphorisms. On the one hand there is "Be temperate in wine, in eating, girls, and cloth, or the Gout will seize you and plague you both," and on the other hand is "Beer is living proof that God loves us and wants us to be happy." His wine cellar contained more than a thousand bottles of wine and he wrote to Abbé Morellet in 1779, suggesting that God made wine for our rejoicing and that mankind was destined to drink it because he is able to move the glass to his mouth. "Let us adore and drink," he urged.

Probably influenced by memories of delicious Thanksgiving dinners, Benjamin Franklin was particularly fond of the American turkey, writing to Sarah Bache from Paris in 1784: "For my own part I wish the Bald Eagle had not been chosen as the Representative of our Country. He is a Bird of bad moral Character...For in Truth the Turkey is in Comparison a much more respectable Bird, and withal a true original Native of America. Eagles have been found in all Countries, but the Turkey was peculiar to ours, the first of the Species seen in Europe being brought to France by the Jesuits from Canada, and serv'd up at the Wedding Table of Charles the ninth. He is besides, tho' a little vain and silly, a Bird of Courage, and would not hesitate to attack a Grenadier of the British Guards who should presume to invade his Farm Yard with a red Coat on."

Franklin, who preceded Jefferson as U.S. minister to France, was well respected by Frenchmen for his prowess as an inventor and a diplomat, but it was the women of French society who adored him. Jeanne Louise Henriette Campan, in her 1823 book *Memoirs of Marie Antoinette*, gave this description of Franklin's appearance and reception at court:

Franklin appeared at court in the dress of an American cultivator. His strait un-powdered hair, his round hat, his brown cloth coat, formed a contrast with the laced and embroidered coats, and the powdered and perfumed heads of the courtiers of Versailles. This novelty turned the enthusiastic heads of the women of France. Elegant entertainments were given to Dr. Franklin, who to the reputation of a most skilful physician, added the patriotic virtues which had invested him with the noble character of an apostle of liberty. I was present at one of these entertainments, when the most beautiful woman out of three hundred was selected to place a crown of laurels upon the white head of the American philosopher, and two kisses upon his cheeks.

One legacy of Franklin's days in Paris is the role he played in Parmentier's potato crusades. Antoine-Augustin Parmentier was a French pharmacist and inspector general of the Health Service. He was a very vocal promoter of the potato and famous for his potato-promoting publicity stunts. In 1772, he successfully persuaded the Paris Faculty of Medicine to declare the potato edible. Because the potato was a member of the Solanaceae family, or nightshade, it was incorrectly thought to be as poisonous as the deadly nightshade belladonna. Parmentier was an enthusiastic potato promoter because he believed that as a crop it could end hunger among France's impoverished rural population.

A story in *Harper's Magazine* in the 1850s told of Parmentier's famous "all-potato dinners," which he organized from 1778 to 1785:

A short time after he gave a dinner, every dish of which consisted of the potato disguised in some variety of form, and even the liquids used at table were extracted from it. Among other celebrated persons, Franklin and Lavoisier were present. And thus, to the persevering efforts of one individual was France indebted for a vegetable which soon took its place in the first rank of its agricultural treasures. By naturalizing the potato in that country, Parmentier diffused plenty among thousands, once the hapless victims of privation and misery during the seasons of scarcity hitherto frequently recurring to desolate its provinces.

According to legend, Franklin was quite enamored with potatoes himself and actually suggested the dinner to Parmentier. However, a search of the Franklin Papers reveals only twenty-two mentions of potatoes, and six of *pommes de terre* ("apples of the earth"), and these were mostly in passing.

JEFFERSON AND FRENCH FRIES

Another common potato legend is that it was Jefferson, after returning from France, who introduced deep-fried potatoes to America. Legend says that Jefferson served his guests potatoes fried in the French manner (as French fries were once known as) at a state dinner in 1802. However, there is most likely no truth to this rumor. Jefferson knew of potatoes and that they originated in South America, but there are only scant mentions of the vegetable in his papers, and most of those related to the Irish dependence on potatoes.

Another legacy of Franklin's years in Paris are sixteen pages of his handwritten recipes, some in English and some in French, including recipes for orange shrub, spruce beer, oyster sauce for boiled turkey, raisin wine, and the recipe "To Roast a Pig." Gilbert Chinard of the American Philosophical Society edited a slim volume titled *Benjamin Franklin and the Art of Eating*, first published in 1958. He discovered that the recipes were from *The Art of Cookery, Made Plain and Easy*, by Hannah Glasse, which was first published anonymously in London in 1760. Chinard commented, "Obviously it was Franklin's *vade mecum* [book for ready reference] when he was in France and the main source of his gastronomic inspiration." Franklin's adaptation of Glasse's recipe "To Broil Steaks" is one of the first known recipes for what would now be charcoal-grilled steaks.

To Broil Steaks, by Benjamin Franklin

First have a very clear brisk fire; let your gridiron be very clean; put it on the fire, and take a chaffing-dish with a few hot coals out of the fire.

Put the dish on it which is to lay your steaks on, then take fine rump steaks about a half an inch thick; put a little salt and pepper on them. Lay them on the gridiron, and (if you like it) take a shallot or two, or a fine onion and cut it fine; put it into your dish. Don't turn your steaks till one side is done, then when you turn the other side there will soon be fine gravy lie on the top of the steak, which you must be careful not to lose. When the steaks are enough [done], take them carefully off into your dish, that none of the gravy be lost; then have ready a hot dish and cover, and carry them hot to the table, with the cover on.

Gout eventually proved to be Franklin's undoing in Paris. In his essay "Dialogue between the Gout and Mr. Franklin," published in 1780, Franklin, playing the role of gout, described his own eating habits: "Why, instead of gaining an appetite for breakfast by salutary exercise, you amuse yourself with books, pamphlets, or newspapers, which commonly are not worth the reading. Yet you eat an inordinate breakfast, four dishes of tea with cream, and one or two buttered toasts, with slices of hung beef, which I fancy are not things most easily digested." By July 1785, when he finally returned to America after Jefferson had replaced him as minister, he could not walk, so King Louis XVI provided his personal litter for Franklin to use.

LET HIM EAT BACON: JEFFERSON LEAVES PARIS

Jefferson returned from his final wine sojourn to Champagne in April 1788 and found Paris to be a "furnace of politics." America was too because the Constitution was being debated and Jefferson, from afar, was urging the adoption of a Bill of Rights, which caused Patrick Henry to comment, "[Jefferson] thinks yet of bills of rights while living in splendor and dissipation." Jefferson wrote a private letter to James Madison protesting this assertion and compared his reduced standard of living to his predecessors John Jay, John Adams, and Franklin. This kind of long-distance politicking made him yearn for his Virginia home after nearly five years away from it, and that same year he wrote to his fellow wine lover Alexander Donald, "I had rather be shut up in a very modest cottage, with my books, my family and a few old friends, dining on simple bacon, and letting the world roll on as it liked." Jefferson soon decided to return to America for a visit of six months.

His visit was delayed, however, so Jefferson planted the Riesling vines he had collected on a trip to Germany in his garden at the hotel. Unfortunately, he was never able to make wine with those grapes because, surrounding him, civil disobedience was rampant and a peasant insurrection was beginning. Starving people began to hunt and kill their own game, and they mounted attacks on the nobility and clergy and their property. Jefferson, fearing that the situation was getting out of hand, wrote to Governor Rutledge of South Carolina that "the cloven hoof begins to appear."

The winter of 1788–1789 was extraordinarily cold, exacerbating the deteriorating situation with food, as the price of bread nearly doubled, forcing peasants to spend nearly all of their little money on food. The River Seine froze over, and people drove their carriages over the ice. All social activity in Paris ceased for two months, and some observers later blamed the unusually cold winter for the French Revolution that followed.

In February 1789, Jefferson's eventual successor as minister arrived in Paris and immediately contacted him. This was Gouverneur Morris (his unusual first name came from his Huguenot mother), a Philadelphia lawyer, former senator, and the man who had been Congress's envoy to General Washington at Valley Forge. It was Morris who had brought Madeira and claret to Washington during that unpleasant winter eleven years before. At first glance, Morris seemed an unlikely friend for Jefferson, as he was a Federalist who was wildly extravagant in his behavior, but both of them loved wine, food, and botany. With the possible exception of Lafayette, Morris was Jefferson's closest companion during his last months in Paris. Together they witnessed severed heads on poles being carried down the streets in the midst of the Revolution, and Morris comforted Jefferson after three burglaries at the Hôtel de Langeac threatened Jefferson's wine supply.

On October 23, 1789, Jefferson, with two years remaining on his ministerial appointment to France, left Europe for Norfolk aboard the *Clermont* for what he believed would be a six-month leave of absence. However, he would return to France. With him were his two daughters and two "servants," plus his collected booty from five years in Paris. The packing list of master Parisian box maker Grevin shows that, among other things, Jefferson took back to America eighty-six crates containing European art, books, silver, furniture, and porcelain; more than sixty pieces of copper cookware and iron utensils; plus mustard, vinegar, raisins, nectarines, macaroni, cheese, almonds, anchovies, olive oil, and 680 bottles of wine.

JEFFERSON AND CULINARY "FAKELORE"

Jefferson's five years in Paris left a legacy of culinary "fakelore," according to the food historian Andrew F. Smith. One of these was the myth that he introduced vanilla and macaroni to the United States and invented ice cream. Small quantities of vanilla beans had been imported to the United States from France prior to Jefferson's time there, but he did enjoy it and later imported it to Monticello. Macaroni, an early generic term for pasta, came to the United States from England as noodles in early colonial times; however, Jefferson may have been the first American to import a pasta machine from Italy. Italians had invented ice cream in the sixteenth century, but both Washington and Jefferson imported ice-cream makers. These myths are all false, but what is true is that Jefferson was a passionate student of various foods, wines, and cooking techniques. For example, in his letter to John Adams on November 27, 1785, he wrote extensively about chocolate and Portuguese wine and the impact these two items could have in America:

Chocolate. This article, when ready made, as also the cocoa, becomes so soon rancid, and the difficulties of getting it fresh, have been so great in America, that its use has spread but little. The way to increase its consumption would be, to permit it to be brought to us immediately from the country of its growth. By getting it good in quality, and cheap in price, the superiority of the article, both for health and nourishment, will soon give it the same preference over tea and coffee in America, which it has in Spain, where they can get it by a single voyage, and, of course, while it is sweet. The use of the sugars, coffee, and cotton of Brazil, would also be much extended by a similar indulgence.

Wines. The strength of the wines of Portugal will give them always an almost exclusive possession of a country, where the summers are so hot as in America. The present demand will be very great, if they will enable us to pay for them; but if they consider the extent and rapid population of the United States, they must see that the time is not distant, when they will not be able to make enough for us, and that it is of great importance to avail themselves of the prejudices already established in favor of their wines, and to continue them, by facilitating the purchase. Let them do this, and they need not care for the decline of their use in England. They will be independent of that country.

Jefferson also wrote extensively on cooking methods he discovered while making some of his favorite dishes. In his essay "Observations on Soup," Jefferson outlined the processes for creating a soup base:

Always observe to lay your meat in the bottom of the pan with a lump of fresh butter. Cut the herbs and roots small and lay them over the meat. Cover it close and put it over a slow fire. This will draw forth the flavors of the herbs and in a much greater degree than to put on the water at first. When the gravy produced from the meat is beginning to dry put in the water, and when the soup is done take it off. Let it cool and skim off the fat clear. Heat it again and dish it up. When you make white soups never put in the cream until you take it off the fire.

There are ten surviving recipes that Jefferson recorded in his own hand, such as *biscuit de Savoyé* (small cakes); wine jellies; his famous ice cream; and blancmanger, a "white dish," which was a sweet dessert similar in style to Mexican or Spanish flan and flavored with almonds. It is a particularly interesting dessert because of its striking appearance on the table for festive occasions when colored by various agents such as saffron (golden yellow), fresh herbs (green), and sandalwood (russet). In medieval French cooking, the use of two bright, contrasting colors on the same plate was very popular.

The surviving Jefferson recipes give us an indication of how much his European travels influenced him. When he returned to Monticello, he transformed the food served there to reflect the French and Italian culinary techniques that he had experienced.

Two of Jefferson's Most Famous Recipes

Blancmanger Mold

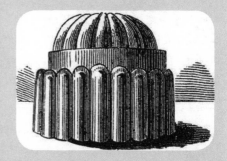

Put a quart of sweet cream into a stew-pan, with two ounces of isinglass [a pre-gelatin ingredient made of fish bladders], a stick of cinnamon, a little lemon peel, a few coriander [s]eeds, two or three laurel leaves, sweeten it with sugar to your palate, boil it

Mold for Blanc Mange

gently till the isinglass is dissolved, in the mean time blanch one ounce of sweet almonds, and two bitter ones, beat them fine in a mortar, and put them in, stir it well about, then drain it through a fine sieve into a bowl, let it stand till it is half cold, then pour it from the settlings into another bowl.— Let your moulds be ready, fill them, let them stand to be cold; when they are thoroughly cold, raise them with your fingers from the sides, dip the bottom of the mold in warm water, and turn them out into a dish: garnish with jellies of different colours; or currant jelly or Seville orange cut in quarters, or flowers, or any thing you fancy.

From Richard Briggs, *The English Art of Cookery*, 1788

Jefferson's Recipe for Ice Cream

2. bottles of good cream.

6. yolks of eggs.

1/2 lb. sugar

mix the yolks & sugar

put the cream on a fire in a casserole, first putting in a stick of Vanilla.

when near boiling take it off & pour it gently into the mixture of eggs & sugar.

stir it well.

put it on the fire again stirring it thoroughly with a spoon to prevent [its] sticking to the casserole.

when near boiling take it off and strain it thro' a towel.

put it in the Sabotiere.

then set it in ice an hour before it is to be served. put into the ice a handful of salt.

put salt on the coverlid of the Sabotiere & cover the whole with ice.

leave it still half a quarter of an hour.

then turn the Sabotiere in the ice 10 minutes

open it to loosen with a spatula the ice from the inner sides of the Sabotiere.

shut it & replace it in the ice

open it from time to time to detach the ice from the sides

Jefferson's ice cream recipe
in his own hand

when well taken (prise) stir it well with the Spatula.

put it in moulds, justling it well down on the knee.

then put the mould into the same bucket of ice.

leave it there to the moment of serving it.

to withdraw it, immerse the mould in warm water, turning it well till

it will come out & turn it into a plate.

Jefferson's Recipe for Ice Cream. Courtesy: Library of Congress

Chapter Five

BOMBASTIC BARBECUES, PRESIDENTIAL PALATES, AND SCURRILOUS SCANDALS

GREAT BOARS OF FIRE

George Washington was no stranger to barbecue. In May 1769, he wrote in his diary that he attended a barbecue in Alexandria that kept him out all night playing cards. While playing, he feasted on smoked meat, most likely from a whole hog or from an ox, the two

A political barbecue

most commonly barbecued animals of the day. Similarly, it was a five-hundred-pound ox he was eating with Congress on September 25, 1793, when Washington presided over the laying of the cornerstone of the Capitol. The historian Robert Shackleton wrote a wonderful description of that event in 1922:

Like the ancient Romans we modern Americans have our Capitol as well as our Appian Way; and whereas the first formal founding feast of Rome itself, was the lupine luncheon of Romulus and Remus with their four-footed hostess, the first formal founding feast of our Capitol, which accompanied the laying of its corner-stone, was also a feast out of doors. It was a barbecue. A great ox was roasted in what the newspapers of the day delightfully referred to as a "cavazion [trench]," into which George Washington descended and from which he emerged, presiding over all of the ceremonies, at which, according to a narrative of the time, there was "every abundance of other recreation"—which was not meant to be a doubtful statement!

Although Americans take credit for barbecue and claim it as their own indigenous food, like many popular foodstuffs, it was imported. The lineage, from the Aztecs to Caribbean natives and their *barbacoa*, to imported pigs (see chapter 1) and African slaves, and then to the American South went like this: Cooking meat over fire was basic to early Native Americans like the Maya and the Aztecs. This technique, along with chili peppers, spread throughout the Caribbean as the Native Americans colonized the islands. When the Spanish arrived and witnessed them cooking meat over a grill made from thin branches, they called it *barbacoa*, which later was Anglicized to *barbecue*. African slaves, brought from the Caribbean to what is now the United States and particularly the South, brought the technique with them and further refined the technique of smoking meat.

But it is sometimes forgotten how much the British love their roasted pork as well. One of the earliest—and best—barbecue recipes around comes from Surrey and was written by a professor of botany at Cambridge University in 1732.

The British and Pork

The British loved pork because of its flavor. You might think that the following quote was from a pork lover from the American South, but the English essayist Charles Lamb wrote it in his "Dissertation upon Roast Pig" in 1874: "He must be roasted…there is no flavour comparable, I will contend, to that of the crisp, tawny, well-watched, not over-roasted, crackling, as it is well called—the very teeth are invited to their share of the pleasure at this banquet in overcoming the coy, brittle resistance—with the adhesive oleaginous…fat and lean (if it must be so) so blended and running into each other, that both together make but one ambrosian result, or common substance."

An Hog Barbecued, or Broil'd Whole, from Vaux-Hall, Surrey

Take an Hog of five or six Months old, kill it, and take out the Innards, so that the Hog is clear of the Harslet [heart and liver]; then turn the Hog upon its Back, and from three Inches below the place where it was stuck, to kill it, cut the Belly in a strait Line down to the Bottom, near the joining of the Gammons, but not so far, but that the whole Body of the Hog may hold any Liquor we would put into it.

Then stretch out the Ribs, and open the Belly, as wide as may be; then strew into it what Pepper and Salt you please.

After this, take a large Grid-Iron, with two or three Ribs in it, and set it upon a stand of Iron, about three Foot and a half high, and upon that, lay your Hog, open'd as above, with the Belly-side downwards, and with a good clear Fire of Charcoal under it. Broil that side till it is enough, flouring the Back at the same time often. Memorandum, This should be done in a Yard, or Garden, with a Covering like a Tent over it.

When the Belly-part of the Hog is enough and turned upwards, and well fix'd to be steady upon the Grid-Iron, or Barbacue, pour into the Belly of the Hog, three or four Quarts of Water, and half as much White-Wine, and as much Salt as you will, with some Sage cut small, adding the Peels of six or eight Lemons, and an Ounce of fresh Cloves whole.

Then let it broil till it is enough, which will be, from the beginning to the end, about seven or eight Hours; and when you serve it, pour out the Sauce, and lay it in a Dish, with the Back upwards. Memorandum, The Skin must not be cut before you lay it on the Gridiron, to keep in the Gravey; neither should any of the Skin be cut, when you have any Pork roasted for the fame Reason.

From *The Country Housewife*, by Richard Bradley, 1732

Barbecue historians—and there are plenty of them—have not been able to pinpoint precisely when outdoor cooking hooked up with politics in the United States, but the start may be the end of the Revolutionary War. In his book *General History of Dutchess County* [New York], Phillip Henry Smith, writing in 1877, described the reaction after Cornwallis surrendered at Yorktown:

When a herald passed through the country announcing the surrender...the tidings met with a hearty response from every patriot. Bonfires, illuminations, and the thunder of artillery everywhere demonstrated the joy that was felt throughout the land. The people of Pawling Precinct instituted a barbecue in commemoration of the event. A hole was dug in the bank near the site of the residence of Richard Chapman, Esq., a fire was built therein, and a fine, full-grown bullock was spitted before it. The cooking was not a pronounced success, and the flesh was either raw or burned to a crisp, [but] the patriotism of the people led them to pronounce it excellent. Patriotic speeches were made, patriotic songs sung, and patriotic toasts drank in profusion; and nothing prevented the thundering of cannon, but the want of cannon and powder.

Patriotism, politics, and pigs (or oxen) were a perfect combination. "These functions, in the day of poor roads and few settlements, were a means of luring voters to a meeting with the promise of free food," wrote Meredith Nicholson in *The Valley of Democracy*. "It was only by such heroic feats of cookery as the broiling of a whole beef in a pit of coals that a crowd could be fed. The meat was likely to be either badly burnt, or raw, but the crowds were not fastidious, and swigs of whiskey made it more palatable. Those were days of plain speech and hard hitting, and on such occasions orators were expected to 'cut loose' and flay the enemy unsparingly." Perhaps surprisingly, despite the confluence of barbecue, alcohol and spirited debate, violence rarely broke out at political barbecues.

In many cases, the rule of thumb was "any political excuse for a barbecue." In his book *Campaigning in America*, Robert Dinkin quoted David Hackett Fischer:

"Try as they might, the young Federalists were probably never able to equal in volume the electioneering of their opponents." On the same day that the party arranged a barbecue in Anne Arundel County, Maryland, in 1809, Fischer notes, the "Jeffersonians sponsored no fewer than nine barbecues in the same county." Just as the Federalists celebrated Washington's birthday and inauguration day, so the Republicans developed festivities commemorating what they considered big occasions and often in a more elaborate fashion.

Easily the most notable event on their calendar was that honoring Jefferson's inauguration on March 4. "The 4th of March forms an epoch in the political history of the United States, which ought to awaken the purest sensations of the American Patriot," announced a Virginia Republican.

Most campaign spending did not involve posting signs or door-to-door canvassing but buying votes with booze and barbecue.

It's difficult to discern, in some of the early definitions of political barbecues, if the observers were being sarcastic. This one is from 1883: "A barbecue is a festival the most prominent features of which are political speeches and roasted hog. A barbecue is usually given by the inhabitants of some rural district desirous of giving candidates an opportunity to state, that, if elected, all their energies will be devoted to the interests of their constituents and the public weal, and that they pledge themselves, that, when their tenure of office shall expire, they will restore the high trust committed to their hands unsullied, etc." Certainly, the upper class looked down their noses at "primitive" barbecues.

Sometimes, because of hard drinking, the barbecues could get out of hand: "For, let me tell you, the Barbecue is one of the ancient and honorable insti-tutions of Virginia—one of the few that have survived the innovation of parties and the wreck of constitutions! It belongs to the people—theoretically, practically, and emphatically—and its social influences upon the body politic are altogether beneficial and conservative when they are not perverted from their legitimate objects by brawling drunkards and blarneying demagogues!" Thus, we see that the hard drinking discussed in the earlier chapters ties in to the growing popularity of barbecue.

And then there was the practical aspect of the barbecue, as Hamilton Pierson pointed out in 1881:

It is the simplest possible manner of preparing a dinner for a large concourse of people. It requires neither building, stove, oven, range, nor baking-pans. It involves no house-cleaning after the feast. It soils and spoils no carpets or furniture. And in the mild, bountiful region where the ox and all that is eaten are raised with so little care, the cost of feeding hundreds, or even thousands, in this manner is merely nominal. Hence barbecues have been for a long time so common and popular in the Southwest. There have been unnumbered political barbecues, where the eloquence peculiar to that region has been developed, and where vast audiences have been moved by its power, as the trees beneath which they were gathered have been swayed by the winds.

But not all of the early barbecues were political in nature; barbecues were made at home as well, both for social gatherings and for everyday cooking. And who were the champions of nonpolitical barbecue? Southern women, of course. Mary Randolph, Lettice Bryan, and Sarah Rutledge were the authors, respectively, of *The Virginia Housewife* (1824), *The Kentucky Housewife* (1838), and *The Carolina Housewife* (1874). Mary Randolph had the broadest scope and the most recipes, giving directions for barbecuing mutton, fish, turkey, and calf heads. She described in detail how to roast a pig, "To Barbecue Shote [shoat]."

Whole hogs smoked over a deep pit, c. 1890

Shote is the name given in the Southern states to a fat young hog, which, when the head and feet are taken off, and it is cut into four quarters, will weigh six pounds per quarter.

To Barbecue Shote

Take a fore-quarter, make several incisions between the ribs, and stuff it with rich forcemeat; put it in a pan with a pint of water, two cloves of garlic, pepper, salt, two gills of red wine, and two of mushroom catsup, bake it, and thicken the gravy with butter and brown flour; it must be jointed, and the ribs cut across before it is cooked, OR it cannot be carved well; lay it in the dish with the ribs uppermost; if it be not sufficiently brown, add a little burnt sugar to the gravy, garnish with balls.

(Note that Randolph called an oven-roasted shoat "barbecue," and she invented one of the earliest known barbecue sauces, with water, garlic, black pepper, red wine, mushroom, catsup, butter, and brown flour. But she also added the following recipe.)

To Roast a Fore-quarter of Shote

Joint it for the convenience of carving, roast it before a brisk fire; when done, take the skin off, dredge and froth it, put a little melted butter with some caper, vinegar over it, or serve it with mint sauce.

Bryan is noted for her use of an early barbecue rub, consisting of salt, pepper, and molasses, and she finished her pork barbecue with lemon juice, melted butter, and wine. Rutledge offered beef and oyster sausages, side dishes like pickled mangoes, and twenty different styles of one of the most popular barbecue accompaniments: corn bread.

As the years rolled on, barbecued beef—especially brisket—shifted to Texas, and barbecued pork came to rule the South.

HERCULES WASHINGTON AND THE FIRST WHITE HOUSE KITCHEN

When George Washington married Martha Dandridge Custis, a widow with two children, he benefited from the property, slaves, and elite social status she brought to their union. A self-described "old-fashioned Virginia house-keeper," Martha knew how to entertain and how to manage a large household. When George became president, Martha was fifty-eight and a grandmother, but she had no trouble managing the first two presidential mansions, in New York City and then in Philadelphia.

The First Presidential Fruitcake

Among the surviving papers of Martha Washington is a recipe for a "great Cake," that her granddaughter Martha Parke Custis wrote for her. This type of rich, fruit-filled cake was the traditional accompaniment for Twelfth Night festivities during the Christmas season.

Martha Washington's Black Great Cake Recipe

Take 40 eggs and divide the whites from the yolks and beat them to froth. Then work 4 pounds of butter to a cream and put the whites of eggs to it a Spoon full at a time till it is well work'd. Then put 4 pounds of sugar finely powdered to it in the same manner then put in the Yolks of eggs and 5 pounds of flour and 5 pounds of fruit. 2 hours will bake it. Add to it half an ounce of mace and nutmeg half a pint of wine and some fresh brandy. Five and a half hours will bake it.

The tradition of good food and service at the White House started during Washington's first administration. "You can't even consider the history of the White House without realizing that the common denominator of White House life is the dinner table," noted the historian William Seale, author of *The President's House*. "When George Washington took office, he wasn't the king, he wasn't the sovereign. He was a combination of head of state and prime minister. It never happened before; nobody ever had one of those. So it was very delicate with him how to proceed in terms of diplomatic tradition. So food became very important."

Although she was adept at managing the mansion, Martha couldn't do all the work herself, so she brought her Mount Vernon slave, Hercules Washington (slaves were often named for classical heroes and then given the surname of their owners) to the presidential mansion to run the kitchen. And even Hercules needed help, to the tune of eight assistants who served as butlers, assistant cooks, and waiters. Martha Washington's grandson George Washington Parke Custis remembered Hercules as "highly accomplished and proficient in the culinary arts as could be found in the United States."

Like James Hemings in Paris, Hercules earned money to buy fancy clothes by selling leftovers and kitchen waste, and so he was always well dressed, immaculate, and impeccable in the kitchen. George Washington Parke Custis described Hercules as follows:

Hercules Washington

The chief cook would have been termed in modern parlance, a celebrated artiste. "[He] was, at the period of the first presidency, as highly accomplished and proficient in the culinary art as could be found in the United States… The chief cook gloried in the cleanliness and nicety of his kitchen. Under his iron discipline, woe to his underlings if speck or spot could be discovered on the tables or dressers, or if the utensils did not shine like polished silver. With the luckless wights [human beings] who had offended in these particulars there was no arrest of punishment, for judgment and execution went hand in hand…

It was while preparing the Thursday or Congress dinner that [he] shone in all his splendor. During his labors upon this banquet he required some half-dozen aprons, and napkins out of number. It was surprising the order and discipline that was observed in so bustling a scene. His underlings flew in all directions to execute his orders, while he, the great master-spirit, seemed to possess the power of ubiquity, and to be everywhere at the same moment. When the steward in snow-white apron, silk shorts and stockings, and hair in full powder, placed the first dish on the table, the clock being on the stroke of four, 'the labors of Hercules' ceased.

Although there is no written evidence of menus or meals that Hercules served at the presidential mansions in New York and Philadelphia, the food was likely similar to that served at Mount Vernon after Washington retired. The family ate ham, ducks, turkeys, and geese at Mount Vernon, and Washington himself was fond of barbecue. In a footnote in his memoirs, George Washington Parke Custis noted:

> The Reverend Andrew Burnaby, who travelled quite extensively in America, in the years 1759 and 1760, and visited Mount Vernon two or three times during the first year of Washington's married life, says in a note, "In several parts of Virginia, the ancient custom of eating meat at breakfast still continues. At the top of the table, where the lady of the house presides, there is constantly tea and coffee; but the rest of the table is garnished out with roast fowls, ham, venison, game, and other dainties. Even at Williamsburg, it is the custom to have a plate of cold ham upon the table; and there is scarcely a Virginian lady who breakfasts without it."

Joshua Brookes, a young Englishman who visited Mount Vernon in 1799, recorded in his journal a list of foods he was served: "Leg of boiled pork... goose...roast beef, round cold boiled beef, mutton chops, hommony [sic], cabbage, potatoes, pickles, fried tripe, onions...mince pies, tarts, cheese." After the main courses were removed, Brookes wrote, the crumbs were brushed off the table and mince pies, tarts, and cheese were placed on it. Mince pies would have been made with leftover meat plus suet, fruits, brandy, and the imported spices that came into the port at Philadelphia. After dessert, Washington's favorite wine, Madeira, was served with nuts, apples, and raisins.

Although similar foods were likely cooked in the presidential mansions as at Mount Vernon, Hercules did not prepare the Mount Vernon meals.

When Washington was getting ready to leave Philadelphia to return to Mount Vernon in 1797, Hercules disappeared. Washington sent out search parties and offered rewards, but Hercules was never found. A visitor, Prince Louis-Philippe of France, told Hercules' daughter she must be very unhappy because she would never see her father again. "Oh, sir, I am very glad," she is reported to have said, "Because he is free now."

PARIS REDUX IN PHILADELPHIA

After Jefferson left France, Washington named him secretary of state and he moved to New York, then a city of thirty-three thousand people (finally surpassing Philadelphia in size), in March 1790. Compared to the excitement of Paris, with a population of about half a million, New York was a letdown for Jefferson, and he began to feel out of place in his own country. "Instead of the lively dinner parties of Paris," wrote John Hailman, "there were the stiff, formal dinners of President Washington." On top of that, Jefferson's eighty-six crates of furnishings and personal affects had not yet arrived from France and he greatly missed Paris.

His brief time in New York marked the beginning of a rift between Jefferson and his longtime friend John Adams, then vice president. Jefferson deplored Adams's failure to support the French Revolution and was embarrassed by Adams's attitude, believing that it undermined everything they had worked for in France. This was an ongoing struggle that had a very great effect on both Jefferson and Adams.

But at least Jefferson still had his cook. Hemings returned with Jefferson to New York and followed him to Philadelphia when Congress moved the capital there in August 1790. Philadelphia's growth had been stagnant since 1776, stuck at about twenty-eight thousand people. Of these, there were 2,150 blacks of which 210 were slaves. Because Washington and Jefferson lived a mere three blocks away from each other on High Street (now Market Street), it is highly likely that James Hemings and Hercules Washington knew each other.

Jefferson remodeled the house he was renting; seventy-eight of his eighty-six crates arrived from France, including his two Parisian goblets; and he went about re-creating Paris in Philadelphia. Hemings moved from a boarding house into Jefferson's house on High Street and resumed his duties as chef and servant in charge. He was, as Gordon-Reed put it, living "his odd existence between slavery and freedom." She also has speculated that Jefferson was going out of his way to make Hemings feel comfortable because he realized that his servant had given up his freedom to return to America with him.

Jefferson himself was "noticeably Frenchified," in the words of John Hailman, "wearing silk suits, ruffles, and an unusual topaz ring." Jefferson, apparently reacting to criticism from the secretary of the treasury, Alexander Hamilton, did a complete reversal, dropped French clothes, and switched to American garb. But he overdid it and was then criticized by Senator William Maclay (of his own party) for wearing "ill-fitting, much worn clothes" and for his "vacant look." Hailman noted: "It is easy to see that with his multiple cellars full of wines, his exotic house at Monticello, his French-trained chef, his esoteric library, and his high-minded intellectual interests, Jefferson came off as a tad phony as a 'mountain man from Virginia.' "

President Washington didn't take much issue with Jefferson's dress; in fact, realizing that Jefferson was extraordinarily knowledgeable about French wines, he turned to him for assistance in selecting and ordering them for his own house down the street. Jefferson's longtime assistant, William Short, was still in Europe, so he assisted in the effort. In September 1790, the president wanted forty dozen bottles of champagne, thirty dozen of Sauterne, twenty dozen of Bordeaux, and ten dozen of Frontignan. Jefferson, of course, ordered even more for his own household.

In July 1791, Jefferson reverted again to his French ways with the arrival of Adrian Petit from Paris to be his housekeeper at a very substantial salary. Petit, who had been the maître d' of the Hôtel de Langeac where Jefferson, his daughters, and the Hemingses had lived, reinforced Jefferson's re-creation of his Parisian environment, bringing French language and sophistication to the food, furniture, fine art, and wines that Jefferson had already installed.

However, Petit was not the only French influence to arrive in Philadelphia. Because of the French Revolution and the slave rebellion in Haiti that threatened French settlers there, many new French émigrés arrived in the city, including pastry chefs and ice-cream vendors, and they helped the Philadelphia restaurant kitchens achieve the quality of those in Europe—especially in confectionery and fine pastries. The cookbook *La Cuisinière Bourgeoise* (*The French Family Cookbook*, as it's sometimes translated) by Menon (first name unknown), first published in Paris in 1746, became the standard reference for Philadelphia caterers. The book and the new French chefs influenced the fine restaurateurs of the day, like Charles Schroeder, who opened the Swan Hotel at the time Washington and Jefferson lived in Philadelphia.

It is important to note that Menon was breaking away from the aristocratic tradition of French cuisine that Hemings was trained in. Instead of using the term *cuisinier*, or "chef," he called for a *cuisinière*, or "cook," which included women, who had previously been banned from professional kitchens except for scullery maids. The title of the first English translation, *The French Family Cookbook*, reveals the total abandonment of what food historian Priscilla Parkhurst Ferguson has called "the sphere of the aristocracy, its elaborate preparations, and its elite customers."

Biscuits Ordinaries [Cookies] by Menon

According to the size & the quantity of cookies which you will want to make, you will increase & decrease the amount here marked. Take eight eggs which you put in a balance, & as much weight of sugar of the other side; weigh also flour by the weight of four eggs, & put the flour and sugar on separate plates. Break eight eggs; put the whites aside in a pot, & the yellows in another pot with sugar & a little lime peel chopped [zested] very-fine. Beat the yellows with sugar during half an hour [until they are almost white and form a ribbon]; then whip the whites until they hold soft peaks. Fold them into the yolk mixture; then carefully fold in the flour little by little. Prepare paper [baking cups] or tinplate moulds, which are very carefully and completed coated with butter; fill molds with paste no more than half full: sprinkle fine [confectioner's] sugar over tops, & cook in a soft furnace [slow oven 300°F] for half an hour. Withdraw moulds from oven when they are of a beautiful golden color, and remove from moulds when half-cooled.

JEFFERSON AND HIS MAPLE SUGAR OBSESSION

Around this time, Dr. Benjamin Rush, a friend of Benjamin Franklin and an ardent campaigner for the abolishment of distilled spirits (see chapter 2), published the essay "Advantages of the Culture of the Sugar Maple Tree" in a Philadelphia magazine. Rush was a supporter of American maple sugar as well as a slavery abolitionist. These two passions eventually dovetailed, and Rush managed to lure Jefferson into a wacky plan.

In 1789, a year after his article was published, Rush and a group of Philadelphia Quakers founded the Society for Promoting the Manufacture of Sugar from the Sugar Maple Tree. Like Parmentier in Paris with his potatoes, Rush staged promotional events to promote maple sugar, including a "scientific tea party." He invited Alexander Hamilton, the Quaker merchant Henry Drinker, and "several Ladies" to tea, and they sipped cups of hyson tea that were sweetened with equal amounts of cane and maple sugar. Everyone who tasted agreed that the sugar from the maple was just as sweet as cane sugar.

The Quakers, of course, were abolitionists, and someone in the group—probably Rush—came up with the idea that the production of American sugar from the maple would reduce the consumption of West Indian sugar, "and thus indirectly…destroy negro slavery." The French abolitionist J. P. Brissot de Warville joined the maple sugar chorus and trumpeted that American sugar would "drive out the sugar produced by the tears and blood of slaves." Because of his love for American-produced goods and his fascination with plants, after a meeting with Rush, Jefferson climbed aboard the sugar train.

In an astonishing letter to Benjamin Vaughn, a friend in England, Jefferson seems to prefer the labor of children to that of slaves, writing that the maple tree "yields a sugar equal to the best from cane, yields it in great quantity, with no other labor than what the

Gathering maple syrup, Vermont, c. 1900

women and girls can bestow…What a blessing to substitute a sugar which requires only the labour of children, for that which it is said renders the slavery of the blacks necessary."

Jefferson began buying maple sugar refined from the syrup in November 1790, and he shipped it to Monticello. This action prompted Rush to write, "Mr. Jefferson uses no other sugar in his family than that which is obtained from the sugar maple tree." Then Rush introduced Jefferson to the maple sugar producer Arthur Noble, who convinced Jefferson that he had enormous production capabilities. As secretary of state, Jefferson envisioned American companies competing with British sugar companies in the Caribbean by exporting surplus maple sugar. A triumphant Noble wrote to his associate William Cooper that Jefferson "is as Sanguine as you or I about the Maple Sugar, he thinks in a few years we shall be able to Supply half the World."

Indeed, a rather naive Jefferson was so sold on the idea that he wrote to President Washington that "evidence grows upon us" that the United States could become an exporter of sugar and "I confess I look with infinite gratification to [its] addition to the products of the U.S." What Rush began to call the maple sugar bubble was actually an association of self-deluded land speculators and abolitionists. Cooper, the founder of Cooperstown and father of James Fenimore Cooper, was trying to use what he called "these diamonds of America"—maple sugar crystals—to lure settlers to Otsego County in upstate New York. But the bubble was not limited to New York. According to the Massachusetts Maple Producers Association, in 1791, a Dutch company bought twenty-three thousand acres of Vermont land and tried to hire local workers to tap the trees, but the Vermonters, living free as usual, preferred to work their own land. The Dutch project was a complete failure, and the bubble had almost burst.

But Jefferson, if he even knew of those developments, was unfazed. In May 1791, he set off with James Madison on a journey to Lake Champlain in New York and then on to New England to check out sugar maples for himself. In Bennington, Vermont, he preached the idea of landholders planting orchards of maples in the same manner as apple trees, and this concept garnered some newspaper coverage.

Maple Sugar Sauce, by Jennie June, 1870

Take half maple sugar and half light brown sugar, boil them together with a little water, clarify the syrup with an egg, strain it and melt a small piece of butter in it. All maple sugar, or all common sugar can be used. It is very good on puddings.

Rush published a pamphlet in 1792 that extensively quoted Jefferson and noted "the impatience of the gentlemen interested in the sugar lands." It was widely reprinted in the United States and Europe. The pamphlet's contents were repeated in books and encyclopedias, but it was all for naught. The New York maple sugar enterprises failed because of lack of support—people simply preferred sugar from sugarcane and couldn't care less about its origin. Rush's Pennsylvania company of Quakers lost £1,400 and disbanded. The "large plantations" of maples that Jefferson planned for Monticello had only eight little saplings in 1794, and one of them is believed to be the ancient tree still standing today near the West Lawn.

Arthur Noble tried one other maple product, maple whiskey, and Jefferson sampled it but noted that there was "less profit made by converting the juice into spirit than into sugar." Afterward, Jefferson abandoned his dream of a national sugar industry. Rush, reverting back to his hatred of distilled spirits, promoted weaker maple beverages instead and never wrote about maple sugar again in his lifetime. He advised that a maple sap could be made into "a cool and refreshing drink in the time of harvest" and "a pleasant summer beer [that] could be made from its syrup."

HEMINGS LOSES EVERYTHING

At the age of fifty-one, Thomas Jefferson moved from Philadelphia back to Monticello, arriving on January 16 along with his cook James Hemings. He was about to enter what one historian called the most boring period of his life, and he soon realized that farming would not bring in the funds needed to support his family.

He found that his farmlands, after a decade under the care of overseers, were nearly ruined. As he put it, there was "a degree of degradation far beyond what I had expected." He had about ten thousand acres, a thousand of which were in riding distance of Monticello, and he was determined to restore them through a new system of crop rotation and a transition from growing tobacco to growing wheat and other crops. That August, he fell so ill that his family feared he would die, and he had to take a break from farming and turn down Washington's request that he return to the government to help with the crisis of the Whisky Rebellion.

Finally, the pressure of debts that his wife had incurred before the Revolution made him realize that he needed a government salary again, so he decided to run for president after Washington retired. Of course, John Adams defeated him, and Jefferson by law became vice president. Still, the job paid $5,000 a year, which would help him greatly.

Meanwhile, within eleven days of returning to Monticello, James

Hemings began his brother Peter's culinary training per his agreement with Jefferson. Hemings had all of his fancy copper cookware that Jefferson had shipped from Paris and was well equipped to train Peter. Unlike the time in Paris when Jefferson made daily notations about Hemings, he now ceased writing about him entirely. No one knows exactly where Hemings lived—with the other slaves on Mulberry Row, in the mansion under renovation, or even in Charlottesville.

In April 1796, Peter's training was completed, and Jefferson freed Hemings. He left Monticello, leaving behind only a well-written inventory of the kitchen and some recipes, both composed in his own hand. His destination was Philadelphia, a city he probably liked—he knew it from when he had been Jefferson's cook during his stint as secretary of state. Hemings also had connections there, namely Benjamin Rush, who had dined many times on Hemings's culinary creations. Rush also had a reputation for assisting blacks in Philadelphia.

Hemings's return to Philadelphia as a free man may have encouraged Washington's cook, Hercules, to run to his own freedom. For a time, before Hemings left to travel to Spain, they lived in the same city and probably had some contact with each other. Washington wanted Hercules back and authorized a former steward, Frederick Kitt, to hire someone to find him, but Hercules was never recaptured or heard from again.

Jefferson spoke with Hemings in Philadelphia, and he wrote to his daughter Maria in May 1797: "James is returned to this place, and is not given up the drink as I had been informed. He tells me his next trip will be to Spain. I am afraid his journeys will end in the moon. I have endeavored to persuade him to stay where he is and lay up money." Considering Jefferson's habit of reckless spending on wine and luxury items, his comment to Hemings to save money is highly ironic. But he wasn't far off with his prediction about where Hemings's journeys would end, as we shall see.

Hemings couldn't make a go of things, and after some European travel- ing, he returned to Monticello as a cook, earning $20 a month. But that lasted only a month and a half, and Jefferson's daughter's son-in-law, Thomas Mann Randolph, commented that Hemings seemed disconcerted by being "among strange servants." After only six weeks on the job, Jefferson paid the $30 he owed him and Hemings moved to Baltimore.

In the fall of 1801, Jefferson learned of the suicide of James Hemings. Incredulous, Jefferson had a friend in Baltimore, William Evans, make inqui- ries, and on November 5, Evans wrote back: "The report respecting James Hemings having committed an act of suicide is true. I made every inquiry at the time this melancholy circumstance took place. The result of which was, that he had been delirious for some days prior to committing the act, and it was the general opinion that drinking too freely was the cause." Although proslavery advocates at the time used this incident to demonstrate that slaves supposedly "weren't ready to be freed," there are more personal reasons for Hemings ending his own life—loneliness and alcoholism. As Annette Gordon-Reed observed, "Hemings's life was probably more difficult because he had no wife and family to succor him and to support him in return. He seems to have been on his own—alone—in the most profound way."

PRESIDENT JEFFERSON: DINNER-PARTY ANIMAL

Jefferson may not have liked the vice presidency, but it must have inspired him to move up, for he ran against Aaron Burr and John Adams for the presidency in 1800–1801 and won. As the wine historian John Hailman commented, "The United States had just elected the greatest wine lover ever to hold office." One of the first letters Jefferson received as president was from the wine dealer Thomas Newton, who offered him some of the finest Madeira ever seen in the United States. The president wrote back that he would "gladly take a pipe [about four hundred bottles]." The pipe cost $350 in 1801 dollars, about $5,000 today. [Note: Comparative dollar values here and following are extremely approximate.]

And that was just the beginning. Exactly one hundred years after Jefferson took office, the first book was published that detailed his wine expenditures, *The True Thomas Jefferson*, by William Eleroy Curtis. In it, Curtis examined the account book owned by Samuel J. Tilden, former governor of New York, titled *Jefferson's Financial Diary*, and calculated the money spent by Jefferson that came out of his $25,000 annual salary. (He had to pay all his own expenses.) From 1801, when he spent $2,622.33 on wine, to 1808, when he spent a mere $75.58, his total expenditure for his administration was $10,955.90 on wine alone, a figure that would roughly be about $175,000 in modern terms.

Curtis is the first biographer to document Jefferson's wine buying, and he uses that as a platform to portray our third president as an opponent of "ardent spirits." He uses Jefferson's famous quote about it: "No nation is drunken where wine is cheap; and none is sober where the dearness of wine substitutes ardent whisky or spirits as the common beverage. It is in truth, the only antidote to the bane of whisky." It should be noted that Jefferson sounds exactly like Benjamin Rush here and in another statement where he refers to "the loathsome and fatal effects of whisky, destroying the fortunes, the bodies, the minds and morals of our people."

The President's House was an unfinished stone mansion when Jefferson moved in, and in the spring of 1801, Jefferson began his first order of business: assembling a large domestic staff that included a butler, cook, coachman, valet-porter, housekeeper, apprentice cooks, stable boy, and washerwoman—a total of ten to twelve servants at all times. He had wanted to hire James Hemings as the President's House chef and passed the word on to friends to ask him, but Hemings wanted Jefferson to detail the conditions and wages of his employment. The president never did this, probably expecting Hemings to still be loyal to him, even in his state as a free man. Essentially there was a standoff; Hemings never accepted the position, and Jefferson moved on.

Jefferson proceeded to host three dinners a week for both Republicans and Federalists alike (but never together at the same dinner), plus numerous other guests. There was not much else to do in the new federal city, for there were no theaters and very few inns, and the congressmen did not have their wives with them. So Jefferson spent fifty dollars a day to wine and dine his guests, serving them such dishes as, in the words of guest Manesseh Cutler, "rice soup, round of beef, turkey, mutton, ham, loin of veal, cutlet of mutton, fried eggs, fried beef…and a pie called macaroni." For dessert, Cutler enjoyed "ice cream very good, crust wholly dried" and a "dish somewhat like a pudding—inside white as milk or curd, very porous and light, covered with cream sauce—very fine. Many other jimcracks, a great variety of fruit, plenty of wine and good."

At President's House dinners, Jefferson always used dumbwaiters. Margaret Bayard Smith wrote, "When he had any persons dining with him, with whom he wished to enjoy a free and unrestricted flow of conversation, the number of persons at table never exceeded four, and by each individual was placed a dumb-waiter, containing everything necessary for the progress of the dinner from beginning to end, so as to make the attendance of servants entirely unnecessary, believing as he did, that much of the domestic and even public discord was produced by the mutilated and misconstructed repetition of free conversation at dinner tables, by these mute but not inattentive listeners."

Some guests reported that, in addition to using dumbwaiters, Jefferson himself served the guests. No servants, meaning slaves, were allowed to serve, for fear they would spread gossip. "Our walls have no ears," Jefferson would tell his guests. In his typical egalitarian way, Jefferson did not seat the guests according to rank or diplomatic status but according to how fast they approached the table.

A longtime tradition that Jefferson banned was toasting, or "drinking healths," as it was called. Toasting was passed on from the British to the colonists and was common at upper-class functions. Even George Washington would occasionally lead his guests in toasts using wine. But not Jefferson, who probably objected to the "forced" nature of compulsive toasting. He may have banned it at the President's House, but even his popularity could not prevent the practice.

Yet even without toasting, the alcohol flowed freely at Jefferson's dinner parties. Dinner began at four in the afternoon, and the feasts were served with beer, porter, and hard cider. After dinner, the tablecloths were removed and various wines were poured to accompany the dried fruits, nuts, and confections. Champagne, Sauterne, claret, Margaux from Bordeaux, and Chambertin from Burgundy were among the wines most commonly served. Additionally, there were many dessert wines, such as sherries and Madeiras, to choose from.

Presidential dinner records, now held at the Massachusetts Historical Society in Boston, run from November 5, 1804, through March 6, 1809. In his meticulous manner, Jefferson kept a tabulation of every guest who dined with him at the President's House. "Correctly deciphered, this extensive list of names and dates provides not only an intimate picture of those seated at the president's table but also insights on the political culture of early Washington," wrote social historian Merry Ellen Scofield. The greatest number of dinners occurred when Congress was in session. The dinners were a form of social lobbying because Jefferson believed that power was not the result of public debate but of social networking. "Politics, cloaked in the informality and congeniality of an intimate dinner, produced results." She added that those presidential dinners were unlike anything before or since.

Although many of his dinners were politically focused, Jefferson set aside Sundays for dining with family and friends, and he abandoned the formal balls and birthday celebrations so popular with the first two presidents. Women were occasional guests and usually attended only the parties for New Year's and the Fourth of July. Scofield points out that Republican philosophy, especially among Southerners, did not encourage the participation of women in the political process. Men also far outnumbered women in the new capital.

Not much is known about Jefferson's chef, Honoré Julien, who prepared all the dinners in a coal-fired stove in the basement of the President's House, but Jefferson's maître d', Étienne Lemaire, did the food purchasing and kept meticulous records in a daybook that Jefferson examined and signed monthly. So, it's well known what ingredients were going into the meals that Julien prepared. In a kind of "Franglish," Lemaire recorded *roquefish* (rockfish), *esturgeon* (sturgeon), *melon d'eau* (watermelon), and *gallon d'huitres* (gallon of oysters). His shopping budget when Congress was in session was $500 a month, but on special occasions, it was not unusual for him to spend $50 or more per day. For a dinner honoring the Tunisian ambassador Mellimelli and his retainers in 1806, Lemaire purchased 120 pounds of beef, 90 pounds of mutton, 35 pounds of veal, 27 pounds of pork, plus 30 pounds of rice, 25 pounds of butter, 17 dozen eggs, 3 turkeys, 30 "small birds," and plenty of vegetables at the Georgetown market. Lemaire was also responsible for decanting Jefferson's wines into bottles, so he was butler, or "bottler," in the truest sense of the word. After Jefferson retired from politics the second time, he asked Lemaire for his recipe for raspberry vinegar, which Lemaire mailed to him. A translated and modified version of the vinegar, for use in a recipe for asparagus, appears in chapter 7. In addition to the American foodstuffs, Lemaire was able to buy imported foods such as Havana chocolate, olives and olive oil, three kinds of almonds, seedless raisins, figs, prunes, Bologna sausage, artichoke hearts, Maille mustard, tarragon vinegar, and Parmesan cheese.

One of the odder moments in Jeffersonian food history occurred on New Year's Day, 1803, when a huge wheel of cheese weighing 1,235 pounds was delivered to the President's House. The brainstorm of Baptist church elder John Leland of Cheshire, Massachusetts, the four-and-a-half-foot-diameter cheese was engraved with the motto "Rebellion to tyrants is obedience to God." At the ceremony, Leland pointedly told Jefferson that the cheese "was produced by the personal labor of freeborn farmers with the voluntary and cheerful aid of their wives and daughters, without the assistance of a single slave."

This "mammoth cheese," as it was called, because archaeologists funded by Jefferson had uncovered the bones of a woolly mammoth in New York City, used the milk of nine hundred cows, and soon became the talk of Washington. It was, of course, ridiculed by the Federalists and some newspapers. The *Norwich Packet* sarcastically reported that bakers in New York were making "a loaf of bread proportionate to the cheese," and a glass manufacturer in Albany had "already blown a bottle of sufficient size to contain one tun, which they intend to fill with the best American Porter" so that "Mr. Jefferson's convivial friends…may not only have cheese, but bread, cheese, and Porter."

Jefferson, worried about accepting gifts as president, paid Leland $200 for the cheese, and it was placed on display in the East Room at the President's House for all to see for more than a year. Jefferson probably had a servant responsible for scraping off the accumulating mold. Two months after the mammoth cheese was delivered, Jefferson hosted a feast in a Senate chamber that featured pieces of the cheese, a large sirloin roast, and a "mammoth loaf," which a navy baker prepared from an entire barrel of flour. Some sources say the remains of the cheese were eventually dumped in the Potomac River. The mammoth cheese was imitated many times, including an even larger one delivered to President Andrew Jackson in 1837.

The cheese was so inspiring that poems—or at least doggerel—were written about it, like this one by Moses Guest that was published in 1824:

When Mammoth Cheese shall be no more;
Millions unborn shall catch the flame,
That raised to honour Leland's name;
From east to west, from north to south,
Each patriot's offering shall come forth;
Brewers no doubt will take the hint,
As they will see it now in print,
Inspired by a reverend sir,
No doubt to me they'll make a stir,
And quickly send on at a word,
A tun as large as Heidleberg;
So that with store of cheese and beer,
Our President may have good cheer;
For surely it would be a pity,
Not to live well in fed'ral city.

President Andrew Jackson slicing another
Mammoth Cheese, 1837

During his eight years in office, Jefferson purchased more than twenty thousand bottles of wine for use at the President's House. However, his wine buying declined from more than $2,600 in 1801 to $75.58 in 1808, with the exception of a $2,600 spike in 1804. The radical drop in wine expenditures during his last three years in office seem to be the result of Jefferson's increasing worries about his financial situation, which was grim, but he didn't cut back on the food he served at his now-famous dinner parties.

In the spring of 1808, Jefferson, despite his being worn "down to a state of almost total incapacity for business," entertained 104 guests at seven dinners. Historian Fawn Brodie commented, "His daughters, knowing the precarious nature of his finances and the frightening escalation of his debts, must have been appalled at the cost of the daily presidential hospitality." But money problems weren't the only thing on Jefferson's mind. He was just as worried about pirates.

BLACK PEPPER RELAUNCHES SALEM AND JEFFERSON'S "WICKED TYRANNICAL EMBARGO" SINKS IT

As seen in chapter 1, cod fishing was the original major industry of New England, particularly from the ports of Gloucester, Marblehead, and Salem. Later, the Revolutionary War broadened the horizons of the fishermen by giving them a new enterprise: privateering. The private navy of Massachusetts, given permission to go raiding by the Continental Congress, was enormously profitable during the early stages of the war, and it was a common practice for merchants to subscribe to a profiteering cruise by speculating on the coming prizes. They actually bought shares in advance from the privateering captains. But during the last years of the war, the

British Navy tightened its blockades of the privateering ports and captured most of the fleet.

As maritime historian Samuel Morison observed, "But it was a great war while it lasted! Then came the worst economic depression Massachusetts has ever known. By 1786, the exports of Virginia had more than regained their pre-Revolutionary figures. At the same date the exports of Massachusetts were only one-fourth of what they had been twelve years earlier." Most of the fishing ships had been destroyed, so both the cod and whaling industries were in ruin. It took so long to rebuild the fishing fleets that the captains turned to other opportunities, namely two commodities that were immensely more profitable: slaves (as seen in chapter 1) and—of all the most unlikely U.S. food commodities—black pepper.

Soon after the popular introduction of the spice, Salem, Massachusetts, became the black pepper capital of the New World and rivaled trading centers like London and Amsterdam. That small town was the focal point of a reexporting business in pepper that saw about 8 million pounds a year of the spice pass through New England to other countries aboard clipper ships. Hundreds of fast schooners were built exclusively for the pepper trade, which greatly helped the economy of the colonies.

Considering that Britain had a complete monopoly on the spice trade in general and black pepper in particular, how was Salem's pepper trade possible and profitable? There were two principal factors: the desire of Americans to first defeat and then compete with the British and the speed of the spice-trading ships. The black pepper from both the East Indies and India was brought to America, and then most of it was exported to Europe at great profits because the enterprising Americans could undercut British pepper prices.

The origins of the American pepper trade began in 1778, when Captain

Jonathan Carnes sailed to Sumatra, bought pepper, and attempted to bring it back. Apparently, he went off course, and his ship was wrecked on a reef in the West Indies. But he did not give up even though his second voyage took nearly twenty years to set up. Times were still tough in Salem, but he gained backing from the Jonathan Peele family and the *Rajah*, with Carnes aboard, left Salem and sailed to Sumatra to buy pepper. In 1797 (some sources say 1799), the *Rajah* returned with 158,544 pounds of bulk pepper that had been shoveled into the hold. The cargo sold for thirty-seven cents a pound and yielded a profit of 700 percent. Carnes and the Peeles kept quiet about the origin of their pepper and made two more voyages in 1798 and 1801, each bringing back about the same amount of pepper. In 1799, Captain Benjamin Crowninshield sailed the *America* to Calcutta and returned with ninety-five thousand pounds of pepper. More voyages followed as the Crowninshields began to compete with the Peeles.

The Crowninshield family was one of the most prominent and wealthy families in New England. They had helped settle Salem and soon turned to trading rather than fishing, and they exported cod, rum, and salt while importing molasses, Madeira wine, oranges, and grapes. Their trade grew so large that they built Crowninshield's Wharf to accommodate all their ships.

It didn't take long for the family to hear about Sumatran pepper, and under the leadership of patriarch George Crowninshield and his son John, who actually made the fourteen-thousand-mile voyage, they began to trade in what they called "our pepper gardens." They were blessed with phenomenal luck at first, avoiding both storms and pirates, and in 1801, two Crowninshield ships brought more than a million pounds of pepper back to Salem. They had to pay enormous duties at the Salem Custom House—roughly the value of the ship plus the bartering money they left with—but it was worth it because the cargo usually sold in Europe for five times the amount of the duties.

One pepper shipment aboard Crowninshield's flagship *America* sold for $140,000 in gold. The Crowninshields quickly gained a virtual monopoly on Sumatran pepper that caused a dramatic increase in pepper growing. Between 1797 and 1822, pepper production in Aceh, Sumatra, increased from 2.13 million pounds a year to 18.6 million pounds.

The import duties at Salem at one time had paid for 5 percent of the gross revenue of the U.S. government. Salem had so many ships plying Asian waters that many Asian traders thought it was a sovereign country. It was the nation's sixth-largest city in 1790 and the richest per capita. The quantity of pepper being brought back from the East Indies steadily increased. The *Concord* returned in 1803 with 261,937 pounds of pepper. The next year the *Belisarius* arrived with 295,824 pounds. The most brought back on one voyage was probably *America*'s load of 844,918 pounds in 1801. By 1805, annual reexporting had topped 7.5 million pounds. This would be the all-time high for the Salem pepper trade.

In the East Indies, the Americans began trading with the smaller ports, where they could buy pepper from the growers for less than from the rajas, who acted as middlemen. A major problem was cheating; often the raja middlemen demanded advance payment for the pepper and then sold it to some other English or Dutch captain so that the Americans never saw their pepper or the return of their money. After a few such transactions, the Americans decided to deal with the growers at the pepper plantations. Another problem was pirates. In 1805, Malays hijacked the *Putnam*, and it was never seen again, alerting the Americans to be on their guard. Other American ships were attacked in the years that followed, but the pepper trade continued.

By the end of 1807, Salem had completely recovered from its economic depression, and business was booming, not only from pepper but also from a new import that had become popular: coffee from the Caribbean and Brazil. The town was truly one of the most important commercial cities in the United States. Then, all trade to and from Salem came to an abrupt halt. Napoleon Bonaparte's French ships, plus those of Great Britain hovered off the U.S. coast and patrolled the Caribbean to enforce blockades, capture ships, and seize sailors. Essentially, they were privateer pirates—if the countries' navies had taken such steps, they would have been an act of war. President Jefferson, who had taken few measures for national defense, took a radical course of action and on December 29 invoked an embargo: no American ships could leave for any foreign port.

Historian James Duncan Phillips notes, "Jefferson believed that he was punishing Great Britain, but actually he was aiding her to enforce the blockage of all Europe, and giving her 'a triumphant monopoly of the commerce of the world.'" Phillips was quoting Joseph Story, who later became a Supreme Court justice. Story noted that the embargo was not temporary but intended to be a "permanent measure of retaliation." Is it possible that Jefferson did not realize the financial impact that the embargo would have—not only on Salem traders but also on the wheat farmers of Pennsylvania and Maryland and the cotton planters and tobacco growers of the South? Additionally, some thirty thousand seamen were immediately unemployed, creating great hardship along the East Coast.

Finally, in July 1808, some interstate coastal trade was allowed, but by then bread had become scarce and soup kitchens were full of hungry people. Riots broke out in Beverly on the first anniversary of the embargo, and a letter in the *Salem Gazette* stated, "This law leaves but one horrible alternative: Civil War or Slavery." The Federalists in Congress led the revolt against Jefferson and the Republicans and organized the repeal of most provisions of the "wicked, tyrannical embargo," as the Massachusetts representative Benjamin Pickman called it on March 1, 1809. This happened just three days before Jefferson's term was up and he was to leave Washington for Monticello. Despite the repeal, trade with England and France was still prohibited.

Salem's pepper trade with Sumatra revived after the repeal, but true pirates rather than privateer pirates attacked many ships. Between 1795 and 1873, clipper ships had made nearly a thousand trips to Sumatra and back. But by 1843, pepper prices had dropped in the United States to less than three cents a pound. Somehow, despite the low price, trading in black pepper continued. Thirty years later, the United States formally ended the pepper trade with Sumatra.

One of the results of the Salem black pepper trade was the popularity of the spice in the United States, which to this day is the world's largest importer of black pepper. Thanks to those founding foodies, who of course were more oriented toward making money than loving spices, black pepper became ubiquitous on American tables and in American restaurants.

BLACK PEPPER IN EARLY AMERICAN COOKERY

The popularity of black pepper in America probably began with Hannah Glasse, whose cookbook *The Art of Cookery Made Plain and Easy* was first published in London in 1747 and went through twenty editions during the next fifty years. The book became very popular in the colonies and the British edition was advertised in the *Virginia Gazette* in the 1760s and 1770s. It was one of the first cookbooks published in America, with two Virginia editions published in Alexandria in 1805 and 1812. Glasse's cookbook has exactly 100 mentions of pepper, both black and white, in its 384 pages, including one for pepper cakes.

To Make Pepper-Cakes, by Hannah Glasse

Take half a gill of sack [1/2 cup of dry white wine], half a quarter of an ounce of whole white-pepper, put it in, and boil it together a quarter of an hour; then take the pepper out, and put in as much double refined-sugar as will make it like a paste; then drop it in what shape you please on plates, and let it dry itself.

The embargo failure and resulting recession were a depressing way for Jefferson to leave his eight-year presidency, but he would soon cheer up: he was returning to his two true loves, gardening and farming.

Chapter Six

FOOD AND WINE AT MONTICELLO

E x-president Thomas Jefferson, sixty-five years old, couldn't wait to retire again and return to his beloved Monticello. He began planning his liberation from politics many months before he attended the inauguration of his successor, President James Madison. He was ordering seeds for his new garden and writing to many friends about his "freedom from the hated occupation of politics," as he had said in 1793 after resigning as secretary of state. "I am tired of a life of contention and of being the personal object for the hatred of every man who hates the present state of things," he wrote to his daughter, Martha Randolph, as early as November 1807. His main goal was to return to farming, as he wrote to Robert Livingston, his minister to France, in 1808: "It is now among my most fervent longings to be on my farm, which, with a garden and fruitery, will constitute my principal occupation in retirement."

Jefferson's slaves shared his eagerness to return to Monticello, because their lives were always better when he was living there. He was a humane owner compared to other planters or their overseers, was accessible to his slaves, and acted as a buffer between the slaves and even his own overseers. During his long absences, slaves were often separated from their families and friends when they were hired out to other plantations. Jefferson's return to Monticello after a second long absence would reunite them.

Martha Jefferson recalled in a letter the reaction of the slaves as their carriage approached Monticello: "The shouting, etc., had been sufficiently obstreperous before, but the moment [we] arrived at the top, it reached the climax. When the door of the carriage was opened, they received him in their arms and bore him to the house, crowding round and kissing his hands and feet—some blubbering and crying—others laughing." After this display of subservience and a great degree of love, the crowd parted when Martha and Maria, dressed in their finest clothes, stepped from the carriage and walked up to the decaying mansion.

Jefferson often threw parties and celebrations at Monticello, and he occasionally ordered oxen to be slaughtered for his slaves. According to food historian James E. McWilliams, "Jefferson's slaves were unique in receiving even a sporadic supply of beef. Other plantation owners never fed it to slaves. But, then again, Jefferson butchered oxen after they had been worn down as beasts of burden, thus insuring that their meat would be tough and sinewy (unlike the tender meat on yearlings and calves), and thus not suitable for the big house." What better excuse was there for a celebration and the slaughtering of an ox and a yearling than the president's retirement? If two such celebrations upon his retirement ever occurred, one with the slaves and one with the Jeffersons, here's how they probably happened.

A Beef Treat: How the Slaves Celebrated

The actual slave celebration probably included a half-day off from working to cook and eat pepper pot or other meals using stewed ox, and there would have been singing, dancing, and storytelling well into the night. All the celebration activities were part of African traditions. "In Africa, music was a key essential of life. It was like breathing. With African music, everybody sang whether they were good or bad singers.

Everybody participated. There was no audience," said Art Johnson, a veteran African American interpreter and site manager of the Raleigh Tavern in Williamsburg, Virginia.

Other dishes they made included stewed collard greens, corn bread, pigs' feet, rabbit stew, rutabaga stew, black-eyed peas, fried okra, or fried chicken; and for dessert, fritters, sweet potato pie, or watermelon.

Jefferson supplied his slaves with some food, clothing, firewood, and shelter. Each week, one slave might have received eight quarts (a peck) of cornmeal, a half-pound of pork, and four salted fish for sustenance. But they were partly self-sufficient, raising chickens for meat and eggs; cultivating squash, cucumbers, peas, melons, and other vegetables; and hunting, trapping, and fishing to add to the variety of their food. They were also entrepreneurs, selling vegetables, fish, fruit, and walnuts to the "great house" (the Monticello mansion) to earn money. On Sundays, they took extras to Charlottesville to sell at the market.

Vegetables were extremely important to the slaves' diet, and they grew so many that Monticello's kitchen came to depend on them. Jefferson's memorandum books, which detailed virtually every financial transaction that he engaged in between 1769 and 1826, documented hundreds of transactions involving the sale of produce by Monticello slaves: twenty-two species of fruits and vegetables from as many as forty-three different individuals. Most of the produce harvested from slaves' gardens at Monticello was intended for the out-of-season table and could be stored for the winter, such as cabbages and potatoes, rather than the gourmet vegetables, like artichokes and sea kale, found in Jefferson's garden.

Peter Hatch, the director of gardens and grounds at Monticello, noted, "Other vegetables grown by Jefferson and associated with African American culture include okra, used liberally around Charleston and New Orleans;

eggplant, an African native; sweet potatoes…peanuts, often associated with the African groundnut; and the West Indian gherkin, a spiny, round cucumber commonly pickled and grown in the Jefferson kitchen garden. Some historians have also attributed the earliest distribution of tomatoes in the deep South to African introductions."

JEFFERSON AND TOMATOES

Beginning in 1809, the first year of his second retirement, Jefferson started planting tomatoes in the Monticello garden. According to Peter Hatch, "Jefferson grew a variety described as 'Spanish tomato,' probably typical of the heavily-loved, ribbed, and flattened tomatoes generally grown in the early 19th century."

Despite rumors of the time that tomatoes were poisonous because they were members of the nightshade family of vegetables, which included the poisonous jimson weed and henbane, Jefferson never worried about eating tomatoes.

There is a legend that, on a visit to Lynchburg, he shocked one of the locals by snacking on a tomato in public, but Monticello researchers have been unable to confirm the story.

The Virginia Housewife, *by Mary Randolph (1824), has seventeen recipes for tomatoes, including gazpacho, gumbo, and catsup.*

Mary Randolph's "To Scollop Tomatoes," 1824

Peel off the skin from large, full, ripe tomatoes—put a layer in the bottom of a deep dish, cover it well with bread grated fine; sprinkle on pepper and salt, and lay some bits of butter over them—put another layer of each, till the dish is full—let the top be covered with crumbs and butter—bake it a nice brown.

An archaeological study of the dry well at Monticello, where the slaves tossed kitchen remains, is quite revealing about the nature of slave cooking. Pigs' bones were the most common remains in the well (30 percent), followed by beef (5 percent), and the remaining 65 percent were of fish, game, chickens, and sheep. Food historian James E. McWilliams has noted that "animal bones from Jefferson's slave quarters were frenetically chopped with four or five different instruments, including chops, saws, and shears. A single rib had 21 cuts, five chops, three saw marks, and one shear." This suggests that the slaves cooked their meals in a single pot shared by many slaves in Mulberry Row, the slave quarters. In addition to an iron pot, many slaves' quarters had a frying pan and an iron kettle, and some even had brass pots, beer barrels, pot racks, bowls, jars, and other owner cast-offs. In fact, 20 percent of the ceramic vessels at Mulberry Row were Chinese porcelain teacups, sauces, plates, and bowls.

ICE CREAM FOR THE GUESTS: HOW THE JEFFERSONS CELEBRATED AT MONTICELLO

As seen in chapter 4, Jefferson formed his culinary preferences mostly during his years as minister to France. After he learned of his diplomatic appointment, Jefferson decided to bring his slave James Hemings with him to study the art of French cookery. Dozens of Jefferson family recipes have survived—eight in Jefferson's own hand—and they include *boeuf à la mode*, blancmanger (almond cream), and *nouilly à macaroni* (a pasta dough).

On his return to America, many of his recipes, including ice cream, were considered novelties. He regularly imported a variety of foods, including Italian olive oil, French mustard, Smyrna raisins, Parmesan cheese, almonds, macaroni, anchovies, artichoke hearts, figs, Bologna sausage, and French and Italian wines. The French influence was a part of Jefferson's table for the rest of his life: in 1824, the statesman Daniel Webster noted that dinners at Monticello were "served in half Virginian, half French style, in good taste and abundance."

Thomas Jefferson and his family ate only two meals a day at Monticello: breakfast, typically at eight, and dinner in the late afternoon, about three-thirty. Both meals were served in the dining room, and, if guests were present, in the adjoining tearoom. Before every meal, two bells rang to alert family and guests, one to call them to the table and one when the meal was served.

Edith Fossett and Frances Hern were the main cooks at the President's house, and Fossett became the head of the kitchen at Monticello after Jefferson retired from politics in 1809. Peter Hemings moved on to other duties, including becoming Monticello's assistant brewer. It was Fossett's cooking, in the French-Virginia style that Jefferson liked so much, that impressed visitors to Monticello like Daniel Webster.

Several guests recorded accounts of breakfast at Monticello. One visitor in particular, Margaret Bayard Smith, spent time with Jefferson both in Washington, D.C., during his presidency, and in Charlottesville, in the summer of 1789. Her accounts of the visits are included in the book *The First Forty Years of Washington Society*, and they reveal details of daily life at Monticello. Smith wrote, "Our breakfast table was as large as our dinner table...we had tea, coffee, excellent muffins, hot wheat and corn bread, cold ham and butter." Fifteen years later, Daniel Webster enjoyed a very similar breakfast at Monticello, partaking of "tea or coffee, bread always fresh from the oven...with a slight accompaniment of cold meat."

Near the end of his life, in 1824, Jefferson, forgetting about wine for the moment, wrote that coffee was "the favorite drink of the civilised world." He had enjoyed the coffeehouses of Williamsburg and Paris, and he regularly served coffee at the President's House and Monticello. He preferred beans imported from the East and West Indies, and he despised the green, or unripe, beans that were popular in America at the time. He estimated that a pound of coffee a day was consumed at Monticello during his retirement, and the cellar at Monticello was stocked with unroasted beans in barrels weighing as much as sixty pounds. "Bourbon or E. India would always be preferred," he wrote, "but good West India will give satisfaction."

The beans were roasted and ground in the Monticello kitchen as needed and then prepared according to the recipe of Adrien Petit, Jefferson's French maître d'hôtel at the President's House: "On one measure of the coffee ground into meal pour three measures of boiling water. Boil it on hot ashes mixed with coal till the meal disappears from the top, when it will be precipitated. Pour it three times through a flannel strainer. It will yield 2 1/3 measures of clear coffee." Coffee was served at breakfast, and likely after dinner, in a silver coffee urn fashioned from Jefferson's design.

The coffee urn, displayed in the tearoom at Monticello, is the only surviving example of several tea and coffee urns that Jefferson owned. It is marked by the silversmith Jacques-Louis Auguste Leguay, and it is thought to be the "silver coffee pot" that Jefferson purchased in February 1789, before he left Paris to return to America.

No menus of main meals at Monticello have survived, but letters and published observations from guests give a good idea of what was served. There have been two cook-books published that explore the cuisine of

Jefferson's coffee urn

Monticello. In addition to *Thomas Jefferson's Cookbook*, by Marie Kimball, which has been in print since 1938, in 2005, the Thomas Jefferson Foundation published *Dining at Monticello*, the most complete analysis of Monticello food yet.

Recipes in *Thomas Jefferson's Cookbook* include French soup maigre; French roast beef; beef a la daube; fillet of veal with Madeira sauce; roasted duck; oyster pie; bread puddings; chocolate cream; and, of course, ice creams flavored with raspberries, strawberries, and peaches.

Dining at Monticello features Monticello muffins (a family favorite), ver-micelli soup, beef a la mode, beef a la daube Lemaire, roast duck with onion sauce, chicken fricassee, fried asparagus, roasted corn, baked macaroni and cheese, glazed turnips, trifle, brandied peaches, and wine jelly.

Desserts served at Monticello included trifle, various kinds of fritters, gin-gerbread, bread pudding, various tarts, custards, creams, and the ubiquitous ice cream. Beth L. Cheuk notes in *Dining at Monticello*, "If Jefferson didn't introduce the confection in America, he certainly promoted it. Visitors to the President's House frequently noted ice cream in their observations... The family cookery manuscripts contain a wide array of ice cream and ice [sherbet] recipes, all of which would suggest that the Jefferson family enjoyed ice cream regularly."

And what wine might Jefferson have served during his retirement party? Financial difficulties forced Jefferson to shift from the Bordeaux, champagnes, and Burgundies to lesser-known wines from southern France, such as Claret de Bergasse, Limoux, Ledenon, and Muscat de Rivesaltes. Only one American wine was purchased after his second retirement: scuppernong from North Carolina. Jefferson wine expert James M. Gabler notes, "Jefferson cut back on the quality of his wines—but not the quantity—and his dinner guests continued to eat heartily—duck, oysters, cheese, lamb, beef, turkey, chicken and herring were standard dinner foods."

If his slaves were singing and dancing to banjo music, the guests at the Monticello great house were probably more subdued. Family would be there: Martha Randolph; her husband, Tom, visiting from Edgehill; Martha's daughter Anne Bankhead and her husband, Charles; and Martha Carr, Jefferson's widowed sister, and her five children. Other guests could have been any of the hundred of well-wishers who would drop by at Monticello expecting food and lodging. As with Washington at Mount Vernon, guests constantly inundated Monticello. Jefferson's daughter and Monticello's first lady, Martha Randolph, recalled having as many as fifty overnight guests at one time in the twelve-bedroom house.

The burden of maintaining Monticello's gracious level of hospitality had always been the responsibility of the Jefferson family and the talented slaves they supervised. Beginning with Jefferson's wife, Martha Wayles Skelton Jefferson, three generations of women managed the Monticello household, and they worked hard at it. In addition to supervising the preparation and serving of the meals, they also managed other domestic activities like making dairy, salting, curing, and smoking meats, and brewing and bottling beer. During one month in 1772, for example, Martha Jefferson recorded in her account book that she opened a barrel of flour; used two loaves of sugar; had seven ducks, one lamb, and one pig killed; bought six pounds of coffee and eleven pounds of butter; and supervised the brewing of one cask (fifteen gallons) of beer. Jefferson valued his wife's managerial ability, writing "the order and economy of the house are as honourable to the mistress as those of the farm to the master, and if either be neglected, ruin follows."

After Jefferson's retirement from the presidency, even more guests and curious sightseers descended on Monticello, ranging from family members who stayed for weeks at a time to international figures. James and Dolley Madison visited so often that the family came to call one of the first-floor bedrooms the Madison Room. Overseer Edmund Bacon recalled, "After Mr. Jefferson returned from Washington, he was for years crowded with visitors, and they almost ate him out of house and home...I have killed a fine beef, and it would all be eaten in a day or two." While entertaining his guests, Jefferson was "learning how to be a farmer."

"THE MOST ARDENT FARMER IN THE STATE": JEFFERSON'S FIRST RETIREMENT, 1790–1796

After Jefferson retired as secretary of state in 1790, he left Washington and returned to face the conditions of his fields and gardens at Monticello. He wrote to George Washington in 1794 that, now that he had a chance to really examine his land, "a ten years' abandonment of them to the ravages of overseers has brought on them a degree of degradation far beyond what

I had expected." But despite that, he claimed an "ardour" for the love of farming that surpassed his "love of study."

To bring his land back to optimum productivity, Jefferson had to learn how to be a farmer for the first time in his life, because previous attempts had not been very productive. "I am too little familiar with the practice of farming to rely with confidence on my own judgment," he wrote in 1793. To help alleviate his lack of farming experience, he turned to his agricultural mentor, George Washington, a highly successful farmer and rancher. Besides exchanging letters, they met frequently even after Jefferson left Washington's administration. "In short," wrote historian Barbara McEwan, "Jefferson found considerable inspiration from his President to challenge conventional farming practices."

Jefferson adopted and added to Washington's techniques of crop rotation and adding organic material to the soil on a seven-year rotation plan. He wrote to Washington about his method of rotation: "1. wheat, followed by winter vetch. 2. corn, followed by winter vetch. 3. fallow pease. 4. wheat. 5.6.7. three years of clover. I mix potatoes with my corn, on your plan." In 1792, Jefferson traveled to Mount Vernon to discuss rotation and adding manure, which he was unsure about. "Manure does not enter into this [his farming plan]," he wrote to Washington after his visit, "because we can buy an acre of new land cheaper than we can manure an old acre."

He eventually changed his mind about manure and finally embraced Washington's concept, using manure in all stages of decomposition, from fresh to well decomposed. He wrote in a letter to his daughter Martha in 1793, "We will try this winter to cover our garden with a heavy coating of manure. When earth is rich it bids defiance to droughts, yields in abundance, and of the best quality. I suspect that the insects which have harassed you have been encouraged by the feebleness of your plants; and that has been produced by the lean state of the soil. We will attack them another year with joint efforts."

Part of the problem with restoring the fertility of his land was his earlier cultivation of tobacco. He noted as early as 1781 in his *Notes on the State of Virginia* that tobacco "is a culture productive of infinite wretchedness," and he echoed that sentiment in 1796: "My hills are too rough ever to please the eye, and as yet unreclaimed from the barbarous state in which the slovenly business of tobacco making has left them." Despite such harsh words, financial considerations forced him to return to occasional tobacco cultivation in later years.

Corn also depleted the fields of nutrients. He experimented with more than a dozen different varieties, but they all had the same result: depletion of nitrogen and other nutrients in the soil, and the spacing of the rows left the ground subject to water erosion, especially in hilly regions such as Monticello. Finally, he switched to farming wheat. "Besides clothing the earth with herbage, and preserving its fertility," he wrote, "it [wheat] feeds the laborers plentifully…raises great numbers of animals for food and service, and dif[f]uses plenty and happiness among the whole."

Ice was plentiful at Monticello. In 1802, Jefferson built an icehouse that could store sixty-two wagon loads of ice hauled from the Rivanna River. Often, the ice would last nearly a year, usually running out the following mid-October. Besides ice and some snow, also stored in the icehouse were butter and fresh meat, making it a convenient—if huge—early refrigerator. As Jefferson noted after visiting an icehouse in Italy that was the inspiration for his own, "Snow gives the most delicate flavor to creams, but ice is the most powerful congealer, and lasts longest."

Good plows were the key to good deep farming, and Jefferson's crowning achievement in farm technology was his invention of a moldboard plow of least resistance. He constructed a model of his new design and showed it to his son-in-law, Thomas Mann Randolph, in 1789. He kept on working to improve the design and in 1794 wrote, "I have imagined and executed a mould-board which may be mathematically demonstrated to be perfect." By lowering the degree of soil resistance, farmers could plant deeper, and the plow was easier to pull for the farm animals like mules and oxen. "Ploughing deep, your recipe for killing weeds, is also the recipe for almost every good thing in farming." In 1798, a description of his plow was published in *Transactions of the American Philosophical Society*, and in 1807, the Society of Agriculture of Paris awarded Jefferson a gold medal for it and named him a foreign associate. "The plough," Jefferson pontificated, "is to the farmer what the wand is to the Sorcerer."

"But Though an Old Man, I Am but a Young Gardener"

Jefferson spoke these words to Charles Wilson Peale in 1811, and in many ways, Jefferson is more renowned as a gardener than as a farmer. His thousand-foot-long kitchen-garden terrace was an experimental laboratory, and Peter Hatch has calculated that he grew 70 different species and 330 varieties of vegetables. The garden was designed more for Jefferson's horticultural experiments than to actually provide food for the family, so that's why he often bought produce from his slaves, particularly vegetables that could be stored for long periods of time, like potatoes and onions.

Many writers have attempted to determine Jefferson's favorite vegetable, and some have concluded that the English, or garden pea, was it, given the frequency of planting and the fact that he grew nineteen different varieties. But he also loved lettuce and asparagus. Peter Hatch noted his "unabashed enthusiasm" and "sweeping pronouncements" about his favorites. When his neighbor and wine adviser Philip Mazzei introduced him to fennel, Jefferson effused about it: "The fennel is beyond every other vegetable, delicious…no vegetable equals it in flavor. Indeed, I preferred it to every other vegetable, or to any fruit." As Barbara McEwan commented in *Thomas Jefferson, Gardener*, "Jefferson never met a plant he didn't like."

Although Jefferson loved vegetables, he was quite fond of fruits as well, and his favorite fruit was undoubtedly the peach. At Monticello, they made "mobby," peach juice that was later distilled into brandy. Jefferson recorded that "20 bushels of peaches will make 75 galls. of mobby." Of course, fresh peaches were used in desserts, such as a topping for ice cream, and were made into preserves. "Peach chips" were sliced from peeled peaches, boiled, sugared, and sun-dried. In 1794, Jefferson had his slaves plant nine hundred peach trees, which also made excellent firewood from the deadwood pruned each winter. "I am endeavoring to make a collection of the choicest kind of peaches for Monticello," he wrote to a friend in 1807.

Two Favorite Monticello Peach Recipes, by Mary Randolph, 1824

Peach Chips

Slice them thin, and boil them till clear in a syrup made with half their weight of sugar; lay them on dishes in the sun, and turn them till dry;

pack them in pots with powdered sugar sifted over each layer; should there be syrup left, continue the process with other peaches. They are very nice when done with pure honey instead of sugar.

Peach Marmalade

Take the ripest soft peaches (the yellow ones make the prettiest marmalade), pare them, and take out the stones; put them in the pan with one pound of dry light coloured brown sugar to two of peaches: when they are juicy, they do not require water: with a silver or wooden spoon, chop them with the sugar; continue to do this, and let them boil gently till they are a transparent pulp, that will be a jelly when cold. Puffs made of this marmalade are very delicious.

In 1796, Jefferson had his best farm harvest ever, writing to James Monroe: "We have had the finest harvest ever known in this part of the country. Both the quantity and quality of wheat are extraordinary. Then, as farm historian Barbara McEwan puts it, "His happy world of rebuilding home, gardens, orchards and farms fell apart. On November 4, 1796 he was elected vice president of the United States." This caused him to be away from Monticello most of the time, and his absence got worse after he was elected president in 1801. For his entire eight years as president, he was only at Monticello for a month in the spring and two months in the late summer and early fall.

BEER AND CIDER AT MONTICELLO

Although not as deeply involved in fermenting things as Washington was—he never built a distillery—Jefferson nonetheless was very interested in beer and cider, and of course had a fascination with wine. He collected the following works for his Monticello library: *The London and Country Brewer* (1736), *Combrun's Theory and Practice of Brewing* (1815), *Richardson's Philosophical Principles of Brewing (1788)*, and *Krafft's American Distiller* (1804).

Jefferson, like many of his contemporaries, was partial to cider. This would be hard cider, made with fermented apples and containing about 3–8 percent alcohol. In his usual manner, Jefferson demanded a certain blend of the best of his eighteen varieties of apples among the hundreds of trees in the orchards at Monticello, and each one had to be at the peak of ripeness. He wrote as early as 1776, "Golden Wilding must not be mellowed before pressed; it will yield nothing. It must be pressed as soon as gathered. Mixed with red Hughes they make the best cyder & yield best." His overseer, Edmund Bacon, described the process: "Then every March we had to bottle all his cider. Dear me, this was a job. It took us two weeks. Mr. Jefferson was very particular about his cider. He gave me instructions to have every apple cleaned perfectly."

Jefferson also made cider from the Taliaferro variety, which mixed with the Hughes crab apple, made another fine cider, as described by Jefferson in 1814: "The cyder they constantly made from this was preferred by every person to the Crab or any other cyder ever known in this state. It has more body, is less acid, and comes nearer to the silky Champaigne than any other." At the age of eighty-three, he wrote to his granddaughter Ellen Randolph Coolidge about that particular variety: "Being from a seedling tree discovered by a gentleman of that name near Williamsburg, and yield unquestionably the finest cyder ever known, and more like wine than any liquor I have ever tasted which was not wine." Seventy bushels of Taliaferro and Hughes apples yielded 120 gallons of cider.

How Dr. Chase Made Cider in 1876

Cider.—A beverage made from the juice of the apple, and for which sour and rough-tasted apples are generally preferred. The process of making cider varies in different localities, but in every case essentially consists of the collection of the fruit, and the expression and fermentation of the juice. The collection of the fruit should not be commenced before it has become sufficiently mature. The apples, after being gathered, are usually left for fourteen or fifteen days in a barn or loft to mellow, during which time the mucilage is decomposed, and alcohol and carbonic acid developed. The expression of the juice is the next step in cider-making. The apples are ground to a pulp in a mill, consisting of two fluted cylinders of hard wood or cast iron working against each other. The pulp is afterwards put into coarse strong bags, and pressed with a heavy weight so as to squeeze out all the juice. This is then placed in large, open tubs, and kept at a heat of about sixty degrees. After two or three days for weak cider, and eight or ten days for strong cider, or as soon as the sediment has subsided, the liquor is " racked off" into clean casks. The casks are then stored in a cellar, shaded barn, or other cool place, where a low and regular temperature can be insured, and are left to mature and ripen until the following spring, when it may be re-racked for use. The refuse pulp is an acceptable food for pigs and store cattle.

Preparatory to bottling cider, it should be examined, to see whether it is clear and sparkling. If not so, it should be clarified, and left for a fortnight. The night previous to bottling, the bung should be taken out of the cask, and the filled bottles should not be corked down until the day after; as, if this is done at once, many of the bottles will burst by keeping. The best corks should be used. Champagne bottles are the best for cider. When the cider is wanted for immediate use, or for consumption during the cooler season of the year, a

> *small piece of lump sugar may be put into each bottle before corking it. When intended for keeping, it should be stored in a cool cellar, when the quality will be greatly improved by age.*

Inundated with rum, wine, and beer tales from the time, it is sometimes easy to forget the importance of cider to the colonial and postcolonial citizens. All people in all classes, from planter to slave, consumed cider. Historian Philip Bruce noted how commonly cider was served: "There was hardly a residence of any pretension which did not keep a supply of this liquor on hand; and some planters had as much as one hundred and fifty gallons stored away in their cellars." Jefferson's old friend, antiliquor advocate Dr. Benjamin Rush commented, "In the room of spirits, in the first place, Cyder. This excellent liquor is perfectly inoffensive and wholesome." Cider was regarded as uniquely American and therefore a "democratic drink." Cider proponents writing in *American Farmer* in the 1820s campaigned to make cider the "national beverage," but nothing ever came of it.

L. H. Bailey, author of *The Standard Cyclopedia of Horticulture* (1936), commented on the changing habits of apple consumption after Jefferson's time: "The gradual change in customs, whereby the eating of the apple (rather than the drinking of it) has come to be paramount, is a significant development." That may be so, but today, according to John Hailman, Virginia is "the home of fine apple cider."

If this is true, where is the hard cider? David Williams of George Mason University notes that in the tables of W. J. Rorabaugh, author of *The Alcoholic Republic*, there was a dramatic disappearance of cider as a favored drink in the year 1840, followed by the beginning of beer as a national beverage. His tables, by his own admission, are "based on guess work from anecdotal and 'literary sources.'" Williams concludes that the temperance movement was a "major culprit" in the disappearance of cider, but other contributing factors were "the economics of beer production, growing urbanization, German immigration, a predatory beer industry, and a substitute drink in Coca-Cola."

In reality, beer was always as popular as cider in Jefferson's day. He called it, along with cider, his "table liquor," and it was served with dinner, unlike wine, which was served afterward. In the early years of his marriage to Martha, it was she who brewed fifteen-gallon batches every two weeks. In 1804, Jefferson gave his permission for Michael Krafft to dedicate his book *American Distiller* to Jefferson "as a safeguard against its falling into the general wreck of oblivion." Jefferson enthusiastically agreed, writing (even though the grain could be used to make whiskey), "The art of distilling which you propose to explain, besides its household uses, is valuable to the agriculturist, as it enables him to put his superfluous grain into a form which will bear long transportation to markets to which the raw material could never get."

Sparked by his correspondence with Krafft, the following year, Jefferson bought Michael Combrune's *Theory and Practice of Brewing*, but it took a rather remarkable coincidence for him to begin brewing in earnest at Monticello years later. The War of 1812 had severely interrupted his supply of European wines, so he was eager to make cider and brew beer. Jefferson heard that an English brewer and army captain, Joseph Miller, had been taken prisoner and arranged for him to be interned at Monticello, where he became "a brewer for family use." Miller instructed Peter Hemings in the brewing art, and Hemings became very skilled at it because of what Jefferson termed his "great intelligence and diligence." (So skilled, in fact, that Hemings taught brewing to James Madison's people in 1820.) By the fall of 1814, there was a brewhouse at Monticello and Jefferson began malting his own grain rather than purchasing it from neighbors.

In the fall, Jefferson had Hemings brew three sixty-gallon casks of ale. The process began with malting the germinating grain. Once the precise germination point had been reached—which only an experienced malter could determine—the grain was cooled, dried, and roasted. The heat and duration of the roasting process determined the strength of the beer, as light roasting produced a light beer, and lengthy roasting made porter or stout. Jefferson recommended a bushel of malt for every eight to ten gallons of strong beer, and he noted that "public breweries" made fifteen gallons from every bushel, which "makes their liquor meager and often vapid." Mashing produced wort (the liquid extracted from the mashing process), to which hops grown at Monticello were added. After Hemings was satisfied with the length of time the hops soaked in the wort, they were strained out and replaced with yeast, which began the fermentation process.

After fermenting, the beer was kegged and allowed to rest for about two weeks in a cool place. Jefferson preferred to store the beer in bottles and jugs, which meant that, each year, he had to buy bottles and corks for both beer and cider. He insisted on better corks than his daughter had used earlier with cider, commenting, "It is so provoking to lose good liquor by bad corks." Because Jefferson grew only corn and wheat, but no barley, his beer undoubtedly tasted much different than what we drink today. Jefferson's beer was probably darker, sweeter, heavier, and more alcoholic, and some brewers even added molasses, horseradish, or sassafras to their beer, although there is no evidence of that at Monticello.

Beer historian Stanley Baron commented on Jefferson's brewing: "Jefferson brought to it all his characteristic enthusiasm and curiosity...he was a real champion of the brewing industry. It is particularly interesting that Jefferson took up brewing at a time when, as an industry, it was at its lowest ebb in the national economy."

But Jefferson was not so successful in making wine. His attempts date from 1771 to 1822—all without success. He had two vineyards at Monticello, the northeastern one measured nine thousand square feet, and the southwestern one was sixteen thousand square feet. In 1807, he planted 287 rooted vines and cuttings of twenty-four European grape varieties in his most ambitious planting of many at Monticello. But his planting more resembled a vineyard of a plant collector than that of a serious winemaker. Not one of these plants survived: they were either dead on arrival, not planted properly, or infected with diseases or plant pests. There was no way for those rooted European cuttings to fight off American pests such as black rot and phylloxera, a root-eating louse related to aphids.

"THE CULTURE OF THE EARTH": JEFFERSON'S SECOND RETIREMENT, 1809–1826

While he was still president in 1806, Jefferson was presented with the most authoritative book yet published on American horticulture, *The American Gardener's Calendar*, by Bernard McMahon. McMahon was a Philadelphia nurseryman and America's first landscape gardener. Jefferson later bought plants from him repeatedly, and his self-published book described sixty-seven varieties of vegetables (only corn is mysteriously missing) and twenty-six varieties of herbs. Probably dreaming of his second retirement and immersing himself again in farming and gardening, Jefferson undoubtedly relished the book, writing later, "No occupation is so delightful to me as the culture of the earth, and no culture comparable to that of the garden."

He may have been young in mind and energy, but the reality of his finances made him feel very old. No doubt he envied George Washington, who had established most of his fortune before the Revolutionary War, and thus could survive the economic downturn that occurred after America became a country. Jefferson was not alone—other prominent Virginia planter-politicians were caught in the same financial trap. Close to Monticello were the plantations of James Madison (Montpelier); James Monroe (Ashlawn, adjacent to Monticello); and Jefferson's son-in-law, Thomas Mann Randolph (Tuckahoe), also adjacent to Monticello. Madison and Monroe also would become president, and the Randolphs were among the first families of Virginia. Randolph was a direct descendant of Pocahontas (see chapter 1), whose English-born husband, John Rolfe, developed a variety of tobacco that became Virginia's first cash crop for export. Randolph later became governor of Virginia and was, of course, Jefferson's son-in-law. One of his sisters was Mary Randolph, the author of the best of all the early cookbooks.

All of these farmer friends suffered similar financial disasters in old age, and Jefferson summed up their joint problems in a letter to James Monroe: "To keep a Virginia estate together requires in the owner skill and attention; skill I never had and attention I could not have, and really when I reflect on all circumstances my wonder is that I should have been so long as sixty years in reaching the result to which I am now reduced."

Jefferson tried to emulate Washington's entrepreneurial success, but he had no Potomac River to provide cheap fish that could easily be caught for a profit. Washington switched from growing tobacco to wheat, and so did Jefferson. Washington built a mill to process wheat into flour, and in 1806, while still president, Jefferson followed suit. He spent $10,000 on his mill at Shadwell and was able grind as many as six hundred barrels of flour, but the mill caused more financial problems than it was worth. Not only did Jefferson have to hire millers (mostly incompetent) to work the mill; the dam that provided the waterpower to run the mill repeatedly broke during floods, and Jefferson had to pay for repairs.

The only good news about the mill was that Jefferson could make money by renting it out to other farmers. He took barrels of flour as the rent, which he could sell on the open market. By 1819, Jefferson had stopped growing wheat at Monticello, and he was back to growing corn, which is ironic given his earlier railings against that crop. The differences were that his land was more fertile from continuing applications of manure and he finally had found a variety of corn that he felt was much tastier than before. Corn was less susceptible to pests and diseases than wheat, and again, new technology in the form of corn shellers and crushers improved his bottom line. Even with corn's added farming benefits, nearly one-third of the time he had no significant corn crop—in thirty years of growing it, from 1790 to 1820, he recorded corn crop failures in eight of them.

Jefferson much preferred gardening to farming. After all, introducing new plant varieties and experimenting with them was a lot less stressful and much more interesting than trying to make a profit from his fields. Peter Ling, author of *Thomas Jefferson and the Environment*, wrote in 2004, "Jefferson's fields and gardens at his retirement home of Poplar Forest contained hops, clover, hemp, bent grass, and winter vetch from England; alfalfa from the Mediterranean; Guinea corn and sesame from Africa; Nanking cotton from Asia; field peas, sainfoin, and turnips from Europe; sulla grass from Malta. His buffalo or Kentucky clover came from the inland grasslands of the Ohio Valley. All his prized orchard fruits—apples, pears, cherries and peaches—were introduced from abroad."

It was a similar situation with olive trees. Jefferson planted 1,500 olive stones at Monticello in 1774, but they never sprouted. An olive tree he received from Philip Mazzei in 1778 died, and the olive stones he brought back from Italy did not sprout either. In 1810, more olive stones arrived from a friend in Paris, but Jefferson wrote him back that of the five hundred plants, "if any of them still exist, it is merely a curiosity in their gardens; not a single orchard of them has been planted." He was still pushing the olive in 1822, when a friend wrote him that his single olive tree in South Carolina "looks healthy and well and some years produces fruit." Agricultural historian Barbara McEwan notes, "It is interesting to note that this otherwise astute botanist would not recognize that the olive requires a semi-arid climate to survive."

Jefferson's next kick was sesamum oil, which was processed from sesame seeds. His friend William Few sent him a bottle of the oil in 1807, and Jefferson proclaimed it to be as good as olive oil. He received seeds and attempted to grow it in 1808, finally succeeded in 1811, and wrote to the nurseryman Bernard McMahon, "We raise it and make our own sallad oil preferable to such olive oil as is usually to be bought." His sesamum project failed for the same reason as the rice—there was no efficient manner to mill the seeds from the chaff. He concluded that it could only be grown for home consumption. Peter Ling commented, "So blind was his enthusiasm for exotic sources of cooking oil, such as the olive and sesame, that he ignored the potential of the native American crop, maize, and that of peanuts, a plant which had been introduced by African slaves."

Some historians have taken Jefferson to task for planting invasive species like paper mulberries, which he arranged around "necessities" (outhouses) to hide them. With his usual effusiveness, he described them in 1816 as "the most beautiful & best shading tree to be near the house." But Jefferson was not alone in planting them, and he hardly is responsible for all the problems this tree, which chokes out native trees, has caused in the South. Certainly, it is hindsight to criticize him for something he could not have predicted. That said, there is some degree of accuracy in Ling's observation: "He held to the illusion that the land could be changed to suit human designs much as he changed and developed his house at Monticello. This dream of progress leached into the larger agricultural development of America, thanks in part to Jefferson's colossal influence."

Jefferson raised livestock, of course, but he was not as much of a rancher as was George Washington. He particularly liked sheep, especially the merino breed, which Washington had recommended and was prized for its excellent wool. He also raised the Barbary breed, which Jefferson said was the best-flavored meat that he had ever eaten.

Jefferson liked his lamb—actually mutton—and it was served boiled, broiled, roasted, and fried at Monticello. Jefferson was not a cook, of course, but he had an interesting food and beverage book collection in his library. Not surprisingly, it included the classic book on Roman cuisine that was later published in English as *Apicius: Cooking and Dining in Imperial Rome*. From his days in Paris, he had been a fan of the French potato promoter and friend of Benjamin Franklin, Antoine-Augustin Parmentier, and he owned books by him that ranged in topic from baking to manufacturing grape syrups and preserves to potatoes. Rounding out his food library were *Dictionnaire Domestique* (1762) and *Eale's Cookery*.

Monticello's kitchen was probably the best equipped in Virginia. While he was U.S. minister to France, Jefferson purchased many cooking utensils for his residence in Paris. After he returned to America in 1789, he had the utensils sent to America and later Monticello as part of an eighty-six-crate shipment of goods. Originally, the kitchen was housed in the cellar of the south pavilion; however, by the time Jefferson retired again in 1809, a newer, much larger kitchen was constructed that featured a bake oven, a fireplace, and an eight-opening stew stove.

When he heard about stew holes, the new kitchen technology installed in Madison's President's House, Jefferson ordered eight for the Monticello kitchen. The unit was a waist-high counter made of brick with individual openings and grates below. The temperature of each burner could be adjusted by the amount of coals placed in it. The stew stove was the precursor to nineteenth-century cast-iron ranges, but it did not have flues, so the windows and doors of the kitchen were opened for ventilation. Jefferson also installed a spit jack that didn't use a dog to turn the spit but rather a clock-type invention using weights and counterweights. A tall case clock also stood in the kitchen and Isaac Jefferson, one of Monticello's former slaves, once recalled that the only time Jefferson went into the kitchen was to wind the clock.

When he was president, Jefferson chose Edith Fossett to train to be a cook in the President's House. For nearly seven years, Edith "cooked in the French style" and fixed fancy desserts. Jefferson was so fond of her cooking that he gave her a "gift" of two dollars a month in lieu of a salary. When Jefferson returned to Monticello in 1809, Edith came with him to be head cook in the new kitchen. It was of her cooking that Daniel Webster spoke when he described the meals at Monticello as "in half Virginian, half French style, in good taste and abundance."

THE FOUNDER OF MODERN AGRICULTURE?

Was Jefferson the founder of modern agriculture? That was the claim Claude Wickard made in 1945 in an article in the journal *Agricultural History*. He bases the claim on Jefferson's concern with soil erosion, his advocating of contour plowing, his crop rotation practices, and his international fame as an agricultural scientist. "We may properly regard him as the founder of agricultural research and our modern agricultural extension service," Wickard concluded.

But he wasn't the founder of profitable agriculture—a title that is more fitting for George Washington. "Jefferson was unsuccessful as a farmer, apparently never making a profit from any of his plantations," noted John Hailman. Joseph Ellis phrased it more kindly: "However fortunate he was as a public figure, he was an extremely unlucky farmer."

That said, Jefferson's agricultural legacy is based on his efforts to make the soil more fertile, to reduce soil erosion, to introduce and experiment with new crops, and to create improved crops through plant-breeding techniques. In those senses, he was, indeed the founder of modern agriculture.

Damon Lee Fowler, editor of *Dining at Monticello*, summed up Jefferson's contributions as a founding foodie: "Jefferson made an important impact on our national culinary consciousness as an ever-searching epicure, gathering and incorporating the best elements of the food traditions he encountered in both Old World and New." He added, "Thomas Jefferson resonates with food lovers across the ages not because he mastered haute cuisine, but because he understood its principles."

It is significant that Jefferson's very last letter, written less than a month before he died (June 25, 1826) was to his wine agents. He was restocking his cellar for all occasions, buying aperitifs, white *vin ordinaire* and red clarets to drink with meals, and some muscats for after dinner sipping. In his letter, he directs Bernard Peyton to pay the $18.00 duty for the incoming new wines. Even at the end, he was still a wine enthusiast.

Chapter Seven

RE-CREATING THE RECIPES OF THE FOUNDING FOODIES

I have revised the original recipes that follow into a standard format so today's cook can easily prepare them in the modern kitchen. My technique involved researching the original recipes; taking the best elements from them; and combining them with my own experiences, techniques, and in some cases, additional ingredients. I have organized the recipes by menus that reflect the themes in this book. The menus are not from actual menus of the time but are suggested menus for today that represent the legacies that have been passed down to us. I have selected these particular recipes because I feel that they are the most representative of what people ate and drank during the times of the founding foodies.

A CLASSIC COLONIAL DRINKING PARTY

The thirteen colonies were awash in alcoholic beverages and colonists invented some very creative ways to consume their favorite liquors, as all alcoholic beverages were generically called.

The rum ration was a daily tradition aboard ships of His Majesty's Navy during the eighteenth and nineteenth centuries. In 1740, British Admiral Sir Edward Vernon, returned from the Caribbean possibly carrying Mount Gay Rum, which had been distilled in Barbados since 1663. The admiral, known as

Old Grog because he wore a cloak of a coarse cloth, decided to dilute the daily ration of rum with water. The resulting "cocktail" was known as grog, as many rum drinks were called generically. The water was soon replaced with lemon or lime juice to counteract scurvy. Grog eventually evolved into the rum toddy, which is served hot with brown sugar, butter, and spices.

Hot Rum Toddy

2 teaspoons brown sugar

2 teaspoons freshly squeezed lemon or lime juice

1 teaspoon butter

1/2 teaspoon grated nutmeg

Dash each powdered cinnamon, ginger, and cloves

1 ounce dark rum

1 cup hot water

Lemon peel and cinnamon stick for garnish

In a bowl, combine the brown sugar, lemon or lime juice, butter, nutmeg, cinnamon, ginger, and cloves, and stir into a paste. Add the rum to the hot water in a serving cup and stir in the paste until it dissolves. Garnish with the lemon peel and cinnamon stick. Serve while still hot.

YIELD: 1 SERVING

Related to eggnog but considered a ladies' drink because it contains no strong alcohol, syllabub is essentially a dessert drink. A report of the British Archaeological Society in 1891 reported: "A mystery hangs over both the origin of the name and time of the invention of syllabub, and even the receipts for its compound differ in no small degree. Minshew, who appears to be one of the earliest lexicographers who paid attention to the subject, regards syllabub or sillabub as a corruption of 'swilling bubbles.'" The report goes on to quote Hannah Woolley's recipe from Queen-Like Closet Stored with Rare Receipts *(1684): "To make very fine sillibub.— Take one quart of cream, one pint and an half of wine or sack, the juice of two limons with some of the pill, and a branch of rosemary; sweeten it very well, then put a little of this liquor and a little of the cream into a bason, beat them till it froth, put that froth into the sillibub-pot; and so do till the cream and wine be done, then cover it close, and set it in a cool cellar for twelve hours, then eat it." Here is an updated version of this strange but flavorful drink.*

Whipped Syllabub

1 1/2 cups sweet white wine or Madeira

Juice of 3 lemons

1/2 cup confectioners' sugar

Grated rind of 2 lemons

1 quart half-and-half

3 egg whites beaten and sweetened with sugar to taste

Freshly grated nutmeg for garnish

In a large bowl, combine the wine, lemons, confectioner's sugar, and lemon rind and mix well. Add the cream and whip to a froth with an electric beater. Serve in individual tall glasses topped with the egg white mixture and sprinkled with nutmeg.

YIELD: 10 SERVINGS

There are so many tales about the origin of this drink that it's impossible to determine the source. One source says the Fish House in Philadelphia first served it to George Washington, but the one I like best states that Shippen Willen invented the recipe in 1848, on the occasion of the first women being allowed into the club.

Fish House Punch

30 limes, juiced
15 lemons, juiced
2 parts light rum
1 part brown sugar
1 part dark rum
1 part brandy
Ice cubes as needed

Measure the amount of the lemon juice and lime juice combined. The result constitutes a "part" for the remainder of the ingredients. Combine the juice and the brown sugar in a bowl, and mix well. Add the remaining ingredients, chill, and serve in small glasses.

YIELD: VARIES

"Sangaree" is a variation on sangria, the Spanish punch of wine and fruits, so named because its dark-red color resembles blood, or sangre. *Margaret Carroll served Martha Washington this punch in April 1789, when she stopped in Baltimore on her way to her husband's inauguration as the first president. Carroll picked the fruits from her greenhouse, which George Washington used as a model for his own. Peach and apricot kernels have a minor role as flavorings in early American recipes and were a substitute for bitter almonds. The sparkling water is a recent adaptation because it did not exist in 1789. Also, note that nectarines are a peach cultivar with a smooth skin, not a cross between a peach and a plum as is commonly believed.*

Mrs. Carroll's Iced Sangaree

1 cup brandy

1/4 cup sugar

2 peach kernels

2 nectarine kernels

10 strawberries, sliced

2 ripe peaches, peeled and sliced

2 slices fresh pineapple, crushed

2 ripe nectarines, sliced

1 orange, peeled, seeded, and sliced

1 lemon, peeled, seeded, and sliced

1 bottle red wine, claret preferred

1 pint sparkling water

Mint leaves for garnish

In a small bowl, combine the sugar, brandy, and peach and nectarine kernels, and let the mixture sit for 4 hours. Transfer the mixture to a punch bowl, remove the kernels, and add the remaining ingredients, stirring gently. Serve over ice garnished with mint leaves.

YIELD: 6 SERVINGS

So named because it supposedly warmed up the imbiber during the winter, a yard of flannel is a variation on the rum flip. It was served at Fraunces Tavern in Manhattan, where Washington gave his farewell address to his officers in 1783. The tavern, opened in 1762, still exists at 54 Pearl Street, along with an adjacent museum that features artifacts from the early periods of New York and American history. Traditionally, the drink was warmed up with a red-hot fireplace poker, called a flip-dog in Washington's time.

A Yard of Flannel

1 quart dark ale
4 eggs
1/2 cup sugar
1/2 cup rum
1 teaspoon grated nutmeg

In a saucepan, heat the ale, but do not let it boil. In a bowl, mix all the other ingredients together, and beat well. Add the heated ale to the bowl slowly, stirring constantly. Transfer to warmed mugs and serve.

YIELD: 4 SERVINGS

Food etymologists believe that the term eggnog *descended from*
egg-and-grog, *a colonial term for rum. Eventually, the name was*
shortened to egg 'n' grog *and finally* eggnog. *According to Mary Donovan*
and her friends in The Thirteen Colonies Cookbook, *Washington's*
sister Betty served this recipe at her home, Kenmore, in Fredericksburg,
Virginia. It was traditionally served during the Christmas holidays and
lives on in that fashion today.

Betty Washington Lewis's Eggnog

1 dozen eggs, separated
1 1/2 cups sugar
1 quart Virginia Gentleman bourbon
4 cups half-and-half
1/2 cup rum
1/2 cup brandy
2 cups heavy cream, whipped
Freshly grated nutmeg for garnish

In a large bowl, add the egg yolks, and beat for 2 or 3 minutes. Add
the sugar slowly and continue beating. Beat the egg whites until stiff
and fold them into the yolk and sugar mixture. Add the remaining
ingredients, except whipped cream and nutmeg, stir well, and chill in
the refrigerator for 4 hours. Ladle the mixture into holiday glasses, top
with whipped cream, and sprinkle nutmeg over each glass.

YIELD: 10 OR MORE SERVINGS

A NEW ENGLAND FEAST

Food historian James E. McWilliams wrote, "New England's local traditions converged with the influences of the British invasion to produce the most Anglicized food in America." The local traditions, of course, reflected the most common available foodstuffs available from the founding of the colonies: seafood, wild turkey, and favorite garden crops like beans and strawberries.

Using salt cod (codfish that has been salted and dried), available from online retailers and in some gourmet shops, will transport the cook back to the colonial days of cod fishing in New England, when salt was the only way to preserve the fish. This is a very simple dish that can also be served with eggs for breakfast. To prepare the salt cod, soak the fish all night, then change the water the next morning, and let it sit for about 2 hours. Then boil it for about 10 minutes, which will harden the fish and make it more palatable. Lard was traditionally used as a frying medium, but you can use butter or cooking oil instead.

Codfish Cakes Appetizer

1 cup salt cod prepared as above

1 cup mashed potatoes

1 egg, beaten

1/2 cup milk or half-and-half

2 tablespoons melted butter

Salt and freshly ground pepper to taste

1/2 cup all-purpose flour

Butter or cooking oil for frying

In a bowl, combine all the ingredients except the flour and butter, and mix well. Fashion the mixture into small, round cakes about 1/2-inch thick.

Heat the butter or cooking oil in a skillet, and fry the cakes lightly until they are a delicate brown on each side.

YIELD: 6 TO 8 SERVINGS, DEPENDING ON THE SIZE OF THE CAKES

Seafood chowders were a signature dish during colonial times in New England and still are today. Chowder was often made with cod or other fish like flounder or pollack, but also with lobster or clams. My grandmother, Vera Austin, would prepare a similar chowder when we visited her at her apartment in the beachfront Breakers Hotel in Lynn, Massachusetts, in the 1950s. My family would dig the clams out of the sand on the beach at low tide. This recipe is based on that of Mrs. N. K. M. Lee, published in Boston in 1842, who wrote, "This Receipt is according to the most approved method, practiced by fishing parties in Boston harbor." Salt pork was traditionally used, but I have substituted bacon. Quahog clams can be used for a more robust flavor than the more delicate steamers, or use young quahogs, called cherrystones. If fresh clams are not available, you can use 2 cups of canned chopped clams.

Classic Clam Chowder

1/4 pound bacon, chopped fine
1 cup minced onions
4 cups diced potatoes

3 cups water

1/2 cup crushed plain crackers

2 dozen steamer clams (nanny-noses), removed from the shells and chopped, with their juice

Salt and freshly ground black pepper to taste

3 cloves (optional)

2 cups heavy cream

Paprika for garnish

In a stewpot, sauté the bacon until the first fat is rendered, then add the onions, and fry until they are golden brown. Add the water and potatoes, and simmer until potatoes are cooked but still firm. Add the crackers and clams, salt and pepper, and cloves (if using them), and simmer, covered, for 15 minutes. In a separate pan, heat the cream, but do not allow it to boil. Add the heated cream to the chowder, stir well, and simmer, uncovered, for another 10 minutes. Serve in individual bowls sprinkled with a little paprika for color.

YIELD: 8 SERVINGS

The prototype recipe for all Thanksgiving turkeys seems to be the one that Amelia Simmons included in her 1796 book American Cookery, *published in Hartford, Connecticut. Her recipe is the first one known to pair roasted turkey with cranberry sauce, which has remained the tradition for more than two hundred years. One source has suggested that Simmons directed that the turkey be served with mashed potatoes, but a close reading of her recipe reveals that she was suggesting stuffing the turkey with mashed potatoes in place of bread. Rather, she suggested serving it with "boiled onions and cranberry sauce, mangoes, pickles or celery." This recipe is based on Simmons's original one but updated. Dried sage can also be added to the stuffing.*

Roasted Turkey with Herb and Wine Stuffing

1/4 pound butter

1 large onion, chopped

1/2 cup finely chopped celery

3 cups crumpled corn bread

3 cups stale bread crumbs

1 cup homemade chicken stock or stock made from turkey giblets

1 cup dry white wine

1/2 cup finely chopped celery

1 teaspoon marjoram

Salt and freshly ground black pepper to taste

12-pound hen turkey

Melted butter for basting

Preheat the oven to 350°F.

In a large bowl, mix together all the ingredients except the turkey and melted butter. Stuff the turkey with this mixture and sew the turkey closed. Any excess stuffing can be baked in a separate glass dish.

Roast the turkey uncovered for about 25 minutes per pound, or until a meat thermometer reads 160°F. Baste every 20 minutes with melted butter and pan juices.

YIELD: 10 TO 15 SERVINGS

Boston baked beans use pork and a sauce of molasses, which of course, came from the New England rum trade, where it was the principal distilling ingredient. There are no published colonial recipes for the dish, and the first recipe appeared in Lydia Marie Francis Child's The American Frugal Housewife *in 1829. Soon afterward, Boston baked beans became the Boston recipe that was so popular that the city became known as Beantown. The city experienced many bean festivals, usually connected with political events, much like Southern barbecues. Before the Red Sox, the baseball team was called the Boston Bean Eaters, who won the championship in 1897 and later moved to Milwaukee. Curiously, Boston baked beans are something of a rarity today in Boston, as no companies in the city make them, and only a few restaurants serve them. However, the baked beans are not "has-beans" and live on in canned products and home recipes. This recipe is based on one by Mrs. A. L. Webster that appeared in her 1855 cookbook,* The Improved Housewife, *which was published in Boston. I have increased the amount of molasses based on the volume of the other ingredients, and I have added dry mustard, which evolved in recipes published later than Webster's. These beans can be made more quickly in a slow cooker.*

Boston Baked Beans

4 cups white beans, picked over and soaked in water overnight in a large bowl

1 onion studded with 8 cloves

1/2 pound bacon, chopped

1 cup brown sugar

1/2 cup molasses

1 tablespoon dry mustard

Salt and freshly ground pepper to taste

Preheat the oven to 250°F.

Drain the soaked beans, transfer to a large pot, cover with water, and cook on medium heat until the skins burst. Drain the beans and place in a ceramic bean pot or other bowl suitable for baking. Press the onion down in the center of the beans. Spread the bacon pieces over the top of the beans. Mix together 3/4 cup of brown sugar, molasses, mustard, and salt and pepper in a small bowl, and pour over the beans and bacon. Cover the pot and bake for 4 to 5 hours, uncovered for the last 30 minutes with the remaining brown sugar sprinkled over the top. Stir in water as needed during the baking.

YIELD: 12 SERVINGS

Despite living in northern Virginia, our family would regularly eat B&M Brown Bread made in Portland, Maine. My mother, who grew up in Boston, would open a can, slice the bread, and serve it with just a little butter. It was a steamed bread, and we loved it. Because steaming is an essential part of the history of Boston brown bread and what makes it unique, steaming is the traditional preparation; however, you can also bake it. Save some 12-ounce metal cans for steaming and make sure they are well washed and grease them with butter. Some recipes call for an egg to be added; others suggest 1/2 cup of raisins.

Boston Brown Bread

2 cups buttermilk

1/2 cup rye flour

1 cup whole wheat flour

1/2 cup cornmeal

2 tablespoons melted butter

1/2 cup molasses

1/2 cup brown sugar

1 teaspoon salt

2 teaspoons baking powder

In a bowl, combine all the ingredients in the order listed and mix well. Fill the greased cans with the dough, and cover them with aluminum foil. To seal the cans, fasten two layers of aluminum foil around the can with string or rubber bands.

Fill a pot with water, and put a rack in it for the cans to rest on. Put the pot, with the rack and cans in it, over a burner on low, and add boiling water until the water level reaches halfway to the top of the cans. Cover the pot and bring the water back to a gentle boil. Steam the bread this way—adding more boiling water if necessary—for 2 1/2 to 3 hours, stopping when an inserted toothpick comes out clean. Carefully slide the bread out of the cans. Alternatively, place the dough in greased loaf pans, cover with aluminum foil, and place in a shallow pan with about 1 1/2 inches of water. Bake in a 325°F oven for 1 1/2 hours.

To bake the bread in the usual manner, fill two greased 9-by-5-inch loaf pans with the dough and bake at 350°F for 1 hour.

YIELD: 8 TO 10 SERVINGS

John Adams's wife, Abigail, wrote in 1798, "After walking in the garden we returned and found the table spread with 6 or 8 quarts of the large…Strawberry, gathered from the vines with a proportional quantity of cream, wine and sugar." Jefferson called them "Arcadian dainties" (a reference to rural simplicity and contentment), and Peter Hatch of Monticello wrote, "Cultivated strawberries abounded at Monticello at a time when they were surprisingly infrequent in Virginia kitchen gardens." Early New Englanders often found them growing wild in burned-over areas, and Hatch noted, "Richard Peters reported on an 800-acre strawberry garden, 'in most extraordinary profusion,' that emerged following the burning of a pine forest outside Philadelphia in the late eighteenth century: 'The people of the towns…from distances of more than 20 miles were accustomed to gather and carry off these strawberries, in quantities almost incredible.'"

Here, strawberries are paired with the favorite sweet wine of the colonies, Madeira, in an elegant dessert.

Strawberries in Madeira and Cream

4 cups fresh strawberries, sliced
2 cups Madeira
Confectioners' sugar for sprinkling
1 1/2 cups heavy cream, whipped

In a bowl, combine the strawberries with the Madeira, and mix well. Marinate for two hours. Drain the strawberries, and place in 4 bowls. Sprinkle sugar lightly over them, and top with a dollop of whipped cream.

YIELD: 4 SERVINGS

A DINNER PARTY IN THE MIDDLE COLONIES

Much of the food from the middle colonies, between New York and Virginia, reflects the immigrants to this region, particularly people from the Caribbean, Holland, and Germany. Seafood from the Chesapeake Bay was popular, particularly crabs and oysters, and roasted lamb was on the menu for the reception for George Washington held at Fraunces Tavern in New York in 1783, as were apples.

I noted the popularity of turtle soup in Philadelphia in chapter 2; it was and still is considered a delicacy. Lewis Carroll in his 1897 book, Alice in Wonderland, *included a poem about turtle soup that begins:*

Beautiful soup, so rich and green,

Waiting in a hot tureen!

Who for such dainties would not stoop?

Soup of the evening, beautiful soup!

Because cooks over time have not always been able to find turtle meat, many of them have created mock turtle soup recipes. Suggested substitutes for turtle meat in mock turtle soup over the centuries have included calf's head, pig's face, oxtails, and even turtle beans. However, frozen turtle meat is available from Exoticmeatmarket .com for $29.95 a pound. It is from farm-raised freshwater snapping turtles from Iowa and Georgia. Here is a classic recipe from early Philadelphia.

Philadelphia Turtle Soup

1/2 pound turtle meat, chopped fine

1/4 pound butter

1 cup Madeira wine

1/4 cup cream

1 tablespoon prepared mustard

1/2 teaspoon cayenne pepper

1/2 teaspoon finely ground black pepper

All-purpose flour as needed for thickening

Combine all ingredients except flour in a pot, cover, and simmer for about 1 hour. Dissolve some flour in cold water, and add to the soup and stir until it reaches the desired thickness.

YIELD: 4 SERVINGS

This preparation of crab imperial is often called a classic American dish and was referred to as "a universal favorite" in The Amiable Baltimorean *in 1951. The dish is quite old and has gone by several different names. The common ingredients over the centuries have been crabmeat, breadcrumbs, cream, cayenne, and sometimes onion, bell peppers, sherry, and mustard. The earliest version I could find was titled "Crab Browned and Served in a Shell," which appeared in the 1777 English cookbook,* The Lady's Assistant for Regulation and Supplying Her Table, *by Charlotte Mason. It called for crabmeat, onions, breadcrumbs, and a "good gravy" that was probably a white sauce.*

I discovered that the recipe is also closely related to minced crab, which started appearing in American cookbooks in the 1850s; deviled crab, in 1876 and in 1887; and hot crab, in 1888. "Crab Meat Terrapin-Style" was featured in the Boston Cooking-School Cookbook *in 1916 and used cream and sherry, but the title began its change in 1904 with "Crab Queen-Style" in* The Culinary Handbook. *The use of* imperial *seems to be derived from this, and "Imperial Deviled Crab" appeared in* Eat in Maryland *in 1932. In the 1950s, Maryland restaurants began serving imperial crab, and that title was used in cookbooks like* Coastal Cookery. *The title stuck and the dish not only was served in crab shells but also was used as a topping for steaks and burgers in upscale restaurants. This recipe is derived from many of the sources listed above.*

Crab Imperial

1/4 cup butter

1/4 cup minced onion

1/4 cup minced red bell pepper

1/4 cup sherry

1 teaspoon dry mustard

1 tablespoon freshly squeezed lemon juice

1 cup heavy cream

2 tablespoons all-purpose flour

1/4 teaspoon cayenne powder, or more to taste

1 pound crabmeat

1/8 cup chopped jarred pimento (really, pimiento)

Salt to taste

4 crab shells

Paprika for garnish

In a skillet, melt the butter and sauté the onions and peppers for 1 minute. Add the sherry, mustard, and lemon juice, and cook over medium heat for 1 minute, stirring constantly. Add the flour, cream, and cayenne, and cook until thick, stirring occasionally. Add the crabmeat and pimento and blend well. Transfer to the crab shells and place under the broiler for 1 minute. Garnish with paprika, and serve immediately.

YIELD: 4 SERVINGS

My mother, Babs, served us this dish often, which was unusual in the beef-obsessed 1950s. I seriously doubt that she had any idea that it was very close to Amelia Simmons's recipe that was published in American Cookery *in 1796. Lamb is served this way at City Tavern in Philadelphia. After the lamb leg was removed to a plate, Mom, who was a gravy expert, would add some water or wine to deglaze the pan, taking care to scrape all the drippings off the bottom. Then she would add flour dissolved in cold water to make a gravy that she would serve over the lamb slices and roasted potatoes, which she mashed lightly with a fork.*

Roasted Leg of Lamb with Potatoes

4 to 6 pound leg of young lamb
4 cloves garlic, cut into slivers
1/4 cup butter
All-purpose flour for dusting
6 new potatoes, cut in half and brushed with melted butter or olive oil
5 sprigs fresh thyme, minced

Preheat the oven to 450°F.

Cut slits in the lamb and insert the garlic slivers. In a large pan, melt the butter, and brown the lamb on all sides. Dust the lamb with the flour. Transfer the leg to a roasting pan, and roast in the oven for 30 minutes.

Remove the lamb from the oven and add the potatoes. Reduce the oven heat to 350°F and return the lamb to the oven. Roast until a meat thermometer registers 145 to 150 degrees for medium-rare, about 45 minutes, depending on the size of the leg. During the final roasting, baste the lamb with pan juices.

Slice the lamb and serve with the roasted potatoes.

YIELD: 8 TO 10 SERVINGS

Potato salad originated in Germany, and the recipes were transferred to the parts of Pennsylvania where immigrants settled, particularly Philadelphia. Despite Parmentier's and Benjamin Franklin's enthusiastic support, the potato was slow to gain popularity in American cooking, though a recipe for potato salad appeared in The Gastronomic Regenerator, *published in London in 1847. I could not find any American recipes for this side dish until the early 1880s, when they started appearing with great regularity. Why potato salad became popular in the 1880s and has remained so is a bit of a mystery. This recipe is served hot, which in this case means at room temperature rather than chilled. I have updated this recipe from* Recipes of All Nations *(1935) by Countess Morphy, an amazing book and one of the first world cuisine survey cookbooks published in the United States.*

Hot Potato Salad (Wärmer Kartoffelsalat)

8 russet or Yukon gold potatoes, boiled in their skins until easily pierced by a fork and left unpeeled, cut into large cubes

2 hard–boiled eggs, sliced thinly

1 onion, minced

1 stalk of celery, sliced thinly

1 tablespoon fresh Italian parsley, minced

4 slices of bacon, minced

1/2 cup wine vinegar diluted with 1/2 cup water

2 tablespoons prepared mustard

1 teaspoon sugar

In a large bowl, mix together the potatoes, eggs, onion, celery, and parsley. In a skillet, fry the bacon until crisp, then separate the bacon from the fat. In a bowl, combine the vinegar, mustard, sugar, and hot bacon fat. Pour over the salad and mix well.

YIELD: 10 SERVINGS

Apples, a favorite fruit, were commonly dried in colonial and postcolonial days to preserve them. Because apples contain so much water, the flavor is very concentrated, and I found a number of early recipes for apple pie using dried apples that were "rehydrated" with a combination of whiskey or applejack and apple juice or nonalcoholic cider.

Applejack Apple Pie from Dried Apples

1 cup applejack

1 cup apple juice or cider

12 ounces dried apples

1 cup brown sugar

1 teaspoon cinnamon

1 teaspoon grated nutmeg

9-inch prepared but unbaked pie shell

Butter as needed

Preheat oven to 400°F.

In a bowl, combine applejack and cider, and add the apples. Cover and soak overnight.

Add the brown sugar, cinnamon, and nutmeg to the apples, and stir well. Transfer the mixture to the pie shell, and dot the top with butter to taste. Bake for 20 to 25 minutes, checking the pie for moisture after 15 minutes. Add more cider if necessary. For a more attractive pie, make pie dough, cut it into thin, flat strips, and place it to create a checkerboard-like design over the top of the pie.

YIELD: 6 SERVINGS

A SOUTHERN PLANTATION SUNDAY DINNER

Reflecting the heritage of both white and black Southerners, these recipes contain classic ingredients that help define the cuisine of the region: pumpkins, ham, rice, asparagus, and peaches.

According to Monticello.org, "Pumpkins were grown in Jefferson's fields both for the Monticello table as well as for feeding the workhorses, cattle, sheep, and pigs in late summer." In her Thomas Jefferson Cookbook, *Marie Kimball included a recipe attributed to the slave cook Annette for pumpkin soup, which I have used as a basis for the one here. I have taken the liberty of adding some chili pepper to it, as Jefferson grew bird peppers during his retirement.*

Spicy Pumpkin Soup

1 small pumpkin, peeled and seeds removed, chopped
Water to cover
3 slices white bread
1/4 cup butter, divided
Sugar, salt, and freshly ground black pepper to taste
4 cups milk
1 dried bird pepper or chile piquin, crushed
Freshly ground nutmeg for garnish

Place the pumpkin and water in a pot, bring to a boil, reduce heat, and simmer until tender. While the pumpkin is cooking, cut the bread into cubes and brown in a skillet using half the butter.

Drain and place the pumpkin pieces in a blender, and puree until smooth. Transfer back to the pot, add the remaining ingredients except the nutmeg, and simmer for about 15 minutes until slightly thickened. Serve in bowls and garnish with the nutmeg.

YIELD: 4 TO 6 SERVINGS

Both Washington and Jefferson had smokehouses that processed huge quantities of meat, mainly pork. Country hams are salt cured (and occasionally nitrate cured) for 1 to 3 months. Then they are smoked over hardwood, usually hickory or oak, and aged for several months, and sometimes up to 3 years, depending on the fat content of the meat. Smoking is not legally mandated for making country ham, according to the U.S. Department of Agriculture.

Smithfield is the name most associated with Virginia hams, and the name has protection similar to the European Union status of champagne. In 1926, the Virginia General Assembly passed a law stating that only peanut-fed hogs, cured and processed in the town of Smithfield, could be called Smithfield hams. The peanut stipulation was eventually dropped, and the hogs are now fed a variety of grains. These days, there are only four companies that can legally sell their products as Smithfield hams; all others are called country hams.

Be sure to soak the ham in water for at least 24 hours and to change the water at least once. To shorten this process, buy a precooked ham and follow the manufacturer's instructions.

Baked Virginia Country Ham

1 uncooked Virginia country ham, about 14 pounds, soaked overnight to remove salt

5 cups water

1 cup prepared mustard

1 cup brown sugar

1/2 cup wine vinegar

About 15 whole cloves

6 to 8 pineapple rings

Preheat the oven to 500°F.

Place the ham in a large pan with a tight-fitting lid. Pour 5 cups of water over the ham, cover, and bake for 15 minutes. Then turn off the oven. Do not open the oven, and let sit for 3 hours. Repeat this process and leave the ham in the oven until it is completely cool.

In a saucepan, combine the mustard, brown sugar, and vinegar. Over medium heat, cook the mixture until it thickens to a glaze. Using a brush, paint the ham completely with the glaze. Remove any skin from the ham, and cut uniform diamond shapes on the fat surface of the ham. Insert one clove into each fat diamond and then, using tooth-picks, attach the pineapple rings to the ham.

Bake the ham in the pan, uncovered, for 2 hours at 350°F. Remove from the pan, slice, and serve.

YIELD: 20 OR MORE SERVINGS

After Jefferson authorized and Congress approved the Louisiana Purchase, Creole and Cajun foods soon became one aspect of the ever-increasing melting pot of cuisines influencing American cooks and consumers. Of course, African American cooks from the region played an important role in popularizing dishes like this one, which gets its name from the color chopped chicken livers add.

African American cooking expert Jessica Harris wrote, "Composed rice dishes are one of the hallmarks of African-American cooking in the New World...These dishes are ours." Similar to a pilaf, it also includes the holy trinity of Creole and Cajun cooking: green bell pepper, celery, and onion.

New Orleans Dirty Rice

1/4 cup vegetable oil

1 large onion, finely chopped

1 green bell pepper, diced

1/2 cup finely diced celery

2 cloves garlic, minced

1 cup Louisiana or Carolina rice

3 cups of chicken stock

1/2 pound minced chicken livers, cooked

3/4 teaspoon cayenne pepper or more to taste

1/2 teaspoon freshly ground black pepper

In a large Dutch oven, heat the oil and sauté the onion, bell pepper, celery, and garlic for 2 to 3 minutes until the onions are soft, stirring occasionally. Add the rice and cook for an additional 2 minutes, stirring constantly. Add the chicken stock, chicken livers, cayenne pepper, black pepper, and cover. Cook for 20 to 25 minutes. Fluff the rice with a fork or spoon before serving.

YIELD: 4 TO 6 SERVINGS

Jefferson alluded to this method of cooking one of his favorite vegetables in a letter to his son-in-law. Because he loved herbs and olive oil, we can imagine that this was one of his favorite accompaniments. I have added the raspberry vinegar because Jefferson asked his former maître d' at the

President's House, Étienne Lemaire, for his recipe, which he mailed to Jefferson. Note: This recipe requires advance preparation.

Asparagus in the French Way, with Lemaire's Raspberry Vinaigrette

For the raspberry vinaigrette:

4 cups raspberries, fresh or frozen

2 cups red wine vinegar

For the asparagus:

1 pound fresh asparagus, ends trimmed off and peeled

Water as needed

1/4 cup olive oil

2 tablespoons raspberry vinegar

2 tablespoons chopped fresh mixed herbs, including basil, Italian parsley, and oregano or tarragon

Freshly ground black pepper to taste

Salt to taste

To make the vinegar, place the raspberries in a glass bowl and lightly crush with a pestle or large spoon. Add the vinegar, cover, and let stand for 48 hours. Strain the vinegar through a fine mesh screen.

Cut the asparagus spears all to the same length. Bring a large pot of water to boil. Add the asparagus, reduce the heat to medium, and cook until it is just tender—do not overcook.

While the asparagus is cooking, combine the remaining ingredients in a glass jar, and shake well. Remove and drain the asparagus, place in a bowl, and pour the vinaigrette over it. If the vinaigrette has separated, shake it again just before adding.

YIELD: 4 SERVINGS

A cobbler is a deep-dish fruit pie that consists of a fruit filling poured into a baking dish over a batter that rises through the fruit when baking, forming a crust on the top. Although the earliest cobbler recipes don't appear until 1890, cobblers evolved from a similar English recipe for brown betty. The brown betty was also referred to as a slump, grunt, and pandowdy, and I tracked down a fruit pandowdy recipe from 1848 in Miss Beecher's Domestic Receipt Book. *For some mysterious reason, forty-two years later, cooks had changed the name to* cobbler, *and I found a plum cobbler in* The New Practical Housekeeping *(1890). The first peach cobbler, made from Jefferson's favorite fruit, appeared in* The White House Cookbook *(1890).*
Here is my version of cobbled-together peaches.

Fresh Peach Cobbler

For the crust:
3/4 cup all-purpose flour
1/3 cup white sugar
2 teaspoons baking powder
1/2 teaspoon salt
1/3 cup brown sugar

3/4 cup milk

1/2 teaspoon grated lemon zest

The filling:

6 fresh ripe peaches, peeled, pitted, and sliced into thin wedges

1/4 cup white sugar

1/4 cup brown sugar

2 teaspoons cornstarch

1 teaspoon fresh lemon juice

1/4 teaspoon ground cinnamon

1/8 teaspoon ground nutmeg

Preheat the oven to 400°F.

To make the crust, in a bowl, sift the flour, sugar, baking powder, and salt together, and stir in the brown sugar; add the milk and lemon zest, and mix well. Let sit while making the filling.

In a large bowl, combine the peaches, sugars, corn starch, lemon juice, cinnamon, and nutmeg. Toss to coat evenly and pour into a 2-quart baking dish. Cover and bake for 10 minutes.

Grease an 8-inch square, glass baking dish with 2 tablespoons of butter. Pour the batter into the dish.

Remove the peaches from the oven and place them on the batter. Bake until the topping is golden, about 40 minutes.

YIELD: 8 SERVINGS

GALA DAY FOR JEFFERSON A LA EDITH FOSSETT

Imagine that you were a guest at Monticello during Lafayette's two-week visit in 1824 and were invited to join the table for some of the meals served. Also imagine that Jefferson wanted to impress the French former general with the quality of his Virginia-French amalgamation cooking and the talent of his African American cook, Edith Fossett. In such a fantasy scenario, here's what you might have been served.

This recipe has an intriguing backstory. The original version was published in 1990 (the first publication of a family recipe) in Kristie Lynn's The Early American Cookbook, *which was dedicated to her great-great-grandmother, Huldah Radike Horton. Lynn claims—and I can find nothing to contradict her—that Horton prepared this for breakfast when Lafayette visited her house in Newburgh, New York, in 1824. Lafayette was in the United States for many months that year, and he probably stayed in or visited the houses of hundreds of Americans, especially the ones who worshipped him for helping the colonies win the Revolutionary War. This recipe is heavy on the fresh herbs, so feel free to adjust the quantity to your liking. Jefferson would have loved this for breakfast—and maybe he ordered it to be prepared for Lafayette when he visited Monticello that same year.*

Lafayette's Favorite Herb Omelet

6 eggs, separated
1 cup whipping cream
Salt and freshly ground black pepper to taste
2 tablespoons minced fresh Italian parsley

2 tablespoon minced fresh thyme

2 tablespoons minced marjoram

2 tablespoons minced onion

Preheat the oven to 400°F.

In a bowl, combine the egg yolks, cream, salt, and pepper, and whisk the mixture thoroughly. With an electric beater, beat the egg whites until they stand. Fold the egg whites into the yolk mixture.

Heat a skillet until hot, using a lightly greased cast-iron one (for authenticity). Add the herbs and onion to the egg mixture and stir well. Pour the mixture into the skillet, and cook for 10 minutes on medium heat without stirring until the eggs set. Then remove the skillet to the hot oven and bake for 10 minutes.

Carefully remove the omelet from the skillet using a small spatula. Fold half the omelet over the other half so that the browned side shows. Serve and eat immediately.

YIELD: 2 TO 4 SERVINGS

Both of these recipes survive in Jefferson's own hand, and his great-granddaughter Ellen Coolidge recalled, "He liked boiled beef, Bouilli, better than roast." Jefferson quaintly titled his potato recipe "To Dress Potatoes." My version of one of Jefferson's favorite beef recipes is more like a traditional pot roast, because it's cooked in the oven rather than boiled on top of the stove, which is how my mother made this dish when my brother Rick and I were growing up. In the Monticello kitchen, the slaves would have forced the cooked potatoes through a colander to mash them, but today a potato ricer

does a fine job. Jefferson would add some freshly grated nutmeg to the potatoes,
and though my mom never did that, it's up to you.

Bouilli (Beef Pot Roast), with Jefferson's Own Mashed Potatoes

For the roast:

1/4 cup bacon fat or vegetable oil

3-pound beef rump roast

3 cups beef stock or water

4 carrots, cut to 1-inch length

2 celery stalks, cut to 1-inch length

1 large onion, quartered

1 bay leaf

Flour as needed for the gravy

Salt and freshly ground black pepper, to taste

For the potatoes:

4 large potatoes, peeled and cut in eighths

1/4 pound (1 stick) butter

1 cup half-and-half

Salt and freshly ground black pepper, to taste

Preheat the oven to 350°F.

Heat the fat or oil in a large Dutch oven, and brown the beef on both sides. Add the beef stock, bring to a boil, and turn off the heat. Cover and transfer to the oven and cook for 2 hours. Add the carrots, celery, onion, and bay leaf; cover; and cook in the oven for another

1 to 1 1/2 hours until the meat is very tender and the vegetables are cooked. Transfer the meat and vegetables to a large bowl, and keep warm in the oven. Reserve the stock and pan juices and cook on top of the stove over medium heat until reduced by half. Season the gravy with salt and pepper.

In a large pot, cover the potatoes with water, and boil until they are pierced easily with a fork, about 15 to 20 minutes. Drain the potatoes, and force them through a ricer in a bowl. Add the butter and half-and-half, stir well, and whip them lightly with an electric mixer until they are smooth. Season with salt and pepper.

Mix the flour with cold water until smooth, and add slowly to the reduced stock to make a thick gravy.

To serve, slice the roast thinly, and arrange with the vegetables on individual plates. Add the mashed potatoes, and ladle the gravy over the sliced roast and the potatoes.

YIELD 6 TO 8 SERVINGS

After he returned from Europe, Thomas Jefferson was so fond of macaroni that he ordered it to be delivered along with his wine shipments from Marseilles. Historical sources show that a basic baked macaroni dish with Parmesan cheese was served at Monticello. The additional ingredients in this version were all grown in the garden at Monticello. This recipe is adapted from "Macaroni" in Mary Randolph's The Virginia Housewife *(1824).*

Macaroni and Spinach Bake

1 (7-ounce) package uncooked dried elbow macaroni

1/4 cup dried breadcrumbs

1 tablespoon butter

1 medium onion, finely chopped

1 teaspoon fresh garlic, minced

1/2 teaspoon marjoram

1/4 teaspoon black pepper, coarsely ground

1 (10-ounce) package chopped fresh spinach

1 1/2 cups freshly grated Parmesan cheese

Preheat the oven to 350°F. In an uncovered pot full of salted, boiling water, cook the macaroni for 10 minutes. Drain the pasta, and set aside. Sprinkle the breadcrumbs into a buttered, 3-quart casserole, and set aside.

Melt the butter in a medium skillet until sizzling, and add the onion, garlic, marjoram, and pepper. Cook over medium-high heat, stirring constantly, until the onion is soft (2 to 3 minutes). Stir in the spinach. Stir constantly until the spinach is heated through (about 3 minutes). Stir in the cooked macaroni and cheese, and remove from the heat.

Spoon the mixture into the prepared casserole, pressing gently. Bake for 20 to 25 minutes.

YIELD: 6 SERVINGS

The first macaroons originated in Italy; they were almond meringue cookies similar to today's amaretti, with a crisp crust and a soft interior. They were made from egg whites and almond paste. The name of the cookie comes from the Italian word for paste, maccarone. Today, most macaroons are made with coconut rather than almonds. Jefferson wrote recipes for both of these desserts, and although his recipe for ice cream works, the one for macaroons is "hopeless," as food historian Karen Hess observed. Thankfully, Mary Randolph has a good one that this recipe is based on. I have modernized both recipes considerably.

In colonial and postcolonial days, women were in charge of the desserts not only because they reflected the status of the family but also because sugar was so expensive. "Controlling sugar must have been especially important at Monticello," wrote Damon Lee Fowler, "where a large family and a steady stream of visitors put a continual strain on the household budget."

The macaroons are heavy with almond flavor, so you might want to eliminate the Amaretto and almond extract. Also, don't use marzipan in place of the almond paste, which is available from gourmet shops and online food retailers. The macaroons must be baked on parchment or a silicone baking sheet to ensure that they don't stick to the pan.

Almond Macaroons with Chocolate Ice Cream

For the macaroons:

6 ounces blanched almonds

1 1/4 cups sugar

7 ounces almond paste

3 egg whites from 3 large eggs (reserve the yolks for use in the ice cream)

1 tablespoon Amaretto

1 teaspoon almond extract

For the ice cream:

1/2 cup unsweetened cocoa powder

3 cups half-and-half

1 cup heavy cream

8 large egg yolks (3 reserved from above)

9 ounces sugar

2 teaspoons pure vanilla extract

To make the macaroons, preheat the oven to 325°F. Cover 2 cookie sheets with parchment paper or silicone baking sheets, and set aside.

Place the almonds in a spice mill or food processor, and grind until roughly chopped. Add the sugar, and continue processing until the almonds are finely ground. Add the almond paste, and continue processing until the mixture is uniform. Add the egg whites, Amaretto, and almond extract, and continue processing until smooth.

Remove the dough from the food processor with a spoon, and let sit in a bowl for 20 minutes.

Drop level tablespoons of the mixture onto a cookie sheet, leaving about 1 1/2 inches of space between each cookie.

Bake for 20 to 25 minutes, rotating the cookie sheets in the oven occasionally. The cookies should be golden on top. Take care not to overbake them, as they will become too hard.

Remove the cookies from the oven with a thin spatula, and allow them to cool. Store in an airtight container. You can also freeze them; they will last for 3 to 4 months.

To make the ice cream, place the cocoa powder and 1 cup of the half-and-half in a medium saucepan over medium heat, and whisk to combine. Add the remaining half-and-half and heavy cream.

Bring the mixture to a simmer, stirring occasionally, and remove from heat.

In a mixing bowl, whisk the egg yolks lightly, and gradually add the sugar and whisk to combine. Gradually add the cream mixture to the eggs and sugar in small amounts; return the mixture to the saucepan, and cook over low heat, stirring frequently, until the mixture thickens and reaches 170 to 175°F. Pour the mixture into a container, and let sit for 30 minutes. Stir in the vanilla extract, place the mixture in the refrigerator, and cool until the temperature reaches 40°F or less.

Pour the mixture into an ice cream maker and process according to the manufacturer's instructions for 25 to 35 minutes. You can serve it fairly soft or freeze for another 3 to 4 hours until it hardens.

Yield: About 3 dozen cookies and 1 1/2 quarts of ice cream

JEFFERSON'S SLAVES CELEBRATE THE FOURTH OF JULY

I mentioned in chapter 6 that some slaves were allowed to celebrate the holidays free from work, particularly on the plantations of the relatively benevolent planters like Thomas Jefferson. After the revolution, July 4 was a particularly poignant and unique time for feasting and celebration. Jessica Harris, an African American food historian, writes that

Peanut harvest, Virginia c. 1870

"African-Americans have a love affair with food perhaps unequaled in the history of this country," and she may well be right. I don't think anyone has told that tale better, and I highly recommend her books *The Welcome Table* and *Iron Pots and Wooden Spoons*.

Pecan orchards were first planted near New Orleans about three hundred years ago because of the demand for thin-shelled pecan nuts. Both George Washington and Thomas Jefferson planted pecan trees called "Illinois nuts" on their plantations, but the credit for development of a superior, hybrid pecan that was the beginning of commercial orchards goes to an African American slave gardener known only as Antoine, who successfully grafted a superior wild stock to a cultivated seedling pecan plant on Louisiana's Oak Alley Plantation in 1846. His hybrid was dubbed "Centennial" because it won the Best Pecan Exhibited award at the Philadelphia Centennial Exposition in 1876. After that, hybrid pecans became the standard tree of pecan orchards, mostly in the South and West. The pecan became the Texas state tree by an act of the Texas Legislature in 1919, undoubtedly because former governor James "Big Jim" Hogg (1890–1895) favored the tree so much that he requested that one be planted at his gravesite.

Chile-Spiced Pecans

1/8 pound butter (1/2 stick)
1 pound shelled pecan halves, as fresh as possible, picked over to remove any shell parts
Salt and New Mexican red chile powder, mixed in equal parts, to taste

Melt the butter in a skillet, add pecans, and cook for 3 to 4 minutes, stirring occasionally. Drain the nuts on paper towels, place in a bowl, sprinkle with the salt–chile mixture, and toss to coat.

YIELD: 8 OR MORE SERVINGS

Peanuts originated in South America and migrated to the Caribbean with chile peppers, carried by Native Americans, where they were commonly eaten when the first Europeans arrived. Portuguese traders in Brazil took peanuts to Africa, where they were equally popular. The slave trade brought peanuts to North America along with their Kimbundu name, nguba, *which became* goober *in popular American English.*

Because African Americans did the cooking on Southern plantations and in some Northern urban homes, it is probable that they introduced the peanut into American cookery. African Americans were also the first peanut vendors, selling them raw and boiled on street corners in cities like Wilmington, North Carolina. The first peanut soup recipe in an American cookbook appeared in Sarah Rutledge's Carolina Housewife *in 1847 and combined, of all things, peanuts and oysters. It wasn't until the 1890s that peanut soup recipes began appearing in food magazines, and the most common recipes featured peanuts and milk rather than shellfish.*

Peanuts caught the attention of another food-loving polymath, George Washington Carver, whose skill as a scientist and developer of food products made him famous. In addition to his work in agriculture experimentation and his advocacy of sustainable farming, Carver made important contributions to the improvement of racial relations and was an accomplished painter, poet, and religious scholar.

In 1897, Booker T. Washington, founder of the Tuskegee Normal and Industrial Institute for Negroes in Alabama, invited Carver to serve as the school's director of agriculture. His peanut-related food products included eleven peanut flours, and his sweet potato–related products included fourteen candies, five breakfast foods, four starches, four flours, and four types of molasses. The most popular of his forty-four practical bulletins for farmers, How to Grow the Peanut, *contained numerous recipes that used peanuts. Published in 1921, the bulletin featured three peanut soups, a peanut bisque, and a peanut consommé, all of which contained ingredients such as butter, flour, milk, onions, celery seed, bell pepper, and cayenne. I have used those elements to develop the following recipe.*

Cream of Peanut Soup with Cayenne

1/4 cup (1/2 stick) unsalted butter
1 onion, minced
2 stalks celery, minced
1/4 cup red bell pepper, minced
3 tablespoons flour
2 quarts homemade chicken stock
2 cups prepared smooth peanut butter
1 1/2 cups half-and-half
1/2 teaspoon cayenne pepper
Salted peanuts, finely chopped, for garnish

In a soup pot, melt the butter over medium heat. Add the onion, celery, and bell pepper, and cook, stirring often, until soft, 3 to 4 minutes. Stir in the flour, and cook for 2 minutes.

Add the chicken stock, stir well, increase the heat to high, and bring to a boil, stirring constantly. Then reduce the heat to medium and cook, stirring often, until slightly reduced and thickened, about 15 minutes. Pour into a sieve set over a large bowl, and strain the mixture, forcing the vegetables through to extract as much flavor as possible. Return the liquid to the pot; add the peanut butter, half-and-half, and cayenne. Warm over low heat, stirring often for about 5 minutes, taking care not to let the soup boil. Serve garnished with the chopped peanuts.

YIELD: 10 TO 12 SERVINGS

African slaves who were brought to America considered chicken a prestigious food, and because it was more expensive than pork, it was considered a special treat for holiday cooking and a symbol of gentility.
This dish is part of the heritage of African American Southern cookery but has become universal. This is the recipe my mom used to make fried chicken. Her cooking style was heavily influenced by where we lived in Virginia. Traditionally, a cast-iron skillet must be used to fry chicken and hoecakes.

Southern Fried Chicken with Cornmeal Hoecakes and Thick Gravy

For the chicken:
1/2 cup bacon fat or lard for frying (vegetable oil may be substituted but is not authentic)
1/2 cup flour

1/2 cup yellow cornmeal

1 tablespoon poultry seasoning (1/2 teaspoon each of rosemary, oregano, sage, ginger, marjoram, thyme, and pepper, mixed)

Salt and freshly ground black pepper to taste

1 frying chicken, cut into pieces

For the hoecakes:

1 cup white cornmeal

1 cup water

1/4 teaspoon salt

For the gravy:

3 tablespoons flour

1 1/2 cups half-and-half

Salt and freshly ground black pepper, to taste

To make the chicken, heat the lard in the skillet. Combine the remaining ingredients except the chicken in a bowl, mix well, and transfer to a brown paper bag. Place the chicken parts in the bag and shake well to cover. Reserve the bag. Fry the chicken in the hot fat for 20 to 25 minutes, turning occasionally. When done, drain the chicken on the bag, and keep it warm in the oven.

To make the hoecakes, combine all ingredients in a bowl and mix well to make a batter. Drop the batter into the same hot fat a table-spoonful at a time, flatten with a spoon, and fry for about 1 minute on each side or until they are well browned. Remove them and add to the same plate as the chicken parts.

To make traditional chicken gravy, pour off all but 2 tablespoons of fat, and set the burner heat to medium. Add the flour to the fat, and using a wooden spoon, stir it into the fat while loosening any brown bits of chicken and hoecakes from the bottom of the skillet. Slowly pour in the half-and-half, and stir well until the gravy thickens. To serve, butter the hoecakes and serve the gravy over mashed potatoes or rice along with the chicken parts.

YIELD: 6 SERVINGS

Okra is a variety of edible hibiscus native to Africa around Ethiopia. Philip Miller described two varieties of okra from the West Indies in 1754 in his book The Gardener's Dictionary, *but mentions of it in colonial America are sparse. However, it must have been common among French colonists because of its use in gumbos in Louisiana. Several distinct varieties were being grown in 1806, and John Low, writing in his* New and Complete American Encyclopedia *(1808), noted, "It is the chief ingredient in the celebrated pepper-pot of the West Indies, which is a rich olla [stew]: the other articles are either flesh meat, or dried fish or capsicum. This dish is very palatable and nourishing." Although a bit slimy in texture, okra has great flavor and thickening properties, and that's why it's a favorite ingredient in various forms of gumbo. Breaded and fried okra is a favorite side dish for barbecue cooking, and the sliminess of the vegetable can be removed by parboiling it before it is fried.*

Fried Okra

1 pound okra pods, stems removed, cut into 1/2-inch rounds
Salted water to cover
1 egg, slightly beaten
2 tablespoons milk
1/2 teaspoon salt
1/2 cup yellow cornmeal (or more as needed)
Bacon fat, for frying

In a medium saucepan, bring salted water to a boil, add the okra, and cook for 5 minutes.

Drain the okra in a colander.

In a bowl, whisk together the eggs, milk, and salt. Place the cornmeal in a paper bag, and heat the bacon fat in a skillet.

Dip the okra pods into the cornmeal, then into the beaten egg mixture, then back into the cornmeal. Fry the okra in the fat until it's golden brown. Serve immediately.

YIELD: 4 TO 6 SERVINGS

The first Louisiana pralines were pink or white coconut patties that echoed the influence of the French colonies in the Caribbean and were sold door-to-door and on the streets by African American women. They continued to sell the more popular native pecan and brown sugar pralines that evolved from the pink ones, and peanuts or coconut shavings occasionally substituted for the pecans. Today, pralines are a popular dessert all over the United States.

Pecan Pralines

2 cups brown sugar, firmly packed
1/4 cup water
1/4 cup evaporated milk
2 cups pecan pieces and halves
3 tablespoons salted butter
2 teaspoons vanilla

Combine the sugar, water, and milk in a 2-quart saucepan. Heat to a boil, stirring constantly. Cook until mixture reaches 228°F on a candy thermometer. Then add pecans, butter, and vanilla stirring constantly. Cook until the temperature reaches 235°F and remove from the heat. Cook for 3 minutes, then, with a wooden spoon, beat the mixture for 1 minute. Drop by tablespoons onto wax paper or aluminum foil, and cool.

YIELD: ABOUT 12 PRALINES

Appendix

RECOMMENDED HISTORICAL SITES AND RESTAURANTS

MONTICELLO, THOMAS JEFFERSON VISITOR CENTER, AND MICHIE TAVERN—CHARLOTTESVILLE, VIRGINIA

Monticello is Thomas Jefferson's masterpiece, designed and redesigned, and built and rebuilt, for more than forty years. The Monticello plantation of five thousand acres was a center of agriculture and industry and was home not only to the Jefferson family but also to workers black and white, enslaved and free. The gardens at Monticello were a botanic showpiece, a source of food, and an experimental laboratory of ornamental and useful plants from around the world. Jefferson grew 170 fruit varieties, including apples, peaches, and grapes, in Monticello's two orchards, and he cultivated more than 330 vegetable varieties in his thousand-foot-long garden terrace, which today is kept in impeccable order during the growing season. Exhibits related to food and drink include the Monticello dining room, tearoom, beer cellar, and restored kitchen.

After nearly a decade of planning, the Thomas Jefferson Visitor Center and Smith Education Center held their grand opening on April 15, 2009. The new center serves as the twenty-first-century gateway to Monticello, with multiple components that transform the visitor experience by presenting fresh perspectives on Monticello and the enduring significance of Jefferson's life and ideas.

Nearby Michie Tavern has welcomed travelers for more than two hundred years and features homemade Southern fare based on recipes from the period. After dining, guests can continue their tour through various outbuildings and down a winding path through the woods that leads to the Meadow Run Mill and General Store. Along the path are the Clothier Shop and the Metal Smith Shop.

MOUNT VERNON, MOUNT VERNON INN RESTAURANT, AND GADSBY'S TAVERN AND MUSEUM—ALEXANDRIA, VIRGINIA

Mount Vernon is the most popular historic estate in America and is located just sixteen miles south of Washington, D.C., and eight miles south of Old Town Alexandria, Virginia, on the banks of the Potomac River. Visitors can tour the mansion house and more than a dozen outbuildings, including the slave quarters, kitchen, stables, smokehouse, and greenhouse. The sixteen-sided barn and reconstructed gristmill and distillery are particularly fascinating.

The Donald W. Reynolds Museum and Education Center and the Ford Orientation Center include twenty-five theaters and galleries that detail George Washington's life. More than five hundred original artifacts, eleven History Channel videos, and immersion theater experiences vividly recreate the story of the first American hero and entrepreneur. The upper garden includes a wide variety of flowers and trees, some boxwoods that have survived since 1786, and a few vegetable beds. The beds have been restored to their original size, on the basis of archaeological excavations. The lower garden supplied fresh produce for the busy Mount Vernon kitchen. Vegetables and herbs are grown in the beds today, as well as cherry, apple, and other fruit trees espaliered along the walls and cordoned to fences. Washington used the fruit garden and nursery to experiment with new seeds and plants before using them elsewhere on the estate. The large size of the garden and its protective fence also made it an ideal site to grow tree-ripened apples, pears, plums, peaches, and cherries.

The Pioneer Farmer Site is home to a variety of heritage breeds that are similar to those owned by Washington in the eighteenth century, including hogs, sheep, turkeys, chickens, horses, oxen, cattle, mules, and livestock. Wild turkeys, deer, and other wildlife are also seen on the plantation and along the forest trail. The farm site stretches over four acres, and it has a rebuilt wharf on the river. Visitors can watch horses tread wheat in the sixteen-sided barn or listen to a dramatic surround-sound interpretation, plus enjoy a variety of eighteenth-century farming and cooking demonstrations.

The Mount Vernon Inn restaurant serves lunch daily and candlelit dinners Monday through Saturday. The inn offers six intimate dining rooms, two with fireplaces, all with colonial charm, servers in colonial garb, and regional and colonial cuisine.

Gadsby's Tavern and Museum in Old Town, Alexandria, consists of two buildings, a 1785 tavern and the 1792 City Hotel. The buildings are named for the Englishman John Gadsby, who operated them from 1796 to 1808. Gadsby's establishment was a center of political, business, and social life in early Alexandria. The tavern was the setting for dancing, theatrical and musical performances, and meetings of local organizations. George Washington enjoyed the hospitality of tavern keepers and twice attended the annual Birthnight Ball held in his honor. Other prominent patrons included John Adams, Thomas Jefferson, James Madison, and the Marquis de Lafayette. In the restaurant section of the tavern, dishes include corn-bread-stuffed roast duck in Madeira sauce, colonial game pie, and traditional English desserts.

COLONIAL WILLIAMSBURG AND THE KING'S ARMS TAVERN—VIRGINIA

In Williamsburg, scores of original buildings and hundreds of homes, shops, and public buildings are reconstructed over 301 acres—most on their original foundations. Rare animal breeds, trades, and gardens add layers of authenticity to the re-created town. Historians and horticulturists have combined historically accurate native plants with exotics that tolerate the hot, humid summers to create gardens and green spaces. The Colonial Nursery offers heirloom seeds and plants, herbs, flowers, seasonal greens, wreaths, eighteenth-century clay flower pots, and bird bottles. The Department of Historic Foodways was created in 1983 with the purpose of researching and re-creating the foods of the eighteenth century. The department currently operates daily in the Governor's Palace and Peyton Randolph kitchens. In addition to cooking programs, Foodways also offers special programs such as From Hog to Ham, which demonstrates the butchering process and the curing of hams; Arts and Mysteries of Brewing, which re-creates the world of colonial brewing; and Secrets of the Chocolate Maker, which shows the processing and use of chocolate in colonial and postcolonial times.

After Jane Vobe opened King's Arms Tavern in 1772, it became one of the town's most genteel establishments. Present-day diners can savor traditional Southern fare, desserts, and after-dinner cordials in surroundings that an eighteenth-century traveler would recognize.

HISTORIC PHILADELPHIA AND CITY TAVERN—PENNSYLVANIA

Historic Philadelphia features Independence Hall, the meeting place for the Second Continental Congress. The Declaration of Independence was debated and signed here in 1776. During the summer of 1787, delegates from twelve states assembled to revise the Articles of Confederation but instead rewrote the document, completing the U.S. Constitution on September 17, 1787. The Liberty Bell, the old state house bell, hung in the Independence Hall steeple during the formative years of the young United States. It was rung to announce the opening of the first Continental Congress in 1774, and after the Revolutionary battles of Lexington and Concord in 1775. Later, in the 1800s, it was adopted as a symbol of the abolitionist (antislavery) movement. The Archaeology Laboratory is a working facility dedicated to processing materials recovered from archaeological excavations conducted between 2000 and 2003 at the site of the National Constitution Center, as well as ongoing excavations by the National Park Service. The almost 1 million artifacts recovered from excavations tell the diverse stories of everyday Philadelphians during the eighteenth and nineteenth centuries. The laboratory presents a behind-the-scenes view of the work conducted by archaeologists and invites the public to observe Philadelphia's buried history.

Called "the most genteel tavern in America" by John Adams in 1774 while dining there during the first Continental Congress, City Tavern hosts chef and cookbook author Walter Staib to re-create and update classic colonial food in an exact replica of the original tavern, which was razed in 1854. Located in the nation's most historic square mile—Independence National Historical Park—City Tavern features candlelit dining, colonial-garbed staff, and tables set with pewter ware. Favorite dishes include West Indies pepper pot, Chesapeake crab cakes, sweet potato biscuits, and chocolate mousse cake.

VALLEY FORGE NATIONAL HISTORICAL PARK—VALLEY FORGE, PENNSYLVANIA

Valley Forge National Historical Park is located in southeastern Pennsylvania at the site where the Continental Army spent the winter of 1777–1778 during the American Revolutionary War. The park encompasses 3,500 acres and is visited by more than 1.2 million people each year. Visitors can see restored historical structures, reconstructed structures such as iconic log huts, and monuments erected by the states from which the Continental soldiers came. Visitor facilities include a welcome center and museum featuring original artifacts that provide a concise introduction to the American Revolution and the Valley Forge encampment. Programs, tours, and activities are available year-round. The park also provides twenty-six miles of hiking and biking trails, which are connected to a robust regional trails system.

The park's newly renovated welcome center has a museum with artifacts found during excavations of the park, an interactive muster roll of Continental soldiers encamped at Valley Forge, ranger-led gallery programs and walks, a storytelling program, a photo gallery, a visitor information desk staffed by the Valley Forge Convention and Visitors' Bureau, and the Encampment Store for books and souvenirs. A snack bar and bike rentals are available in season. A short eighteen-minute film, *Valley Forge: A Winter Encampment*, is shown in the park's theater next door. A ninety-minute trolley tour of the entire park also arrives and departs from this location. A key attraction of the park is the restored colonial home used by George Washington as his headquarters during the encampment.

FRAUNCES TAVERN MUSEUM AND FRAUNCES TAVERN RESTAURANT—NEW YORK, NEW YORK

Fraunces Tavern Museum is a survivor of the early days of New York City. It was built in 1719 as an elegant residence for the merchant Stephan Delancey and his family. In 1762, the home was purchased by the tavern keeper Samuel Fraunces, who turned it into one of the most popular taverns of his time, rivaled only by City Tavern in Philadelphia. Although it is best known as the site where Washington gave his farewell address to the officers of the Continental Army in 1783, the tavern also played a significant role in pre-Revolutionary activities. After the war, when New York was the nation's first capital, the tavern was rented to the new government to house the offices of the Departments of War, Treasury, and Foreign Affairs. It was restored to its colonial appearance in 1907 by William Mersereau in 1907. These days, the three-story, red brick building gives visitors a glimpse into the past with period rooms accompanied by exhibitions on colonial life and the tavern's significant role in New York history. Visitors can dine downstairs on roasted codfish or game hen, shepherd's pie, or pot roast, with sides of fava beans, spinach, or potatoes, and some contemporary fare as well. If the surroundings look familiar, that could be the result of the numerous films that have been shot at Fraunces, like *American Psycho*, *Two Weeks Notice*, and *National Treasure*.

MONTPELIER—ORANGE, VIRGINIA

Montpelier, located in the foothills of the Blue Ridge Mountains in Orange, Virginia, was the lifelong home of James Madison. Madison was raised at Montpelier, lived there after his marriage to Dolley, returned there after his presidency, and died there in his study surrounded by the books and papers that marked so much of his life's work. It was at Montpelier that Madison researched past democracies and conceived of the system of government that became the United States.

The Montpelier estate features the Madison mansion, historic buildings, exhibits, archaeological sites, gardens, forests, hands-on activities, a visitor center, and a freedman's cabin and farm. The visitor center offers an interactive model of the estate and a short presentation in the Alan and Louise Potter Theater about the restoration of Montpelier. The Grills Gallery features treasures of Montpelier, such as Madison's spyglass, a brace of pistols, a snuffbox, and a reproduction of Dolley's red dress. There is lunch available in the Courtyard Café and a museum shop.

JAMESTOWN AND YORKTOWN—VIRGINIA

Jamestown Settlement tells the story of the people who founded Jamestown and of the Virginia Native Americans they encountered, through film, gallery exhibits, and living history. Gallery exhibits and an introductory film trace Jamestown's beginnings in England and the first century of the Virginia colony and describe the cultures of the Powhatan Native Americans, Europeans, and Africans who converged in 1600s Virginia. Outdoors, visitors can board replicas of the three ships that sailed from England to Virginia in 1607; explore life-size re-creations of the colonists' fort and a Powhatan village; and tour a seasonal riverfront discovery area to learn about European, Powhatan, and African economic activities associated with water. In the outdoor areas, costumed historical interpreters describe and demonstrate daily life in the early seventeenth century.

Yorktown Victory Center chronicles America's evolution from colonial status to nationhood through a blend of timeline, film, thematic exhibits, and outdoor living history. An outdoor walkway details events that led to American colonies to declare independence from Britain. Indoor exhibition galleries recount the war's effect on ten ordinary men and women who witnessed the Revolutionary War, highlight the roles of different nationalities in the Siege of Yorktown, and explore the story of the *Betsy* and other British ships lost in the York River during the war. Exhibits also describe experiences of ordinary soldiers, Yorktown's importance as an eighteenth-century port, and the development of a new government with the Constitution and Bill of Rights. Outdoors, visitors can explore a re-created Continental Army encampment, where historical interpreters describe and depict the daily life of American soldiers at the end of the war. A re-created 1780s farm, complete with a house, kitchen, tobacco barn, crop fields, and herb and vegetable garden, shows how many Americans lived in the decade following the Revolutionary War.

Image Credits

❧

Photographs on the following pages courtesy of Sunbelt Archives: 1, 2, 5, 9, 19, 27, 45, 49, 68, 71, 73, 74, 81, 82, 84, 98, 114, 137, 154. Photograph courtesy of the New Hampshire Historical Society: 32. Photograph courtesy of the Medford Historical Society: 25. Photographs courtesy of North Wind Picture Archives: 25, 33, 54, 127, 133. Photograph courtesy of Sturgis Library: 57. Photograph courtesy of the National Park Service: 65. Photograph courtesy of the Mount Vernon Ladies' Association: 80, 91. Photograph courtesy of the National Archives: 125. Photograph courtesy of the Library of Congress: 143. Photograph courtesy of Monticello, by Robert Lautman: 170. Photograph courtesy of The Bettmann Archive: 227.

Bibliography

Author's Note

I researched this book from the summer of 2006 to the fall of 2009 and the website URLs reflect those dates.

On some occasions while researching this book, I first encountered information for a source on Wikipedia.org, and have thus cited Wikipedia as the origin of my information. In every such instance, I checked the original sources of the material and verified their accuracy before citing them in this book.

Recommended Reading

- *A Revolution in Eating*, James E. McWilliams
- *Dining at Monticello*, Damon Lee Fowler, Ed.
- *The Virginia Housewife*, Mary Randolph
- *The Hemingses of Monticello*, Annette Gordon-Reed
- *Thomas Jefferson on Wine*, John Hailman
- *And a Bottle of Rum*, Wayne Curtis
- *The Thirteen Colonies Cookbook*, Mary Donovan, et al.
- *The Welcome Table: African-American Heritage Cooking*, Jessica B. Harris

GENERAL HISTORY

Adams, Charles Francis, ed. *The Works of John Adams*, vol. 2. Boston: Little, Brown, 1850.

"Annapolis, December 25." *Maryland Gazette*. no. 1928, Dec. 25, 1783, 2.

"Antoine-Augustin Parmentier." Wikipedia. www.wikipedia.org.

"Art: Black Leonardo." *Time*. Nov. 24, 1941. www.time.com.

Bartlett, John Russell. *Dictionary of Americanisms: A Glossary of Words and Phrases Usually Regarded as Peculiar to the United States*. Boston: Little, Brown, 1877.

Beach, William Dorance, et al. *Manual of Military Field Engineering for the Use of Officers and Troops of the Line*. Fort Leavenworth, KS: Hudson-Kimberly, 1897.

"Benedict Arnold." Wikipedia. www.wikipedia.org.

"Benjamin Rush." Wikipedia. www.wikipedia.org.

Bierce, Ambrose. *The Enlarged Devil's Dictionary*. New York: Doubleday, 1967.

Bodle, Wayne, and Jacqueline Thibaut. *The Valley Forge Report*. www.nps.gov.

Boorstin, Daniel J. *The Americans: The Democratic Experience*. New York: Vintage Books, 1974.

Boyle, Joseph Lee. "The Valley Forge Fish Story." *Shad Journal*. www.cbr.washington.edu/shadfoundation/.

"Brain Trust." Wikipedia. www.wikipedia.org.

Bremer, Francis J. *John Winthrop: America's Forgotten Founding Father*. New York: Oxford University Press, 2003.

Brisse, Léon. *Menues and 1200 Recipes of the Baron Brisse in French and English*. Translated by Mrs. Matthew Clark. London: Sampson Low, Marston, Searle, & Rivington, 1882.

Brooks, Charles, and William Henry Whitmore. *History of the Town of Medford, Middlesex County, Massachusetts: From Its First Settlement in 1630 to*

1855. Boston: Rand, Avery, 1885. (Originally published by J. M. Usher, 1855.)

Bruce, Franklin Howard. *The Most Important Fish in the Sea: Menhaden and America*. Washington, D.C.: Island Press/Shearwater Books, 2007.

Carroll, Lewis. *Alice in Wonderland*. Boston: Barta Press, 1897.

"Charles Cornwallis." Wikipedia. www.wikipedia.org.

Clary, David. *Adopted Son: Washington, Lafayette, and the Friendship That Saved the Revolution*. New York: Bantam Books, 2007.

Collins, Joseph William. "Evolution of the American Fishing Schooner." *New England Magazine* 18, 1898.

Coolidge, Richard B. "Medford and Her Minutemen." *Medford Historical Society Publications* 28 (1925): 42–51.

Condit, William Ward. "Christopher Ludwick, The Patriotic Gingerbread Baker." *Pennsylvania Magazine of History and Biography* 81, no. 4 (1957): 365–90.

Crews, Ed. "Juba and Djembe: Music Helps Interpret Slavery." *Colonial Williamsburg, Winter 2002–03*. www.history.org/foundation/journal/winter02-03/music.cfm.

Cronin, William. *Change in the Land: Indians, Colonists, and the Ecology of New England*. New York: Hill and Wang, 1983.

"Crowninshield Family." Wikipedia. www.wikipedia.org.

Dinkin, Robert J. *Campaigning in America: A History of Election Practices*. New York: Greenwood Press, 1989.

Donovan, Mary. *The Thirteen Colonies Cookbook*. Santa Barbara, CA: Praerger Publishers, 1975.

Durey, Michael. *"With the Hammer of Truth": James Thomson Callender and America's Early National Heroes*. Charlottesville: University Press of Virginia, 1990.

"Economic Aspects of Tobacco During the Colonial Period 1612–1776."
www.tobacco.org.

Engel, Leo. *American and Other Drinks*. London: Tinsley Bros., 1878.

Ex-Member of Congress. *My Ride to the Barbecue: or, Revolutionary Reminiscences of the Old Dominion*. New York: S. A. Rollo, 1860.

Farquhar, Michael. *A Treasury of Great American Scandals*. New York: Penguin Books, 2003.

Ferling, John. *Setting the World Ablaze: Washington, Adams, Jefferson and the American Revolution*. New York: Oxford University Press, 2002.

Filipski, Jim W. "Boiled Beef & Ash Cake." www.captainselinscompany.org.

Flower, Milton Embrick. *John Dickinson, Conservative Revolutionary*. Charlottesville: University Press of Virginia, 1983.

Galloway, Patricia Kay. *The Hernando de Soto Expedition: History, Historiography, and "Discovery" in the Southeast*. Lincoln: University of Nebraska Press, 2006.

Garland, Joseph E. *Lone Voyager: The Extraordinary Adventures of Howard Blackburn, Hero Fisherman of Gloucester*. New York: Simon and Schuster, 2000.

Gies, Oliver. "The Genius of Oliver Evans." *Invention and Technology* 6, no. 2 (1990). www.AmericanHeritage.com.

"Gilbert du Motier, Marquis de Lafayette." Wikipedia. www.wikipedia.org.

Gleason, Hall. "Captain Isaac Hall." *Medford Historical Society Publications* 8 (1905): 100–103.

Goodwin, Jason. *Greenback: The Almighty Dollar and the Invention of America*. New York: Picador, 2003.

Hawes, Charles Boardman. *Gloucester, By Land and Sea: The Story of a New England Seacoast Town*. Boston: Little, Brown, 1923.

Headley, Phineas Camp. *The Life of General Lafayette*. Auburn, NY: Miller, Orton & Mulligan, 1854.

Henningsen, Vic. "The Key to the Bastille." Vermont Public Radio, July 14, 2009. www.vpr.net.

Historical Society of Pennsylvania. *Pennsylvania Magazine of History and Biography*, vol. 1. Philadelphia: Historical Society of Pennsylvania, 1877.

Holbrook, Stewart H. *Lost Men of American History*. New York: Macmillan, 1948.

Hoobler, Dorothy, and Thomas Hoobler. *Captain John Smith: Jamestown and the Birth of the American Dream*. Hoboken, NJ: John Wiley & Sons, 2006.

Irving, Theodore. *The Conquest of Florida by Hernando de Soto*. New York: Putnam, 1868.

"Jefferson's Financial Diary." *Harper's Magazine Making of America Project*, vol. 70. New York: Harper's Magazine, 1885.

"John Sears Capt," Sears Family Association, www.searsr.com.

"John Smith of Jamestown." Wikipedia. www.wikipedia.org.

"John Winthrop the Younger." Wikipedia. www.wikipedia.org.

Karsch, Carl G. "City Tavern: A Feast of Elegance." www.ushistory.org.

Kulikoff, Allan. *Tobacco and Slaves*. Chapel Hill: University of North Carolina Press, 1988.

Lloyd, Gordon. "Entertainment of George Washington, City Tavern, Philadelphia, September 1787, Menu and Bill." TeachingAmericanHistory .org.

Martin, Joseph Plumb. *Private Yankee Doodle*, edited by George E. Scheer. London: Acorn Press, 1979.

McFarland, Raymond. *A History of the New England Fisheries: With Maps*. State College: University of Pennsylvania, 1911.

McPhee, John. *The Founding Fish*. New York: Farrar, Strauss, and Giroux, 2002.

Middleton, Arthur Pierce. *Tobacco Coast*. Newport News, VA: Mariners' Museum, 1953.

"Minutemen." www.ushistory.org/people/minutemen.htm.

Moore, Virginia. *Virginia Is a State of Mind*. New York: E. P. Dutton, 1942.

Morgan, Philip D. *Slave Counterpoint*. Chapel Hill: University of North Carolina Press, 1998.

Morison, Samuel Eliot. *The Maritime History of Massachusetts*. Boston: Houghton Mifflin, 1921.

"Navigation Acts." Wikipedia. www.wikipedia.org.

National Park Service. "Discovering What Washington's Troops Left Behind at Valley Forge." www.nps.gov/history/logcabin/html/rd_valleyforge.html.

Nicholson, Meredith. *The Valley of Democracy*. New York: C. Scribner's Sons, 1918.

Paine, Ralph Delahaye. *Old Merchant Marine: A Chronicle of American Ships and Sailors*. New Haven, CT: Yale University Press, 1920.

"Paul Revere: The D.U.I. That Roused a Nation." Dec. 19, 2007. www.snopes.com.

Philbrick, Nathaniel. *Mayflower: A Story of Courage, Community, and War*. New York: Viking, 2006.

Pierson, Hamilton Wilcox. *In the Brush; or, Old-time Social, Political, and Religious Life in the Southwest*. New York: D. Appleton, 1881.

Putnam, George Granville. *Salem Vessels and Their Voyages: A History of the Pepper Trade with the Island of Sumatra*. Salem, MA: Essex Institute, 1922.

Rak, Emily. "Salty Air." *Edible Cape Cod* 19. www.ediblecapecod.com.

Randall, Henry Stephens. *The Life of Thomas Jefferson*, vol. 1. New York: J. B. Lippincott, 1871.

Randall, Willard Sterne. "Benedict Arnold—Patriot and Traitor." www.cooperativeindividualism.org/randall_on_benedict_arnold.html.

Rantoul, Robert Samuel, and William O. Chapman. *Old Time Ships of Salem*. Salem, MA: Essex Institute, 1917.

Reed, John F. "Valley Forge Commissariat." *Picket Post*, 1980. www.ushistory .org/valleyforge/history/commissary.html.

Rees, John U. "'As many fireplaces as you have tents'...Earthen Camp Kitchens." www.revwar75/library/rees/kitchen.htm.

Richards, Henry Melchior Muhlenberg. *The Pennsylvania-German in the Revolutionary War, 1775–1783*. Lancaster, PA: Press of the New Era Printing Company, 1908.

Risch, Erna. *Supplying Washington's Army*. Washington, D.C.: Center of Military History, U.S. Army, 1981.

Salisbury, Neal. "Squanto." In *The Human Tradition in America from the Colonial Era through Reconstruction*, edited by Charles W. Calhoun. Wilmington, DE: SR Books, 2002.

Scharf, John Thomas, and Thompson Westcott. *History of Philadelphia, 1609–1884*, vol. 2. Philadelphia: L. H. Everts, 1884.

"Schooner." Wikipedia. www.wikipedia.org.

Seaburg, Carl and Alan Seaburg. *Medford on the Mystic*. Medford, CT: Self-published, 1980.

Shaver, Bob. "Oliver Evans Automated Flour Mill." *Patent Pending Blog*, July 16, 2005. http://patentpending.blogs.com.

Smith, John. *A Description of New England (1616). An Online Electronic Text Edition*. Lincoln: University of Nebraska, 2006.

Society of the Descendants of Washington's Army at Valley Forge. "Valley Forge." www.revolutionarywararchives.org/valleyforge.html.

Sparber, Max. "The Midnight Tipple of Paul Revere." *The Bottle Gang*.www .bottlegang.blogspot.com.

Spears, John Randolph. *The Story of the American Merchant Marine*. New York: Macmillan, 1910.

"Squanto." Wikipedia. www.wikipedia.org.

Staib, Walter. "City Tavern." www.citytavern.com.

Sweet, Alexander Edwin and John Armoy Knox. *On a Mexican Mustang, through Texas, from the Gulf to the Rio Grande*. Hartford, CT: S. S. Scranton, 1883.

Taussig, Charles William and Philip Kappel. *Rum, Romance & Rebellion*. New York: Minton, Balch, 1928.

"Timeline." www.porkopolis.org.

Treese, Lorett. *Valley Forge: Making and Remaking a National Symbol*. University Park: University of Pennsylvania Press, 1995. (Online at www.nps.gov.)

"Townsend Act." Wikipedia. www.wikipedia.org.

"Triangle Trade." Wikipedia. www.wikipedia.org.

"Turnspit Dog." Wikipedia. www.wikipedia.org.

U.S. Census Bureau. "Rank by Population of the 100 Largest Urban Places, Listed Alphabetically by State: 1790–1990." www.census.gov/population/www/documentation/twps0027/tab01.txt.

U.S. Senate. "The Nine Capitals of the United States." www.senate.gov/reference/reference_item/Nine_Capitals_of_the_United_States.htm.

"Valley Forge." Wikipedia. www.wikipedia.org.

"Virtual Jamestown Timeline." www.virtualjamestown.org.

Walbert, David. "The Value of Money in Colonial America." www.learnnc.org/lp/editions/nchist-colonial/1646.

Walton, Joseph Solomon and Martin Grove Brumbraugh. *Stories of Pennsylvania; or, School Readings from Pennsylvania History*. New York: American Book Company, 1897.

"Washington's Resignation; The Centenary of the Event Close at Hand." *New York Times*, Dec. 21, 1883, 6.

Weatherford, Jack. *The History of Money*. New York: Crown Publishers, 1997.

Weedon, George and American Philosophical Society. *Valley Forge Orderly Book of General George Weedon*. New York: Dodd, Mead, 1902.

Webster, Daniel. *The Works of Daniel Webster*, edited by Edward Everett. Boston: Little, Brown, 1853.

Webster, Thomas and William Parkes. *An Encyclopaedia of Domestic Economy*. New York: Harper & Brothers, 1855.

Wildes, Harry Emerson. *Valley Forge*. New York: Macmillan, 1938.

Wills, Garry. *Negro President: Jefferson and the Slave Power*. New York: Houghton Mifflin Harcourt, 2005.

Woods, Thomas E. *33 Questions about American History You're Not Supposed to Ask*. New York: Random House, 2007.

Zacks, Richard. *The Pirate Coast: Thomas Jefferson, the First Marines, and the Secret Mission of 1805*. New York, Hyperion, 2005.

INTERVIEWS, HISTORICAL LETTERS, PAYMENTS, AND ORDERS

Baron de Kalb to the Comte de Broglie, 12, 17 and 25 December 1777, original letter in cipher, deciphered and translated, France, Archives des Affaires Étrangeres, États Unis, vol. 2, no. 153, in Benjamin F. Stevens, ed., *Facsimiles of Manuscripts in European Archives Relating to America, 1773–1783* (London: Issued only to subscribers at 4, Trafalgar Square, Charing Cross, London [Photographed and printed by Malby & Sons], 1889–1895), vol. 8, document 761.

Jedediah Huntington to Washington, 1 January 1778, Washington Papers, reel 46, Library of Congress.

Blagden to Banks, April 20, 1778. In Blagden, Charles. Letters from Sir Charles Blagden to Sir Joseph Banks on American natural history and politics, 1776–1780. Published in *Bulletin of the New York Public Library* 7, no. 11 (1903).

General Orders, 9 January 1778, WGW, 10:284.

Alexander Hamilton to Governor George Clinton, 13 February 1778, Hamilton Papers, 1:426; Clinton Papers, 2:860–62.

Jefferson to John Adams, 27 November 1785, www.familytales.org.

Thomas Jones, Return of Provisions Remaining in Camp, 9 February 1778, RG 93, M 859, roll 75, doc. 22035, f201, National Archives.

Thomas Jones, 13 February 1778, RG 360, M 247, roll 199, p407, National Archives.

Henry B. Livingston to Robert R. Livingston, 24 December 1777, Robert R. Livingston Papers, New York Historical Society; Bancroft Transcript Collection, New York Public Library; quoted in Ryan, *A Salute to Courage*, 111–13.

James Lovell to John Adams, 30 December 1777, LDC, 8:507.

Henry E. Lutterloh, Remarks, 25 December 1777, Washington Papers, roll 46, Library of Congress.

Kerr, Barbara, Medford Historical Society. Interview via email, June 25, 2009.

Ludwick Payment, 26 March 1778. RG 53, M 1014, Treasury Records, roll 1, Waste Book A, 140, National Archives.

Dona McDermott, archivist with Valley Forge National Historical Park. Telephone interview, June 26, 2009.

Jonathan Todd Jr. to Jonathan Todd, 25 December 1777, National Archives, RG15, M806, r1561.

Varnum to Washington, 22 December 1777, Washington Papers, reel 46, Library of Congress.

FOOD AND DRINK HISTORY

Abala, Ken. *Beans: A History*. Oxford, UK: Berg Publishers, 2007.

Adams, C. F., ed. *Letters of Mrs. Adams, Wife of John Adams*. Boston: C. C. Little and James Brown, 1848.

Aidells, Bruce. *Bruce Aidells's Complete Book of Pork*. New York: HarperCollins, 2004.

"Antoine-Augustin Parmentier." Wikipedia. www.wikipedia.org, September 2008.

Ashton, John. *The History of Bread: From Pre-historic to Modern Times*. London: Religious Tract Society, 1904.

Baron, Stanley. *Brewed in America: A History of Beer and Ale in the United States*. Boston: Little, Brown, 1962.

Barr, Ann and Paul Levy. *The Official Foodie Handbook*. New York: Arbor House, 1984.

Barrett, Mary Brigid. "A Taste of the Past: White House Kitchens, Menus, and Recipes." www.ourwhitehouse.org/tasteofpast.html.

Barty-King, Hugh and Anton Massel. *Rum Yesterday and Today*. London: William Heinemann, 1983.

"Blancmange." Wikipedia. www.wikipedia.org.

Bradley, Richard. *The Country Housewife and Lady's Director, in the Management of a House, and the Delights and Profits of a Farm*. London: D. Browne and T. Woodman, 1732.

Brewer, Priscilla J. *From Fireplace to Cookstove: Technology and the Domestic Ideal in America*. Syracuse, NY: Syracuse University Press, 2000.

Briggs, Richard. *The English Art of Cookery, according to the Present Practice: Being a Complete Guide to All Housekeepers, on a Plan Entirely New...* London: G. G. J. and J. Robinson, 1788.

Brisse, Léon. *366 Menus and 1200 Recipes of the Baron Brisse in French and English, translated by Mrs. Matthew Clark*. London: Sampson Low, Marston, Searle & Rivington, 1882.

Carver, George Washington. *How to Grow the Peanut: And 105 Ways of Preparing It for Human Consumption*. Tuskegee, AL: Tuskegee Normal and Industrial Institute Experiment Station, 1921.

Chase, Alvin Wood. *Dr. Chase's Recipes*. Ann Arbor, MI: R. A. Beal, 1876.

"Christmas at Mount Vernon." www.mountvernon.org.

Coulombe, Charles A. *Rum: The Epic Story of the Drink That Conquered the World*. New York: Citadel Press Books, 2004.

Coyle, L. Patrick. *Cook's Books*. New York: Facts on File Books, 1985.

Countess Morphy. *Recipes of All Nations*. New York: Wm. H. Wise, 1935.

"Country Ham." Wikipedia. www.wikipedia.org.

Croly, Jane Cunningham. *Jennie June's American Cookery Book: Containing Upwards of Twelve Hundred Choice and Carefully Tested Receipts...* New York: American News, 1866.

Cuming, D. Syer. "Syllabub and Syllabub Vessels." *Journal of the British Archaeological Association* 47 (1891), 212–216.

Curtis, Wayne. *And a Bottle of Rum: A History of the New World in Ten Cocktails*. New York: Crown Publishers, 2006.

Déliée, Felix J. *The Franco-American Cookery Book; or, How to Live Well and Wisely Every Day in the Year*. New York: G.P. Putnam's Sons, 1884.

DeWitt, Dave and Nancy Gerlach. *Barbecue Inferno*. Berkeley, CA: Ten Speed Press, 2001.

DeWitt, Dave and Nancy Gerlach. *The Spicy Food Lover's Bible*. New York: Stewart, Tabori & Chang, 2005.

DeWitt, Dave, Mary Jane Wilan, and Melissa T. Stock. *Hot & Spicy Caribbean*. Rocklin, CA: Prima Publishing, 1996.

Earle, Alice Morse. *Stage-Coach and Tavern Days*. New York: Macmillan, 1922.

"The Facts on Wild Feral Hogs." www.texasboars.com.

Ferguson, David L. *Cleopatra's Barge: The Crowninshield Story*. Boston: Little, Brown, 1976.

Ferguson, Priscilla Parkhurst. *Accounting for Taste: The Triumph of French Cuisine*. Chicago: University of Chicago Press, 2004.

Forney, John W. "Terrapin." In *The Epicure*. New York: H. K. & F. B. Thurber, 1879, 32.

Fox, Danny. "Pecans: A Growing Tradition." www.foodeditorials.com.

Franklin, Benjamin. "The Drinker's Dictionary." *Pennsylvania Gazette*, Jan. 13, 1737.

Franklin, Howard Bruce. *The Most Important Fish in the Sea: Menhaden and America*. Washington, D.C.: Island Press, 2007.

Fussell, Betty. *The Story of Corn*. New York: Alfred A. Knopf, 1992.

"George Washington Carver." Wikipedia. www.wikipedia.org.

Guest, Moses. *Poems on Several Occasions*. Cincinnati: Looker & Reynolds, 1824.

Harris, Jessica B. *The Welcome Table: African-American Heritage Cooking*. New York: Simon and Schuster, 1995.

Hess, Karen. *The Carolina Rice Kitchen*. Columbia: University of South Carolina Press, 1992.

Hines, Mary Ann, Gordon Marshall, and William Woys Weaver. *The Larder Invaded: Reflections on Three Centuries of Philadelphia Food and Drink*. Philadelphia: Historical Society of Pennsylvania, 1987.

"The History of Hog Island Sheep." http://hogislandsheep.org.

"Hog Wild Problem in Florida: UF Experts Say Feral Pig Problem Here to Stay." *Science Daily*, June 7, 2005. www.sciencedaily.com.

Holland, Barbara. *The Joy of Drinking*. New York: Bloomsbury USA, 2007.

Irving, Theodore. *The Conquest of Florida by Hernando de Soto*. New York: Putnam, 1868.

Johnson, Harry. *The New and Improved Illustrated Bartenders' Manual; or, How to Mix Drinks of the Present Style*. New York: H. Johnson, 1888.

Jones, Evan. *American Food: The Gastronomic Story*. Woodstock, NY: Overlook Press, 1990.

King, Louise Tate and Jean Stewart Wexler. *The Martha's Vineyard Cookbook*. New York: Harper & Row, 1971.

Kitchen Sisters. "Hercules and Hemings: Presidents' Slave Chefs." www.npr .org/templates/story/story.php?storyId=18950467.

Kurlansky, Mark. *Cod: A Biography of the Fish That Changed the World*. New York: Penguin Books, 1997.

Kurlansky, Mark. *Salt: A World History*. New York: Walker & Co., 2002.

Lamb, Charles. *Charles Lamb's Essays*. Boston: Little, Brown, 1892.

Lee, Mrs. N. K. M. *The Cook's Own Book: Being a Complete Culinary Encyclopedia... With Numerous Original Receipts and a Complete System of Confectionery*. Boston: Munroe and Francis, 1832.

Lichine, Alexis. *Alexis Lichine's Encyclopedia of Wines and Spirits*. New York: Alfred A. Knopf, 1968.

Longone, Janice Bluestein. "Introduction to the Dover Edition." In *The Virginia Housewife; or, Methodical Cook: A Facsimile of an Authentic Early American Cookbook*. New York: Dover Publications, 1993.

Louisiana Sugar Planters' Association. *The Louisiana Planter and Sugar Manufacturer*, vol. 28. New Orleans: Louisiana Planter and Sugar Manufacturer Co., 1902.

Low, John. *The New and Complete American Encyclopedia*, vol. 4. New York: Self-published, 1808.

"Macaroons." Wikipedia. www.wikipedia.org.

McDonald, James. *Life in Old Virginia*. Norfolk, Virginia: The Old Virginia Publishing Co., 1907.

McFarland, Raymond. *A History of the New England Fisheries: With Maps*. State College: University of Pennsylvania, 1911.

Miller, Philip. *The Gardeners Dictionary*, vol. 2. London: Printed for the author, 1754.

Mood, Fulmer. "John Winthrop, Jr., on Indian Corn." *New England Quarterly* 10, no. 1 (1937): 121–133.

Neill, E. and James B. Herndon. *What Shall I Eat? The Housewife's Manual*. New York: Home Life Publishing, 1892.

"Okra, or 'Gumbo', from Africa." *Plant Answers*. http://aggie-horticulture.tamu.edu/plantanswers/publications/vegetabletravelers/okra.html.

Parloa, Maria. *Miss Parloa's Kitchen Companion: A Guide for All Who Would Be Good Housekeepers*. Boston: Estes and Lauriat, 1887.

"Parmentier Introduces the Potato Into France." *Harper's Magazine Making of America Project,* vol. 4. New York: *Harper's Magazine,* 1852.

Pinney, Thomas. *A History of Wine in America*. Berkeley: University of California Press, 1989.

"Pumpkins." www.wiki.monticello.org.

Raichlen, Steven. *BBQ USA*. New York: Workman Publishing, 2003.

Root, Waverly. *Food*. New York: Simon and Schuster, 1980.

Root, Waverly and Richard de Rochemont. *Eating in America*. Hopewell, NJ: Ecco Press, 1981.

Rorabaugh, W. J. *The Alcoholic Republic: An American Tradition*. New York: Oxford University Press, 1979.

Sarafin, Justin. "Like Clockwork: French Influence in Monticello's Kitchen." In *Dining at Monticello*, edited by Damon Fowler, 26. Charlottesville: Thomas Jefferson Foundation, 2005.

"Savoy Biscuit and Two Other Dessert Recipes." Monticello Classroom. www .wiki.monticello.org.

"'Shocking' History of Fish House Punch." Great Party Recipes. www .greatpartyrecipes.com/history-of-fish-house-punch.html.

Smith, Andrew F. *Peanuts: The Illustrious History of the Goober Pea*. Urbana: University of Illinois Press, 2002.

Smith, Andrew F. *The Tomato in America*. Columbia: University of South Carolina Press, 1994.

Smith, Andrew F. *The Oxford Companion to American Food and Drink*. New York: Oxford University Press, 2007.

Smith, Andrew F. *The Oxford Encyclopedia of Food and Drink in America*, vols. 1–2. New York: Oxford University Press, 2004.

Smith-Kizer, Carolyn. "Biscuits Ordinaries." 18thccuisine Blog, Feb. 2, 2008. http://18thccuisine.blogspot.com, translated from *La Cuisinière Bourgeoise* by Menon, 1746–1815.

Smoler, Roberta Wolfe. *The Useful Pig*. New York: HarperCollins Publishers, 1990.

Stoney, Louisa (Mrs. Samuel G. Stoney). *Carolina Rice Cook Book*. Charleston, SC: Carolina Rice Kitchen Association, 1901.

"Sugar Maple." Thomas Jefferson Encyclopedia. www.wiki.monticello.org.

Thaxter, Celia. *Making of America Project: Cairns Collection of American Women Writers*. New York: Atlantic Monthly Co., 1909.

Tucker, Susan and S. Frederick Starr. *New Orleans Cuisine: Fourteen Signature Dishes and Their Histories*. Oxford: University Press of Mississippi, 2009.

Watson, Lyall. *The Whole Hog*. Washington, D.C.: Smithsonian Books, 2004.

Whittaker, Anne-Marie. "Pepperpot—The Amazing Story!" http://ezinearticles.com/.

Wilkins, Sharron E. "The President's Kitchen." *American Visions*, Feb.–March 1995. www.pbs.org.

Williams, David. "The Mysterious Demise of Hard Cider." George Mason University. http://mason.gmu.edu/~drwillia/cider.html.

Wilson, Mary Tolford. "The First American Cookbook." In *The First American Cookbook*. New York: Dover Publications, 1984, vii–xxiv.

COLONIAL AND POSTCOLONIAL FOOD AND COOKERY

Brookes, Joshua. "A Dinner at Mount Vernon." *New York Historical Society Quarterly* 31, no. 2 (1947): 72–85.

Bryan, Mrs. Lettice. *The Kentucky Housewife*. Cincinnati, OH: Shepard & Stearns, 1839.

Carson, Jane. *Colonial Virginians at Play*. Williamsburg, VA: Colonial Williamsburg, 1965.

Carson, Jane. *Colonial Virginia Cookery*. Williamsburg, VA: Colonial Williamsburg Foundation, 1985.

Carter, Landon. "Green Corn Stalk Beer." *Virginia Gazette*, Feb. 14, 1775. http://brewery.org.

"Cheshire Mammoth Cheese." Wikipedia. www.wikipedia.org.

"Cornelius Swartwout, Inventor of the Waffle Iron." www.swartoutfamily .org.

"Dining at the President's House." Thomas Jefferson Encyclopedia. www .monticello.org.

"Dining with Congress." Thomas Jefferson Encyclopedia. www.wiki.monticello .org.

"Dinner Etiquette." Thomas Jefferson Encyclopedia. www.wiki.monticello .org.

Earle, Alice Morse. *Home Life in Colonial Days*. Stockbridge, MA: Berkshire Traveller Press, 1974.

Eden, Trudy. *The Early American Table*. DeKalb: Northern Illinois University Press, 2008.

Emerson, Lucy. *The New England Cookery*. Montpelier, VT: Parks, 1808.

Gillette, Fanny Lemira, and Hugo Zieman. *The White House Cook Book: Cooking, Toilet and Household Recipes, Menus, Dinner-Giving, Table Etiquette, Care of the Sick, Health Suggestions, Facts Worth Knowing, etc., etc....* New York: Werner Publishing, 1890.

Glasse, Hannah. *The Art of Cookery, Made Plain and Easy*. London: W. Strahan, J. F. Rivington, and J. Hinton, 1774.

Harbury, Katherine E. *Colonial Virginia's Cooking Dynasty*. Columbia: University of South Carolina Press, 2004.

Hawke, David Freeman. *Everyday Life in Early America*. New York: Perennial Library, 1988.

Hooker, Richard J., ed. *A Colonial Plantation Cookbook: The Receipt Book of Harriott Pinckney Horry, 1770*. Columbia: University of South Carolina Press, 1984.

Lynn, Kristie and Robert W. Pelton. *The Early American Cookbook*. Deerfield Beach, FL: Liberty Publishing, 1990.

"Maple History." Massachusetts Maple Producers Association. www.massmaple .org/history.html.

"Menu, Dinner." City Tavern. www.citytavern.com, 2009.

McWilliams, James E. *A Revolution in Eating: How the Quest for Food Shaped America*. New York: Columbia University Press, 2005.

The Old Foodie. "The Battle for Food." Dec. 29, 2005, http://theoldfoodie .blogspot.com/2005/12/battle-for-food.html.

Oliver, Sandra L. *Food in Colonial and Federal America*. Westport. CT: Greenwood Press, 2005.

"Pepper-Pot: A Scene in the Philadelphia Market, 1811." PBS. www.pbs.org/ wgbh/aia/part3/.

Phillips, James Duncan. Salem in the Seventeenth Century. Boston and New York: Houghton Mifflin Company, 1933.

Randolph, Mary. *The Virginia Housewife; or, Methodical Cook*. Mineola, NY: Dover Publications, 1993. (First published in Washington, D.C. in 1824. Facsimile of the 1860 edition published by E.H. Butler & Co., Philadelphia.)

Rutledge, Sarah. *The Carolina Housewife*. Columbia: University of South Carolina Press, 1979.

Salinger, Sharon V. *Taverns and Drinking in Early America*. Baltimore: Johns Hopkins University Press, 2002.

Simmons, Amelia. *The First American Cookbook, A Facsimile of "American Cookery," 1796*. Mineola, NY: Dover Publications, 1984.

Staib, Walter. *The City Tavern Cookbook*. Philadelphia: Running Press, 2009.

Stanton, Lucia. "Nourishing the Congress." In *Dining at Monticello*, edited by Damon Fowler, 11–18. Charlottesville: Thomas Jefferson Foundation, 2005.

"Sugar Maple." Thomas Jefferson Encyclopedia. www.wiki.monticello.org.

Super, John C. *Food, Conquest, and Colonization in Sixteenth Century Spanish America*. Albuquerque: University of New Mexico Press, 1988.

Taylor, Dale. *The Writer's Guide to Everyday Life in Colonial America*. Cincinnati, OH: Writer's Digest Books, 1999.

Vintage Recipes. www.vintagerecipes.net.

Walsh, Lorena. "Feeding the Eighteenth Century Town Folk." Colonial Williamsburg Research Division Web Site. http://research.history.org.

Webster, Mrs. A. L. *The Improved Housewife*. Boston: Phillips, Sampson, 1855.

"What Is the Difference between Liquor and Spirits?" WikiAnswers. www .wikianswers.com.

Wilson, Mary Tolford. "The First American Cookbook." *William and Mary Quarterly* 14, no. 1 (1957), 493–498.

BENJAMIN FRANKLIN

"Benjamin Franklin." Wikipedia. www.wikipedia.org, May 2007.

Chinard, Gilbert, ed. *Benjamin Franklin on the Art of Eating*. Philadelphia: American Philosophical Society, 1958.

Dubourcq, Hilaire. *Benjamin Franklin Book of Recipes*. Bath, U.K.: Canopus Publishing, 2000.

Ford, Paul Leicester. *The Many-Sided Franklin*. New York: Century, 1899.

Franklin, Benjamin. *The Autobiography of Benjamin Franklin*. New York: Macmillan, 1914.

Franklin, Benjamin. "From the Writings of Benjamin Franklin in the *Pennsylvania Gazette*. 1736–1737." www.historycarper.com, September 2006.

Franklin, Benjamin. *Poor Richard Improved: Being an Almanack and Ephemeris…for the Year of our Lord 1757*. By Richard Saunders, Philom. Philadelphia: Printed and Sold by B. Franklin, and D. Hall, 1757. Yale University Library. www.franklinpapers.org.

Franklin, Benjamin. *The Writings of Benjamin Franklin: London, 1757–1775*. www.franklinpapers.org.

Gabler, James M. *An Evening with Benjamin Franklin and Thomas Jefferson*. Palm Beach, FL: Bacchus Press, 2006.

Goodman, Nathan G. *The Ingenious Dr. Franklin: Selected Scientific Letters of Benjamin Franklin*. Philadelphia: University of Pennsylvania Press, 1931.

Heise, S. K. F. "Benjamin Franklin and Slavery." http://colonial-america.suite101.com, 2008.

Isaacson, Walter, ed. *A Benjamin Franklin Reader*. New York: Simon and Schuster, 2003.

Japiske, Carl, ed. *Fart Proudly: Writings of Benjamin Franklin You Never Read in School*. Marble Hill, GA: Elthea Press, 2003.

Packard Humanities Institute. *Papers of Benjamin Franklin*. www.franklinpapers.org 1988–2009.

Sparks, Jared, ed. *The Works of Benjamin Franklin: Containing Several Political and Historical Tracts Not Included in Any Former Ed., and Many Letters Official and Private, Not Hitherto Published; with Notes and a Life of the Author*. Boston: Hillard, Gray, 1836.

Wilson, Bee. "Gulp Fiction." *New Statesman* 128, no. 4422 (1999): 42.

Woods, Leonard. *The Life of Benjamin Franklin: Including a Sketch of the Rise and Progress of the War of Independence, and of the Various Negociations at Paris for Peace; with the History of His Political and Other Writings*. London: Hunt and Clarke, 1826.

George Washington

Associated Press. "A Taste of George Washington's Whiskey." www.msnbc
.com, April 9, 2007.

Burns, James MacGregor, Susan Dunn, and Arthur M. Schlesinger Jr. *George Washington.* New York: Times Books, 2004.

Chadwick, Bruce. *The General and Mrs. Washington.* Naperville, IL: Sourcebooks, 2007.

Cocktail Times. "Historic Distilling at George Washington's Distillery." http://cocktailtimes.com/news/?p=108, Feb. 14, 2009.

Custis, George Washington Parke and Mary Randolph Custis Lee. *Recollections and Private Memoirs of Washington.* Philadelphia: J. W. Bradley, 1861.

Dalzell, Robert F. and Lee Baldwin Dalzell. *George Washington's Mount Vernon.* New York: Oxford University Press, 1998.

Distilled Spirits Council of the United States. "Recreating George Washington's Distillery—Using Colonial-Era Tools and Techniques." www.discus.org.

Forester, Frank. "Bass and Bass Fishing." *Graham's American Monthly Magazine of Literature, Art, and Fashion*, vol. 36. Philadelphia: G. R. Graham, 1850.

Founders, Washington Committee for Historic Mount Vernon. *The Mount Vernon Cookbook.* Mount Vernon, VA: Mount Vernon Ladies' Association, 1984.

Fusonie, Alan and Donna Jean. *George Washington: Pioneer Farmer.* Mount Vernon, VA: Mount Vernon Ladies' Association, 1998.

George, Phillip Brandt. "George Washington: Patriot, President, Planter, and Purveyor of Distilled Spirits." *American History Magazine.* http://historynet.com.

"George Washington's Gristmill." Wikipedia. www.wikipedia.org.

"George Washington's Recipe for Beer." www.beerhistory.com.

"The Greenhouse Complex." www.mountvernon.org.

Griswold, Mac. *Washington's Gardens at Mount Vernon.* Boston: Houghton Mifflin, 1999.

Haworth, Paul Leland. *George Washington: Farmer: Being an Account of His Home Life and Agricultural Activities*. Indianapolis: Bobbs-Merrill, 1915.

Head, Thomas. "First in War, First in Peace, First in Whiskey: George Washington as Distiller," Southern Foodways Alliance. www.southernfoodways.com.

Hess, Karen. *Martha Washington's Booke of Cookery*. New York: Columbia University Press, 1981.

Kimball, Marie. *The Martha Washington Cook Book*. New York: Coward-McCann, 1940.

"James Anderson, Washington's Plantation Manager." In Archaeology's Interactive Dig. www.archaeology.org/interactive/mtvernon/anderson.html.

"Kitchen." Mount Vernon Explorer. www.mountvernon.org.

"Lafayette's Visits to Mount Vernon." http://xenophongroup.com/mcjoynt/visits.htm.

Mares, Bill. *Fishing with the Presidents*. Mechanicsburg, PA: Stackpole Books, 1999.

McCullough, David. *1776*. New York: Simon and Schuster, 2005.

Mount Vernon Ladies' Association. *George Washington's Mount Vernon: Official Guidebook*. Mount Vernon, VA: Mount Vernon Ladies' Association, 2001.

Petri, Anne. "George Washington and Food." www.house.gov.

Pogue, Dennis J. and Esther C. White. *George Washington's Gristmill at Mount Vernon*. Mount Vernon, VA: Mount Vernon Ladies' Association, 2005.

Pogue, Dennis J. and Robert Arner. "Washington, the Revolutionary Farmer: America's First Composter." Urban Agriculture Notes in City Farmer. http://www.xaia.ca/cityfarmer/, Apr.–Nov. 2003.

Pogue, Dennis J. "Shad, Wheat, and Rye (Whiskey): George Washington, Entrepreneur." Lecture presented at the Society for Historical Archaeology Annual Meeting, St. Louis, Missouri, January 2004, www.mountvernon.org.

Shackleton, Robert. *The Book of Washington*. Philadelphia: Penn Publishing, 1922.

"Smokehouse." www.mountvernon.org.

Washington, George. *Diaries*. Library of Congress. www.loc.gov.

Washington, George, et al. *The Writings of George Washington: From the Original Manuscript Sources, 1745–1799*, vol. 11. Washington, D.C.: Government Printing Office, 1931.

Washington, George. *The Writings of George Washington from the Original Manuscript Sources 1745–1799*, edited by John C. Fitzpatrick (1931–1944). Washington Resources. University of Virginia Library. http://etext.virginia.edu/washington/fitzpatrick/.

THOMAS JEFFERSON

Adams, William Howard. *The Paris Years of Thomas Jefferson*. New Haven: Yale University Press, 1997.

Baron, Robert C., ed. *The Garden and Farm Books of Thomas Jefferson*. Golden, CO: Fulcrum, 1987.

Baron, Stanley. *Brewed in America: A History of Beer and Ale in the United States*. Boston: Little, Brown, 1962.

Bear, James A. Jr., ed. *Jefferson at Monticello*. Charlottesville: University Press of Virginia, 1967.

"Beer." Thomas Jefferson Encyclopedia. www.wiki.monticello.org.

Betts, Edwin Morris, ed. *Thomas Jefferson's Farm Book*. Charlottesville: University Press of Virginia, 1987.

Betts, Edwin Morris, ed. *Thomas Jefferson's Garden Book, 1766–1824*. Philadelphia: American Philosophical Society, 1944.

Betts, Edwin Morris and James Adam Bear Jr., eds. *The Family Letters of Thomas Jefferson*. Charlottesville: University Press of Virginia, 1966.

Bowman, R. "Thomas Jefferson and William Short." www.monticello.org, 1997.

Brodie, Fawn M. *Thomas Jefferson: An Intimate History*. New York: W. W. Norton, 1998.

Cerami, Charles A. *Dinner at Mr. Jefferson's*. Hoboken, NJ: John Wiley & Sons, 2008.

Cheuk, Beth L., ed. *Thomas Jefferson's Monticello*. Charlottesville: Thomas Jefferson Foundation, 2002.

Cheuk, Beth L. "Jefferson and Ice Cream." In *Dining at Monticello*, edited by Damon Fowler. Charlottesville: Thomas Jefferson Foundation, 2005, 29–35.

"Coffee Urn." Thomas Jefferson Encyclopedia. www.wiki.monticello.org.

Crader, Diana C. "The Zooarchaeology of the Storehouse and the Dry Well at Monticello." *American Antiquity* 49 (1984): 542–558.

Crawford, Alan Pell. *Twilight at Monticello: The Final Years of Thomas Jefferson*. New York: Random House, 2008.

Curtis, William Eleroy. *The True Thomas Jefferson*. Philadelphia: J. B. Lippincott, 1901.

"A Day in the Life." Thomas Jefferson Encyclopedia. www.wiki.monticello .org.

"Dining with Congress." Thomas Jefferson Wiki. www.wiki.monticello.org.

"Edith Fossett." Thomas Jefferson Encyclopedia. www.wiki.monticello.org.

Ellis, Joseph J. *American Sphinx: The Character of Thomas Jefferson*. New York: Vintage Books, 1998.

Edwards, Everett, ed. *Jefferson and Agriculture*. New York: Arno Press, 1976.

Foley, John P. *The Jeffersonian Cyclopedia: A Comprehensive Collection of the Views of Thomas Jefferson*. New York: Funk & Wagnalls, 1900.

Fowler, Damon Lee, ed. *Dining at Monticello*. Charlottesville: Thomas Jefferson Foundation, 2005.

Gabler, James M. *Passions: The Wines and Travels of Thomas Jefferson*. Baltimore: Bacchus Press, 1995.

Gordon-Reed, Annette. *The Hemingses of Monticello*. New York: W. W. Norton, 2008.

Gordon-Reed, Annette. *Thomas Jefferson and Sally Hemings: An American Controversy*. Charlottesville: University Press of Virginia, 1997.

Hailman, John. *Thomas Jefferson on Wine*. Jackson: University Press of Mississippi, 2006.

Hamilton, Alexander. *Gentleman's Progress: The Itinerarium of Dr. Alexander Hamilton, 1744*, edited by Carl Bridenbaugh. Chapel Hill: University of North Carolina Press, 1948.

Harrington, John and Alessandro Santarelli. *The Cultivated Life: Thomas Jefferson and Wine*. DVD. Alexandria, VA: Madisonfilm, 2005.

Hatch, Peter J. "African-American Gardens at Monticello." *Twinleaf Journal*. www.twinleaf.org, January 2001.

Hatch, Peter J. *The Gardens of Thomas Jefferson's Monticello*. Charlottesville: Thomas Jefferson Foundation, 1992.

Hatch, Peter J. *The Fruits and Fruit Trees of Monticello*. Charlottesville: University Press of Virginia, 1998.

Hatch, Peter J. "McMahon's Texas Bird Pepper: A Pretty Little Plant." *Twinleaf Journal*. www.twinleaf.org, January 1996.

Hatch, Peter J. "Monticello's Mystery Plants." *Twinleaf Journal*. www.twinleaf .org, January 2004.

Hatch, Peter J. "Thomas Jefferson's Favorite Vegetables." In *Dining at Monticello*, edited by Damon Lee Fowler. Charlottesville: Thomas Jefferson Foundation, 2005, 55–63.

Hatch, Peter J. "Thomas Jefferson's Favorite Vegetables." *Twinleaf Journal*. www.twinleaf.org, January 2000.

Holmes, John M. *Thomas Jefferson Treats Himself.* Fort Valley, VA: Loft Press, 1997.

"Ice House." Thomas Jefferson Encyclopedia. www.wiki.monticello.org.

"Jack Jouett." Wikipedia. www.wikipedia.org, December 2008.

"Jack Jouett's Ride." http://wiki.monticello.org, December 2008.

"James Hemings," Thomas Jefferson Encyclopedia. www.wiki.monticello.org.

"Jefferson Library." Thomas Jefferson Encyclopedia. www.wiki.monticello.org.

Johnson, Eric. "Water Supply." Thomas Jefferson Encyclopedia. http://wiki.monticello.org, 2006.

Kelso, William M. "Mulberry Row: Slave Life at Thomas Jefferson's Monticello." *Archaeology* 39 (1986): 28–35.

Kimball, Marie. *Jefferson: The Scene of Europe 1784 to 1789.* New York: Coward-McCann, 1950.

Kimball, Marie. *Thomas Jefferson's Cook Book.* Greenville, MS: Lillie Ross Productions, 2004.

"Kitchen." http://explorer.monticello.org/text/index.php.

Kukla, Jon. *Mr. Jefferson's Women.* New York: Alfred A. Knopf, 2007.

Ling, Peter. "Thomas Jefferson and the Environment." *History Today* 54, no. 1 (2004): 48ff.

Loewer, Peter. *Jefferson's Garden.* Mechanicsburg, PA: Stackpole Books, 2004.

Lucas, Ann. "The Philosophy of Making Beer." www.monticello.org, April 1995.

"Marquis de Lafayette." Wikipedia. www.wikipedia.org, December 2008.

McEwan, Barbara. *Thomas Jefferson: Farmer.* Jefferson, NC: McFarland, 1991.

McLaughlin, Jack. *Jefferson and Monticello: The Biography of a Builder.* New York: Macmillan, 1990.

"Mediterranean." Thomas Jefferson Encyclopedia. www.wiki.monticello.org.

Merchant, Ismail, James Ivory, and Ruth Prawer Jhabvala. *Jefferson in Paris*. DVD. Hollywood Hills, CA: Merchant Ivory Productions, 1995.

Monticello Research Committee on Thomas Jefferson and Sally Hemings. *The Report of the Monticello Research Committee on Thomas Jefferson and Sally Hemings*. Thomas Jefferson Foundation, January 2000. www.wiki.monticello.org.

Moore, Roy and Alma Moore. *Thomas Jefferson's Journey to the South of France*. New York: Stewart, Tabori & Chang, 1999.

Morgan, Jefferson. "A Weekend at Monticello." *Bon Appetit* 38 (1993): 100–106.

Padover, Saul K., ed. *A Jefferson Profile as Revealed in His Letters*. New York: John Day, 1956.

"Paris Residences." Thomas Jefferson Encyclopedia. www.wiki.monticello.org.

Parton, James. *Life of Thomas Jefferson: Third President of the United States*. Boston: Harvard University, 1883.

"Peaches." Thomas Jefferson Encyclopedia. www.wiki.monticello.org.

Peterson, Merrill D. *Visitors to Monticello*. Charlottesville: University Press of Virginia, 1989.

Peterson, Merrill D., ed. *The Portable Thomas Jefferson*. New York: Viking Press, 1975.

Pierson, Rev. Hamilton Wilcox. *Jefferson at Monticello: The Private Life of Thomas Jefferson (1862)*. In *Jefferson at Monticello*, edited by James A. Bear, Jr. Charlottesville: University Press of Virginia, 1967, 25–117.

Prial, Frank J. "Wine Talk: At Monticello, Bottling Makes History." *New York Times*. www.nytimes.com, April 17, 2002.

Randolph, Sarah N. *The Domestic Life of Thomas Jefferson*. Charlottesville: University Press of Virginia, 1978.

Rayner, B. L. *Life of Thomas Jefferson*. Boston: Lilly, Wait, Colman & Holden, 1834.

Reed, O. E. "Thomas Jefferson in Agriculture." *Journal of Dairy Science* 27 (1944): 613–16.

Revell, Katherine G. "The Order and Economy of the House." www.monticello .org, 1995.

"Sally Hemings." Thomas Jefferson Encylcopedia. www.wiki.monticello.org.

Scofield, Merry Ellen. "The Fatigues of His Table: The Politics of Presidential Dining During the Jefferson Administration." *Journal of the Early Republic* 26, no. 3 (2006): 449–69.

Shackelford, George Green. *Thomas Jefferson's Travels in Europe, 1784–1789*. Baltimore: Johns Hopkins University Press, 1995.

"Sheep." Thomas Jefferson Wiki. http://wiki.monticello.org, April 2008.

Sloan, Herbert E. *Principle and Interest: Thomas Jefferson and the Problem of Debt*. Charlottesville: University Press of Virginia, 1995.

Smith, Margaret Bayard and Gaillard Hunt. *The First Forty Years of Washington Society: Portrayed by the Family Letters of Mrs. Samuel Harrison Smith*. New York: Scribner, 1906.

"The Vegetable Garden." Thomas Jefferson Encyclopedia. www.wiki.monticello .org.

"Vineyard." Thomas Jefferson Encyclopedia. www.wiki.monticello.org.

Wallace, Benjamin. *The Billionaire's Vinegar: The Mystery of the World's Most Expensive Bottle of Wine*. New York: Crown Publishers, 2008.

Wickard, Claude R. "Thomas Jefferson: Founder of Modern American Agriculture." *Agricultural History* 19 (1945): 179–80.

Wills, Garry. *Negro President: Jefferson and the Slave Power*. New York: Houghton Mifflin Harcourt, 2005.

"Wine." Thomas Jefferson Wiki. http://wiki.monticello.org, February 2008.

Endnotes

xii   *In that prescient and hilarious work:* Ann Bar and Paul Levy, *The Official Foodie Handbook* (New York: Arbor House, 1984), 6.

1   *He had but a single hope:* Dorothy and Thomas Hoobler, *Captain John Smith: Jamestown and the Birth of the American Dream* (Hoboken, NJ: John Wiley & Sons, 2006), 1–3.

2   *They didn't know how to farm, fish, or hunt:* David Freeman Hawke, *Everyday Life in Early America* (New York: Perennial Library, 1988), 12; and James E. McWilliams, *A Revolution in Eating: How the Quest for Food Shaped America* (New York: Columbia University Press, 2005), 58.

2   *Smith was not allowed to take the oath of office:* Hoobler, *Captain John Smith: Jamestown and the Birth of the American Dream,* 93–95.

3   *This meager cargo was not nearly enough:* Ibid., 105.

3   *he blamed the illness on lack of proper food:* Ibid., 106–108.

4   *they finally taught themselves minimal hunting skills:* Ibid., 106; and Sandra L. Oliver, *Food in Colonial and Federal America* (New York: Columbia University Press, 2005), 4–6.

4   *History reveals the reason for this peace gesture:* Hoobler, *Captain John Smith: Jamestown and the Birth of the American Dream,* 112; and Oliver, *Food in Colonial and Federal America,* 4–6.

4   *Despite the generosity of the Algonquian people:* McWilliams, *A Revolution in Eating: How the Quest for Food Shaped America,* 62; and Oliver, *Food in Colonial and Federal America,* 12.

5   *He led a series of expedition from Jamestown:* Hoobler, *Captain John Smith: Jamestown and the Birth of the American Dream,* 113–14.

6   *They blamed Smith for the deaths of two of his men:* Ibid., 115, 138.

6   *the captain's first act was to void the judgment against Smith:* Ibid., 138–39.

7   *He didn't search for those minerals, of course:* Ibid., 221; and Mark Kurlansky, *Cod: A Biography of the Fish That Changed the World* (New York: Penguin Books, 1997), 66–67.

7   *Determined to bring a profitable cargo back to England:* Kurlansky, *Cod: A Biography of the Fish That Changed the World,* 66–67.

8   *"The year after the Plymouth landing:* John Smith, *A Description of New England (1616) An Online Electronic Text Edition* (Lincoln: University of Nebraska, 2006), 26; and Kurlansky, *Cod: A Biography of the Fish That Changed the World,* 68.

8   *another legacy of John Smith's food-finding legacy:* Mark Kurlansky, *Salt: A World History* (New York: Walker & Co., 2002), 216.

9   *he helped the Pilgrims survive:* "Squanto," Wikipedia, www.wikipedia.org; and Neal Salisbury, "Squanto," in *The Human Traditions in America from the Colonial Era through Reconstruction* (Wilmington, DE: SR Books, 2002), 6–7.

9   *There was ample food available for the colonists:* Salisbury, "Squanto," in *The Human Traditions in America from the Colonial Era through Reconstruction,* 1–5.

10   *In the spring, the herring began their run:* Nathaniel Philbrick, *Mayflower: A Story of Courage, Community, and War* (New York: Viking, 2006), 101–102; and Salisbury, "Squanto," in *The Human Traditions in America from the Colonial Era through Reconstruction,* 10–11.

10   *It has created a classic battle between historians and scientists:* William Cronin, *Change in the Land: Indians, Colonists, and the Ecology of New England* (New York: Hill and Wang, 1983), 45; and Thomas E. Woods, *33 Questions about American History You're Not Supposed to Ask* (New York: Random House, 2007), 130.

10–11 *Historian Thomas Woods concluded:* Woods, *33 Questions about American History You're Not Supposed to Ask,* 132–33.

10   *And as another historian, William Cronin, pointed out:* Cronin, *Change in the Land: Indians, Colonists, and War,* 45.

11   *In fact, some scientists supported the rotting-fish scenario:* Woods, *33 Questions about American History You're Not Supposed to Ask,* 130; and Franklin Howard Bruce, *The Most Important Fish in the Sea: Menhaden and America* (Washington, D.C.: Island Press/Shearwater Books, 2007), 14–15, 227.

11   *Eventually, the colonists overcame their prejudices about corn:* Oliver, *Food in Colonial and Federal America,* 10; and McWilliams, *A Revolution in Eating: How the Quest for Food Shaped America,* 82–84.

12   *That happened because of the collaboration of two polymaths:* "John Winthrop the Younger," Wikipedia, www.wikipedia.org.

12   *Boyle was interested for two reasons:* Fulmer Mood, "John Winthrop, Jr., on Indian Corn." *New England Quarterly* (1937), 122–23.

13   *Indian corn grew tall:* Ibid., 125–26.

13   *Then Winthrop gave details about the methods of planting the corn:* Ibid., 126–27.

13   *Winthrop described the techniques for weeding:* Ibid., 130–33.

14   *At least one modern historian didn't think so:* McWilliams, *A Revolution in Eating: How the Quest for Food Shaped America,* 55–56.

14   *This is the first recipe for corn bread published in any cookbook:* Amelia Simmons, *The First American Cookbook, A Facsimile of "American Cookery," 1796* (Mineola, NY: Dover Publications, 1984), 34.

14   *Kitchen gardens were common by the 1730s:* McWilliams, *A Revolution in Eating: How the Quest for Food Shaped America,* 64–65.

15   *A writer in your paper comforts himself:* "Benjamin Franklin," Wikipedia (May 2007), www.wikipedia.org; and Benjamin Franklin, "From the Writings of Benjamin Franklin in the *Pennsylvania Gazette,* 1726–1737," (September 2006) www.historycarper.com.

16   *A Recipe for Making Sweet Corn:* Benjamin Franklin, *Poor Richard Improved: Being an Almanack and Ephemeris…for the Year of Our Lord 1757* by Richard Saunders, Philom. (Philadelphia: Printed and Sold by B. Franklin, and D. Hall, 1757, Yale University Library), www.franklinpapers.org.

17   *Franklin discusses Parched corn, later called popcorn:* Nathan G. Goodman, *The Ingenious Dr. Franklin: Selected Scientific Letters of Benjamin Franklin* (Philadelphia: University of Pennsylvania Press, 1931), 76–77.

17   *In his corn essay, Franklin gives one of the first descriptions:* Ibid., 76–77.

17   *This recipe by Mary Randolph:* Mary Randolph, *The Virginia Housewife; or, Methodical Cook* (Mineola, NY: Dover Publications, 1993), 84.

18   *The [corn] stalks, green as they were:* Goodman, *The Ingenious Dr. Franklin: Selected Scientific Letters of Benjamin Franklin,* 76–77; and "What is the difference between Liquor and Spirits?" WikiAnswers, www.wikianswers.com.

19   *Once a sow reaches breeding age:* "Hog Wild Problem in Florida: UF Experts Say Feral Pig Problem Here to Stay," *Science Daily* (Jun 7, 2005), www.sciencedaily.com; and "The Facts on Wild Feral Hogs," www.texasboars.com.

20   *Pig expert Lyall Watson noted in his 2004 study:* Lyall Watson, *The Whole Hog* (Washington, D.C.: Smithsonian Books, 2004), 108.

20   *The Caribbean pigs produced a lot of lard:* John C. Super, *Food, Conquest, and Colonization in Sixteenth Century Spanish America* (Albuquerque: University of New Mexico Press, 1988), 29.

20   *They had grown to three hundred boars and sows:* Watson, *The Whole Hog*, 108.

21   *De Soto continued to explore:* Ibid., 108; and Theodore Irving, *The Conquest of Florida by Hernando de Soto* (New York: Putnam, 1868), 304.

21   *By 1627, settlers could count the number of cattle:* Watson, *The Whole Hog*, 109–10.

22   *It is commonly believed that the Native Americans:* Ibid., 110.

22   *Sheep from England were imported and released:* "The History of Hog Island Sheep," http://hogislandsheep.org.

23   *Curing and exporting hams:* Roberta Wolfe Smoler, *The Useful Pig* (New York: HarperCollins Publishers, 1990), 12.

23   *At Concord, before the pigs were released:* Watson, *The Whole Hog*, 110; and McWilliams, *A Revolution in Eating: How the Quest for Food Shaped America*, 81.

23   *The excess of pork in the northern colonies:* Bruce Aidells, *Bruce Aidells's Complete Book of Pork* (New York: HarperCollins, 2004), 8.

23   *Though not the favorite meat:* McWilliams, *A Revolution in Eating: How the Quest for Food Shaped America*, 81.

24   *This recipe is from Emerson's cookbook:* Lucy Emerson, *The New England Cookery* (Montpelier, VT: Parks, 1808), 45.

24   *In New Amsterdam:* Watson, *The Whole Hog*, 110.

25   *The further legacy of the introduction of corn and pigs:* Trudy Eden, *The Early American Table* (DeKalb: Northern Illinois University Press, 2008), 155.

25–26   *Interestingly, the slaves preferred corn:* Ibid., 155; Philip D. Morgan, *Slave Counterpoint* (Chapel Hill: University of North Carolina Press, 1998), 134; and Betty Fussell, *The Story of Corn* (New York: Alfred A. Knopf, 1992), 236.

26   *Thomas Jefferson told his overseer:* James A. Bear, Jr., ed. *Jefferson at Monticello* (Charlottesville: University Press of Virginia, 1967), 54.

26   *As the tobacco colonies' populations increased:* "Economic Aspects of Tobacco During the Colonial Period 1612–1776," www.tobacco.org.

26   *The negative aspects of tobacco growing:* Ibid., www.tobacco.org.

26   *Captain Andrew Robinson was not overly passionate about food:* Raymond McFarland, *A History of the New England Fisheries: With Maps* (State College: University of Pennsylvania, 1911), 82.

27   *Robinson's place as a founding foodie:* Ibid., 82; Ralph Delahaye Paine, *Old Merchant Marine: A Chronicle of American Ships and Sailors* (New Haven, CT: Yale University Press, 1920), 186–87; and Joseph William Collins, "Evolution of the American Fishing Schooner," *New England Magazine* (1898), 336.

27   *Captain Robinson abandoned square-rigged shipbuilding:* "Schooner," Wikipedia, www.wikipedia.org; McFarland, *A History of the New England Fisheries: With Maps*, 82; and

John Randolph Spears, *The Story of the American Merchant Marine* (New York: Macmillan, 1910), 87.

28   *More schooners were built in the colonies:* "Schooner," Wikipedia; Paine, *Old Merchant Marine: A Chronicle of American Ships and Sailors*, 186–88; and Collins, "Evolution of the American Fishing Schooner," *New England Magazine*, 337.

28–29   *Ten years after he launched his first schooner:* Joseph E. Garland, *Lone Voyager: The Extraordinary Adventures of Howard Blackburn, Hero Fisherman of Gloucester* (New York: Simon and Schuster, 2000), 318.

29   *In 1623, they established a fishing station:* Kurlansky, *Cod: A Biography of the Fish That Changed the World*, 69–70.

29   *The salt demand was driven not only by fishing:* Kurlansky, *Salt: A World History*, 217–19.

30   *This recipe, from* The Virginia Housewife: Randolph, *The Virginia Housewife; or, Methodical Cook*, 65.

31   *Salt cod proved to be the perfect trade item:* Kurlansky, *Cod: A Biography of the Fish That Changed the World*, 81; and Waverly Root, *Food* (New York: Simon and Schuster, 1980), 87.

31   *it was more of a piecemeal operation:* "Triangle Trade," Wikipedia, www.wikipedia.org.

31   *The success of the colonies' trading:* "The Navigation Acts," Wikipedia, www.wikipedia.org.

32   *In 1667, about a hundred years before:* Kurlansky, *Cod: A Biography of the Fish That Changed the World*, 88.

32   *The point was moot, though, because New England:* "Townsend Act," Wikipedia, www.wikipedia .org; Kurlansky, *Cod: A Biography of the Fish That Changed the World*, 94–96.

33   *All it took was one taste of the water:* Charles Brooks and William Henry Whitmore, *History of the Town of Medford, Middlesex County, Massachusetts: From Its First Settlement in 1630 to 1855* (Boston: Rand, Avery, 1885), 390.

33   *A hundred twenty-five years later, Carl and Alan Seaburg:* Carl and Alan Seaburg, *Medford on the Mystic* (Medford, CT: Self-published, 1980), 101.

33–34 *Andrew and those who followed:* Charles A. Coulombe, *Rum: The Epic Story of the Drink That Conquered the World* (New York: Citadel Press Books, 2004), 114–15; and W.J. Rorabaugh, *The Alcoholic Republic: An American Tradition* (New York: Oxford University Press, 1979), 40–41.

34   *After Andrew Hall died:* Brooks and Whitmore, *History of the Town of Medford, Middlesex Country, Massachusetts: From Its First Settlement in 1630 to 1855*, 390–91; and Seaburg, *Medford on the Mystic*, 101.

34   *This was an early example of brand recognition:* Brooks and Whitmore, *History of the Town of Medford, Middlesex Country, Massachusetts: From Its First Settlement in 1630 to 1855*, 390.

34–35 *This recipe appeared in an early bartenders' manual:* Harry Johnson, *The New and Improved Illustrated Bartenders' Manual; or, How to Mix Drinks of the Present Style* (New York: H. Johnson, 1888), 76.

35   *The colonists couldn't have cared less about that term:* Hugh Barty-King and Anton Massel, *Rum Yesterday and Today* (London: William Heinemann, 1983), 13; and Alice Morse Earle, *Stage-Coach and Tavern Days* (New York: Macmillan, 1922), 100.

35   *During the following forty years:* Barty-King and Massel, *Rum Yesterday and Today*, 13, 157–58.

36   *The Largest Rum Punch Bowl in the World:* Alexis Lichine, *Alexis Lichine's Encyclopedia of Wines and Spirits* (New York: Alfred A. Knopf, 1968), 460.

36   *After some unknown sugarcane processor invented:* Barty-King and Massel, *Rum Yesterday and Today*, 159; and McWilliams, *A Revolution in Eating: How the Quest for Food Shaped America*, 264.

37   *New England distilleries were making so much rum:* McWilliams, *A Revolution in Eating: How the Quest for Food Shaped America*, 264; and Brooks and Whitmore, *History of the Town of Medford, Middlesex Country, Massachusetts: From Its First Settlement in 1630 to 1855*, 391.

37   *The colonists hated to drink water:* Dale Taylor, *The Writer's Guide to Everyday Life in Colonial America* (Cincinnati, OH: Writer's Digest Books, 1999), 87; Andrew F. Smith, *The Oxford Companion to American Food and Drink* (New York: Oxford University Press, 2007), 614; Sharon V. Salinger, *Taverns and Drinking in Early America* (Baltimore: Johns Hopkins University Press, 2002), 3; and Rorabaugh, *The Alcoholic Republic: An American Tradition*, 97.

38   *Rum was unique and important:* McWilliams, *A Revolution in Eating: How the Quest for Food Shaped America*, 264–76.

41   *Not only was Isaac Hall one of the:* Brooks and Whitmore, *History of the Town of Medford, Middlesex Country, Massachusetts: From Its First Settlement in 1630 to 1855*, 187; and "Minutemen," www.ushistory.org/people/minutemen.htm.

41   *As a Minuteman, Hall was part of a:* Ibid., "Minutemen"; and Brooks and Whitmore, *History of the Town of Medford, Middlesex Country, Massachusetts: From Its First Settlement in 1630 to 1855*, 187.

41–42   *On the evening of April 18, 1775:* Coulombe, *Rum: The Epic Story of the Drink That Conquered the World*, 115.

42   *Up the road to Menotomy:* Richard B. Coolidge, "Medford and Her Minutemen," *Medford Historical Society Publications* (1925), 42–51.

43   *Rum Flip:* Leo Engel, *American and Other Drinks.* (London: Tinsley Bros., 1878).

43   *Coolidge's account of Revere's meeting:* Ibid., 42–51.

43   *In 2002, an anonymous message:* "Paul Revere: The D.U.I. That Roused a Nation" (December 19, 2007), www.snopes.com; and Charles William Taussig and Philip Kappel, *Rum, Romance & Rebellion* (New York: Minton, Balch, 1928), 78–79.

44   *Many other sources give alternatives to Revere's:* Barbara Kerr, Medford Historical Society, interview via email, June 25, 2009.

45   *In December 1773, Revere brought news:* Coulombe, *Rum: The Epic Story of the Drink That Conquered the World*, 119.

45   *He had ridden from Boston carrying a letter:* Milton Embrick Flower, *John Dickenson, Conservative Revolutionary* (Charlottesville: University Press of Virginia, 1983), 102; and Historical Society of Pennsylvania, *Pennsylvania Magazine and Biography*, vol. 1 (Philadelphia: Historical Society of Pennsylvania, 1877), 192.

45–46   *Later that year, on September 4:* John Thomas Scharf and Thompson Westcott, *History of Philadelphia, 1609–1884*, vol. 2 (Philadelphia: L.H. Everts, 1884), 982.

46   *When the Tavern was completed:* Walter Staib, "City Tavern," www.citytavern.com

47   *Philadelphia at the time was the second largest city:* Mary Ann Hines, Gordon Marshall, and William Woys Weaver, *The Larder Invaded: Reflections on Three Centuries of Philadelphia Food and Drink* (Philadelphia: Historical Society of Pennsylvania, 1987), 21; and Walter Staib, *The City Tavern Cookbook* (Philadelphia: Running Press, 2009), 19.

47–48   *Mary Randolph's Curry, 1824:* Randolph, *The Virginia Housewife; or, Methodical Cook*, 80.

48–49   *Terrapin Soup:* Felix J. Déliée, *The Franco-American Cookery Book; or, How to Live Well and Wisely Every Day in the Year* (New York: G.P. Putnam's Sons, 1884), 272.

49   *Ironically, Daniel Smith, a Loyalist:* Scharf and Westcott, *History of Philadelphia, 1609–1884*, vol. 2, 982; and James M. Gabler, *An Evening with Benjamin Franklin and Thomas Jefferson* (Palm Beach, FL: Bacchus Press, 2006), 7.

49   *Before that, City Tavern had played:* Gabler, *An Evening with Benjamin Franklin and Thomas Jefferson*, 7.

50   *The turnspit dog had short legs:* "Turnspit Dog," Wikipedia, www.wikipedia.org.

50   *Thomas Jefferson, as a delegate to the Continental Congress:* Henry Stephens Randall, *The Life of Thomas Jefferson*, vol. 1 (New York: J.B. Lippincott, 1871), 176–77.

51   *Hannah Glasse's Pretty Side of Roast Beef:* Hannah Glasse, *The Art of Cookery, Made Plain and Easy* (London: W. Strahan, J.F. Rivington, and J. Hinton, 1774), 39.

51   *Taverns were everywhere in the colonies:* McWilliams, *A Revolution in Eating: How the Quest for Food Shaped America*, 245; Rorabaugh, *The Alcoholic Republic: An American Tradition*, 35; and Wayne Curtis, *And a Bottle of Rum: A History of the New World in Ten Cocktails* (New York: Crown Publishers, 2006), 88.

52   *Regular drinking was normal for all ages:* Barbara Holland, *The Joy of Drinking* (New York: Bloomsbury USA, 2007), 61; and Rorabaugh, *The Alcoholic Republic: An American Tradition*, 19, 25.

52   *In 1770, just before the Revolution:* Salinger, *Taverns and Drinking in Early America*, 89–90.

53   *But Rush's antiliquor campaign fell:* Rorabaugh, *The Alcoholic Republic: An American Tradition*, 41, 48.

54   *In 1829, the secretary of war estimated:* Ibid., 7, 10, 15.

54   *Salt was as important to the American Revolution:* Erna Risch, *Supplying Washington's Army* (Washington, D.C.: Center of the Military History, U.S. Army, 1981), 198.

55   *Mary Randolph's Directions for Salting:* Randolph, *The Virginia Housewife; or, Methodical Cook*, 24.

55   *Early in the war, England cut off American trade:* Risch, *Supplying Washington's Army*, 199; and Kurlansky, *Salt: A World History*, 221.

56   *Congress responded by permitting:* Kurlansky, *Salt: A World History*, 221–22; Risch, *Supplying Washington's Army*, 200; and Emily Rak, "Salty Air," *Edible Cape Cod*, www.ediblecapecod .com.

56   *Born in 1744 in Yarmouth, Massachusetts:* "John Sears Capt.," Sears Family Association, www .searsr.com; and Rak, "Salty Air," *Edible Cape Cod*.

57   *The industry was great for the citizens:* Rak, "Salty Air," *Edible Cape Cod*; and "John Sears Capt.," Sears Family Association.

58   *Numerous accounts document the shortages of meat:* Varnum to Washington, December 22, 1777, Washington Papers, Library of Congress; Henry B. Livingston to Robert R. Livingston, December 24, 1777, Robert R. Livingston Papers, New York Historical Society; and Jonathan Todd Jr. to Jonathan Todd, December 25, 1777, National Archives.

58   *General Washington's own officers criticized him:* Baron de Kalb to the Comte de Broglie, December 12, 17, and 25, 1777, in Benjamin F. Stevens, ed., *Facsimiles of Manuscripts in European Archives to America, 1773–1783*, Trafalgar Square, Charing Cross, London; and

George Weedon and American Philosophical Society, *Valley Forge Orderly Book of General George Weedon* (New York: Dodd, Mead, 1902), 31–32.

58 *Washington's political enemies warned of the doom:* James Lovell to John Adams, December 30, 1777, LDC, 8:507.

59 *he described how the shad swam:* Harry Emerson Wildes, *Valley Forge*, (New York, 1938), 174–75.

59 *shad were an important fish in colonial times* "John Winthrop the Younger," Wikipedia, www .wikipedia.org.

59 *In 2002, archaeological excavations of the food remains:* John McPhee, *The Founding Fish* (New York: Farrar, Strauss, and Giroux, 2002), 180, 175; "John Winthrop the Younger," Wikipedia, www.wikipedia.org.

60 *To Bake a Shad:* Randolph, *The Virginia Housewife; or, Methodical Cook*, 58.

61 *In a letter written in April 1778:* Sir Charles Blagden to Sir Joseph Banks, April 20, 1778, in *Bulletin of the New York Public Library*, 1903.

61 *Historian Boyle expected:* "John Winthrop the Younger," Wikipedia, www.wikipedia.org.

61 *During the summer of 1780, Joseph Plumb Martin:* Joseph Plumb Martin, *Private Yankee Doodle* (London: Acorn Press, 1979), 192.

62 *Christopher Ludwick arrived in Philadelphia in 1754:* William Ward Condit, "Christopher Ludwick, The Patriotic Gingerbread Baker," *Pennsylvania Magazine of History and Biography* (1957), 370, 373.

62 *As an army volunteer, Ludwick pulled off:* Ibid., 374–75; and Stewart H. Holbrook, *Lost Men of American History* (New York: Macmillan, 1948), 52.

62 *Ludwick's many accomplishments did not escape:* Henry Melchior Muhlenberg Richards, *The Pennsylvania-German in the Revolutionary War, 1775–1783* (Lancaster, PA: Press of the New Era Printing Company, 1908), 369.

63 *The new baker-general of the army:* Condit, "Christopher Ludwick, The Patriotic Gingerbread Baker," *Pennsylvania Magazine of History and Biography*, 379–80.

63 *Ludwick moved his baking operations to Skipjack:* Ibid., 380.

63 *National Archive records show that on March 26, 1778:* Ludwick Payment, March 26, 1778, Treasury Records, National Archives.

64 *During his renovation of the Washington Inn:* Lorett Treese, *Valley Forge: Making and Remaking a National Symbol* (University Park: University of Pennsylvania Press, 1995), www.nps.gov.

64 *If Ludwick didn't build standing brick ovens:* Jedediah Huntington to Washington, January 1, 1778, Washington Papers, Library of Congress; General Orders, January 9, 1778, WGW; and Google Books browse.

65 *During the mapping phase of a 2000 archaeological dig:* "Discovering What Washington's Troops Left Behind at Valley Forge," National Park Service, www.nps.gov/history/logcabin/html/ rd_valleyforge.html.

65 *Although the order for the brigade masters:* Dona McDermott, activist with Valley Forge National Historical Park, interview via phone, June 26, 2009.

66 *Thomas Webster and William Parkes observed in 1855:* Thomas Webster and William Parkes, *An Encyclopedia of Domestic Economy* (New York: Harper & Brothers, 1855), 759.

66 *Ludwick got to work with his staff:* Henry E. Lutterloh, Remarks, December 25, 1777,

Washington Papers, Library of Congress; and Thomas Jones, Return of Provisions Remaining in Camp, February 9, 1778, National Archives.

66   *Lieutenant Colonel Alexander Hamilton, who was not present:* Alexander Hamilton to Governor George Clinton, February 13, 1778, Hamilton Papers, Clinton Papers; and Thomas Jones, February 13, 1778, National Archives.

67   *The main supply problems, besides letters crossing:* John F. Reed, "Valley Forge Commissariat," *Picket Post* (1980), www.uhistory.org/valleyforge/history/commissary.html.

67   *Of course, as spring arrived in 1778:* Ibid., "Valley Forge Commissariat."

68   *General Washington assigned sutlers:* George Washington, et al., *The Writings of George Washington: From the Original Manuscript Sources, 1745–1799*, vol. 11 (Washington, D.C.: Government Printing Office, 1931), 264.

67   *Another of Ludwick's assumed culinary legacies was:* Condit, "Christopher Ludwick, The Patriotic Gingerbread Baker," *Pennsylvania Magazine of History and Biography*, 381–82.

69   *Philadelphia Pepper Pot:* Fanny Lemira Gillette and Hugo Zieman, *The White House Cook Book: Cooking, Toilet and Household Recipes, Menus, Dinner-Giving, Table Etiquette, Care and Sick, Health Suggestions, Facts Worth Knowing, etc., etc.* (New York: Werner Publishing, 1890).

69   *Mary Randolph has an abbreviated recipe for it:* Randolph, *The Virginia Housewife; or, Methodical Cook*, 81.

69   *Another version of pepper pot:* Mrs. Samuel G. (Louisa) Stoney, *Carolina Rice Cook Book* (Charleston, SC: Carolina Rice Kitchen Association, 1901), 43–44; and Karen Hess, *The Carolina Rice Kitchen* (Columbia: University of South Carolina Press, 1992), 112.

70   *After danger of starvation was over, two soldiers:* "Gilbert du Montier, Marquis de Lafayette," Wikipedia, www.wikipedia.org; and David Clary, *Adopted Son: Washington, Lafayette, and the Friendship That Saved the Revolution* (New York: Bantam Books, 2007), 100.

70   *A month later, the British withdrew from Philadelphia:* "Benedict Arnold," Wikipedia, www.wikipedia.org.

73   *On July 5, 1777, John Adams:* Joseph Solomon Walton and Martin Grove Brumbraugh, Stories of Pennsylvania; or, School Readings from Pennsylvania History (New York: American Book Company, 1897), 187.

72   *After Cornwallis surrendered four years later at Yorktown:* Holbrook, *Lost Men of American History*, 55.

72   *In 1985, Dr. David Kimball, the lead historian:* Gordon Lloyd, "Entertainment of George Washington, City Tavern, Philadelphia, September 1787, Menu and Bill," www.TeachingAmericanHistory.org.

72   *As detailed by Carl G. Karsch in his article:* Carl G. Karsch, "City Tavern: A Feast of Elegance," www.uhistory.org.

73   *As stupendous as that party was:* Staib, *The City Tavern Cookbook*, 25.

73   *After his presidency and farewell party:* Mount Vernon Ladies' Association, *George Washington's Mount Vernon: Official Guidebook* (Mount Vernon, VA: Mount Vernon Ladies' Association, 2001), 11.

74   *In fact, Washington was extremely devoted to his home:* Bruce Chadwick, *The General and Mrs. Washington* (Naperville, IL: Sourcebooks, 2007), 70.

74   *Shortly after the presidential inauguration of John Adams:* Ibid., 322.

74–75   *Washington's life as a farmer had begun:* Alan and Donna Jean Fusonie, *George Washington: Pioneer Farmer* (Mount Vernon, VA: Mount Vernon Ladies' Association, 1998), 6.

75   *At first, Washington had a tobacco dependency:* Fusonie, *George Washington: Pioneer Farmer,* 8.

75   *Washington began to study the principles of the new husbandry practices:* Fusonie, *George Washington: Pioneer Farmer,* 8.

76   *One of the new husbandry principles that Washington followed:* Dennis J. Pogue and Robert Arner, "Washington, the Revolutionary Farmer: America's First composter," Urban Agriculture Notes in City Farmer (April–November 2003), http://www.xaia.ca/cityfarmer.

76   *"When I speak of a knowing farmer:* Ibid., Urban Agriculture Notes in City Farmer; and Fusonie, *George Washington: Pioneer Farmer,* 22–24.

76   *Washington was one of the finest horsemen:* [George, online]

77   *Washington was so enamored with the farming abilities:* Fusonie, *George Washington: Pioneer Farmer,* 35.

77   *Washington the farmer was also ahead of his time:* Fusonie, *George Washington: Pioneer Farmer,* 28-30.

77   *Washington's cattle were the Devon milk breed:* Fusonie, *George Washington: Pioneer Farmer,* 31-2.

77   *Much like the swine of the conquistadors:* Ibid., 32-33.

78   *"Virginia Ladies value":* "Lafayette's Visits to Mount Vernon," http://xenophongroup.com/mcjoynt/visits.htm.

78   *Occasionally a thief would break into the smokehouse:* "Smokehouse," www.mountvernon.org.

78   *Poultry for the kitchen and table:* Fusonie, *George Washington: Pioneer Farmer,* 33.

79   *Immediately upon his retirement:* Mac Griswold, *Washington's Gardens at Mount Vernon* (Boston: Houghton Mifflin, 1999), 131; and Chadwick, *The General and Mrs. Washington,* 71.

79   *On the basis of advice from his library of gardening books:* Griswold, *Washington's Gardens at Mount Vernon,* 113–15.

79   *As did Jefferson, Washington planted a vineyard:* Ibid., 137, 140.

79–80   *Washington wanted to have fresh fruits and vegetables:* Ibid., 94–95, 129; and "The Greenhouse Complex," www.mountvernon.org.

80   *Farming was hardly a hobby; it was a business:* Fusonie, *George Washington: Pioneer Farmer,* 38.

84   *In June 1771, he sold 128,000:* Fusonie, *George Washington: Pioneer Farmer,* 39, 41.

82   *In 1790, a farmer and inventor in Delaware:* Oliver Gies, "The Genius of Oliver Evans," *Invention and Technology* (1990), www.AmericanHeritage.com.

82   *Evans radically modified several different devices:* Ibid., Gies; and Bob Shaver, "Oliver Evans Automated Flour Mill," *Patent Pending Blog* (July 16, 2005), http://patentpending.blog.com.

83   *In the words of Eugene Ferguson:* Gies, "The Genius of Oliver Evans," *Invention and Technology;* and Shaver, "Oliver Evans Automated Flour Mill," *Patent Pending Blog.*

83   *After Evans patented his invention:* Shaver, "Oliver Evans Automated Flour Mill," *Patent Pending Blog;* and Fusonie, *George Washington: Pioneer Farmer,* 40.

83   *In 1793, Washington designed and built a barn:* Paul Leland Haworth, *George Washington: Farmer: Being an Account of His Home Life and Agricultural Activities* (Indianapolis: Bobbs-Merrill, 1915), 125.

85   *The barn, which was so well built that:* Fusonie, *George Washington: Pioneer Farmer,* 20.

85   *He was one of the first American experimental agriculturalists:* Haworth, *George Washington: Farmer: Being an Account of His Home Life and Agricultural Activities,* 6–7.

85   *Washington strongly believed in the new viability:* Fusonie, *George Washington: Pioneer Farmer,* 53.

86   *When on his eastern tour of 1789:* Haworth, *George Washington: Farmer: Being an Account of His Home Life and Agricultural Activities,* 266.

86   *Washington was also a commercial fisherman:* Fusonie, *George Washington: Pioneer Farmer,* 46–47.

86   *Washington allowed the poor people who lived near:* Ibid., 47; and Haworth, *George Washington: Farmer: Being an Account of His Home Life and Agricultural Activities,* 65.

87   *But Washington had farther-reaching goals:* Fusonie, *George Washington: Pioneer Farmer,* 47–49; and Bill Mares, *Fishing with the Presidents* (Mechanicsburg, PA: Stackpole Books, 1999), 5.

87   *After packing enough food for the slaves:* Fusonie, *George Washington: Pioneer Farmer,* 47–49; Mares, *Fishing with the Presidents,* 4; and Dennis J. Pogue, "Shad, Wheat, and Rye (Whiskey): George Washington, Entrepreneur," Society for Historical Archaeology Annual Meeting (January 2004), www.mountvernon.org.

88   *Frank Forester, writing in Graham's:* Frank Forester, "Bass and Bass Fishing," *Graham's American Monthly Magazine of Literature, Art, and Fashion,* vol. 36 (Philadelphia: G.R. Graham, 1850), 408–9.

88–89   *Maria Parloa's Shad Roe Baked:* Maria Parloa, *Miss Parloa's Kitchen Companion: A Guide for All Who Would Be Good Housekeepers* (Boston: Estes and Lauriat, 1887), 204.

89   *On February 15, 1787, just before:* Chadwick, *The General and Mrs. Washington,* 116; and Robert F. and Lee Baldwin Dalzell, *George Washington's Mount Vernon* (New York: Oxford University Press, 1998), 192.

89–90   *It has been estimated that between 1768 and 1775:* Chadwick, *The General and Mrs. Washington,* 78, 93; and Dalzell, *George Washington's Mount Vernon,* 194.

90   *Washington's most famous guest was undoubtedly:* Phineas Camp Headley, *The Life of General Lafayette* (Auburn, NY: Miller, Orton & Mulligan, 1854), 211.

90   *Lafayette arrived in New York:* "Lafayette's Visits to Mount Vernon," http://xenophongroup .com/mcjoynt/visits.htm.

91   *General Washington's step-granddaughter:* "Kitchen," www.mountvernon.org.

91   *In 1981, Columbia University Press published:* Karen Hess, *Martha Washington's Booke of Cookery* (New York: Columbia University Press, 1981), vii, 7.

92   *From the cookbook manuscript used at Mount Vernon:* Ibid., 80.

92   *Martha, in her late fifties when George retired:* Chadwick, *The General and Mrs. Washington,* 78–79.

93   *By the early 1790s, Washington was:* Dalzell, *George Washington's Mount Vernon,* 197–98.

93   *George Washington was a devoted beer lover:* Stanley Baron, *Brewed in America: A History of Beer and Ale in the United States* (Boston: Little, Brown, 1962), 97.

94   *To Make Small Beer, by George Washington:* "George Washington's Recipe for Beer," www .beerhistory.com.

94   *In 1796, again seeking to diversify:* Pogue, "Shad, Wheat, and Rye (Whiskey): George Washington, Entrepreneur," Society for Historical Archaeology Annual Meeting.

95   *They landed in Norfolk, Virginia:* "James Anderson, Washington's Plantation Manager," Archaeology's Interactive Dig, www.archaeology.org/interactive/mtvernon/anderson .html.

95   *It was a simple process to make the whiskey:* Pogue and Arner, "Washington, the Revolutionary Farmer: America's First Composter," Urban Agricultural Notes in City Farmer.

96   *Washington consulted with his friend:* "Recreating George Washington's Distillery—Using Colonial-Era Tools and Techniques," Distilled Spirits Council of the United States, www.discus.org; and "James Anderson, Washington's Plantation Manager," Archaeology Interactive Dig.

96   *The three stills had a capacity of 616 gallons:* Pogue and Arner, "Washington, the Revolutionary Farmer: America's First Composter," Urban Agricultural Notes in City Farmer.

97   *Washington realized the need for varying qualities:* "Recreating George Washington's Distillery—Using Colonial-Era Tools and Techniques," Distilled Spirits Council of the United States.

97   *Sarah McCarty Chichester's 1799 purchase:* Ibid.

97   *Washington's best whiskey customer was:* Ibid.

98   *I have not only retired from all public employments:* Headley, *The Life of General Lafayette*, 211.

98   *Mount Vernon officials began considering:* "A Taste of George Washington's Whiskey," Associated Press (April 9, 2007), www.msnbc.com; and Thomas Head, "First in War, First in Peace, First in Whiskey: George Washington as Distiller," Southern Foodways Alliance, www.southernfoodways.com.

99   *Funded by a $2.1 million grant from:* "Recreating George Washington's Distillery—Using Colonial-Era Tools and Techniques," Distilled Spirits Council of the United States.

99   *The new distillery was dedicated on:* Ibid., Distilled Spirits Council of the United States; and "Historic Distilling at George Washington's Distillery," Cocktail Times (February 14, 2009), http://cocktailtimes.com/news/?p=108.

99   *Visitors to the distillery can watch:* "Historic Distilling at George Washington's Distillery," Cocktail Times.

101   *Thomas Jefferson was an architect:* See Thomas Jefferson section in the bibliography.

102   *Jefferson's situation worsened in June 1781:* B.L. Rayner, *Life of Thomas Jefferson* (Boston: Lilly, Wait, Colman & Holden, 1834), 169; "Jack Jouett's Ride," Thomas Jefferson Encyclopedia, www.wiki.monticello.org; and "Jack Jouett," Wikipedia, www.wikipedia.org.

102   *According to legend, Jefferson offered:* "Jack Jouett's Ride," Thomas Jefferson Encyclopedia, www.wiki.monticello.org; and Fawn M. Brodie, *Thomas Jefferson: An Intimate History* (New York: W.W. Norton, 1998), 146–47.

103   *Considering his financial predicament:* Brodie, *Thomas Jefferson: An Intimate History*, 185.

103   *Rural taverns in Virginia:* McDonald, James, *Life in Old Virginia* (Norfolk, Va.: The Old Virginia Publishing Co., 1907) 302–304.

104   *Four years before Washington's farewell dinner:* "Washington's Resignation; The Centenary of the Event Close at Hand," *New York Times* (December 21, 1883); and Gabler, *An Evening with Benjamin Franklin and Thomas Jefferson*, 11–12.

104   *Annapolis was all abuzz about Washington's visit:* "Annapolis, December 25," *Maryland Gazette* (December 25, 1783); Gabler, *An Evening with Benjamin Franklin and Thomas Jefferson*, 231, 12; and "Washington's Resignation; The Centenary of the Event Close at Hand," *New York Times.*

104   *On May 7, Jefferson was reappointed:* Gabler, *An Evening with Benjamin Franklin and Thomas Jefferson*, 13–14; and John Hailman, *Thomas Jefferson on Wine* (Jackson: University Press of Mississippi, 2006), 73.

105   *During his first month at the hotel, he bought:* James M. Gabler, *Passions: The Wines and Travels of Thomas Jefferson* (Baltimore: Bacchus Press, 1995), 17–18; and Hailman, *Thomas Jefferson on Wine*, 69.

105   *Jefferson and his daughter joined the Adams family:* Gabler, *An Evening with Benjamin Franklin and Thomas Jefferson*, 19; and William Howard Adams, *The Paris Years of Thomas Jefferson* (New Haven: Yale University Press, 1997), 240–41.

106   *After two months in temporary hotel quarters:* Annette Gordon-Reed, *The Hemingses of Monticello* (New York: W.W. Norton, 2008), 164; and Hailman, *Thomas Jefferson on Wine*, 74.

106   *After Hemings's apprenticeship with Combeaux:* Gordon-Reed, *The Hemingses of Monticello*, 166.

106   *Indeed, Hemings was living a charmed life:* Ibid., 171–72, 174.

107   *On July 15, 1787, Hemings's sister Sally arrived:* Annette Gordon-Reed, *Thomas Jefferson and Sally Hemings: An American Controversy* (Charlottesville: University Press of Virginia, 1997), 1.

107   *After his apprenticeships ended, Hemings was hired:* Gordon-Reed, *The Hemingses of Monticello*, 209, 226; "Paris Residences," wiki.monticello.org; and Hailman, *Thomas Jefferson on Wine*, 81, 84.

107   *Despite the opulent food Hemings was preparing:* Hailman, *Thomas Jefferson on Wine*, 161.

108   *Fritters a la Chantilly:* Léon Brisse, translated by Mrs. Matthew Clark, *Menues and 1200 Recipes of the Baron Brisse in French and English* (London: Sampson Low, Marston, Searle, & Rivington, 1882).

109   *Gordon-Reed wrote about the pressure:* Gordon-Reed, *The Hemingses of Monticello*, 226–27.

109   *In addition to Hemings's monthly salary:* Ibid., 209–10.

109   *In turn, Jefferson used his charm and:* Hailman, *Thomas Jefferson on Wine*, 193; and Brodie, *Thomas Jefferson: An Intimate History*, 243.

110   *Perhaps it was all of the above:* Hailman, *Thomas Jefferson on Wine*, 91–92.

110   *Jefferson's European travels were extensive:* Gabler, *The Wines and Travels of Thomas Jefferson*; and Marie Kimball, *Jefferson: The Scene of Europe 1784 to 1789* (New York: Coward-McCann, 1950).

110   *Jefferson spent six days traveling through London:* Gabler, *The Wines and Travels of Thomas Jefferson*, 27, 39.

111   *Regarding English food, Jefferson had defined it:* John P. Foley, *The Jefferson Cyclopedia: A Comprehensive Collection of the Views of Thomas Jefferson* (New York: Funk & Wagnalls, 1900), 372.

111   *In a letter to John Jay, Jefferson described:* Hailman, *Thomas Jefferson on Wine*, 85.

111   *He wrote to his secretary in Paris, William Short:* Kimball, *Jefferson: The Scene of Europe 1784 to 1789*, 191; and R. Bowman, "Thomas Jefferson and William Short," wiki.monticello.org.

112   *The olive is a tree the least known in America:* Foley, *The Jefferson Cyclopedia: A Comprehensive Collection of the Views of Thomas Jefferson*, 872; and "Mediterranean," wiki.monticello.org.

113   *Lafayette loved all things American:* Hailman, *Thomas Jefferson on Wine*, 89; and John Russell Bartlett, *Dictionary of Americanisms: A Glossary of Words and Phrases Usually Regarded as Peculiar to the United States* (Boston: Little, Brown, 1877), 342.

113   *Consuming much more than olives:* Gabler, *The Wines and Travels of Thomas Jefferson*, 82, 90.

114   *He also studied the icehouses there:* Hailman, *Thomas Jefferson on Wine*, 112.

114   *Jefferson succeeded in smuggling the rice out of Italy:* Ibid., 99, 112; and Gabler, *The Wines and Travels of Thomas Jefferson,* 98, 100.

114   *In Amsterdam, Jefferson ate oysters and drank chocolate:* Ibid., 140; and Kimball, *Jefferson: The Scene of Europe 1784 to 1789,* 214.

114   *Jefferson bought four waffle irons:* "Cornelius Swartwout, Inventor of the Waffle Iron," www .swartoutfamily.org.

115   *Benjamin Franklin wrote about food sporadically:* Hailman, *Thomas Jefferson on Wine,* 75–76; and www.ushistory.org.

115   *writing to Sarah Bache from Paris:* Benjamin Franklin to Sarah Bache, 1784, www.franklinpapers .org.

116   *Franklin appeared at court in the dress of:* Leonard Woods, *The Life of Benjamin Franklin: Including a Sketch of the Rise and Progress of the War of Independence, and of the Various Negotiations at Paris for Peace; with the History of His Political and Other Writings* (London: Hunt and Clarke, 1826), 240.

116   *One legacy of Franklin's days in Paris:* "Antoine-Augustin Parmentier," Wikipedia, www .wikipedia.org.

117   *A short time after he gave a dinner:* "Parmentier Introduces the Potato Into France," *Harper's Magazine Making of America Project,* vol. 4 (New York: Harper's Magazine, 1852), 623.

117   *A search of the Franklin Papers:* www.franklinpapers.org.

118   *Gilbert Chinard of the American Philosophical Society:* Gilbert Chinard, *Benjamin Franklin on the Art of Eating* (Philadelphia: American Philosophical Society, 1958), 34–35, 47.

118–19   *To Broil Steaks, By Benjamin Franklin:* Ibid., 47.

119   *Gout eventually proved to be Franklin's undoing:* Walter Isaacson, *A Benjamin Franklin Reader* (New York: Simon and Schuster, 2003), 303; and Hailman, *Thomas Jefferson on Wine,* 77.

119   *Jefferson returned from his final wine sojourn:* Hailman, *Thomas Jefferson on Wine,* 181–82.

120   *Unfortunately, he was never able to make wine:* Gabler, *The Wines and Travels of Thomas Jefferson,* 162; and Hailman, *Thomas Jefferson on Wine,* 184.

120   *The winter of 1788–1789 was extraordinarily cold:* Gabler, *The Wines and Travels of Thomas Jefferson,* 160–61.

120–21   *It was Morris who had brought Madeira and claret:* Ibid., 162; and Hailman, *Thomas Jefferson on Wine,* 186–92.

121   *Jefferson's five years in Paris left a legacy:* Andrew F. Smith, *The Oxford Encyclopedia of Food and Drink in America,* vols. 1–2 (New York: Oxford University Press, 2004), vol. 2, 568; vol. 1, 703; 719.

122   *Chocolate. This article, when ready made:* Thomas Jefferson to John Adams, November 27, 1785, www.familytales.org.

123   *Always observe to lay your meat in the bottom:* Mary Brigid Barrett, "A Taste of the Past: White House Kitchens, Menus, and Recipes," www.ourwhitehouse.org/tasteofthepast.html.

123   *There are ten surviving recipes that Jefferson recorded:* Damon Lee Fowler, *Dining at Monticello* (Charlottesville: Thomas Jefferson Foundation, 2005), 1; "Savoy Biscuit and Two Other Dessert Recipes," Monticello Classroom, wiki.monticello.org; and "Blancmange," Wikipedia, www.wikipedia.org.

124   *Two of Jefferson's Most Famous Recipes:* Richard Briggs, *The English Art of Cookery, according to the Present Practice: Being a Complete Guide to All Housekeepers, on a Plan Entirely New...*

(London: G.G.J. and J. Robinson, 1788); Gabler, *The Wines and Travels of Thomas Jefferson*, 165; Fowler, *Dining at Monticello*, 3, 19.

128 *Like the ancient Romans we modern Americans:* Robert Shackleton, *The Book of Washington* (Philadelphia: Penn Publishing, 1922), 63.

129 *An Hog Barbecued, or Broil'd Whole:* Richard Bradley, *The Country Housewife and Lady's Director, in the Management of a House, and the Delights and Profits of a Farm* (London: D. Browne and T. Woodman, 1732), 165.

130 *When a herald passed through the country announcing:* Steven Raichlen, *BBQ USA* (New York: Workman Publishing, 2003), 8.

131 *Patriotism, politics, and pigs (or oxen):* Meredith Nicholson, *The Valley of Democracy* (New York: C. Scribner's Sons, 1918), 197.

132 *Most campaign spending did not involve:* Robert J. Dinkin, *Campaigning in America: A History of Election Practices* (New York: Greenwood Press, 1989), 27.

132 *It's difficult to discern, in some of the early:* Alexander Edwin Sweet and John Armoy Knox, *On a Mexican Mustang, through Texas, from the Gulf to the Rio Grande* (Hartford, CT: S.S. Scranton, 1883), 436.

132 *Sometimes, because of hard drinking:* Ex-Member of Congress, *My Ride to the Barbecue; or, Revolutionary Reminiscences of the Old Dominion* (New York: S.A. Rollo, 1860), 18.

133 *It is the simplest possible manner of preparing a dinner:* Hamilton Wilcox Pierson, *In the Brush; or, Old-time Social, Political, and Religious Life in the Southwest* (New York: D. Appleton, 1881), 95.

134 *To Barbecue Shote:* Randolph, *The Virginia Housewife; or, Methodical Cook*, 51.

134 *To Roast a Four-quarter of Shote:* Ibid., 52.

135 *Bryan is noted for her use of an early barbecue rub:* Ibid., 52; Mrs. Lettice Bryan, *The Kentucky Housewife* (Cincinnati, OH: Shepard & Stearns, 1839), 95; and Sarah Rutledge, *The Carolina Housewife* (Columbia: University of South Carolina Press, 1979), 19–28, 64, 181.

135 *When George Washington married Martha Dandridge Curtis:* Barrett, "A Taste of the Past: White House Kitchens, Menus, and Recipes."

136 *Martha Washington's Black Great Cake Recipe:* Ibid., Barrett; and "Christmas at Mount Vernon," www.mountvernon.org.

136 *The tradition of good food and service at the White House:* "Hercules and Hemings: Presidents' Slave Chefs," Kitchen Sisters, www.npr.org/templates/story/story.php?storyId=18950467.

136 *Although she was adept at managing the mansion:* Ibid., Kitchen Sisters.

137 *The chief cook would have been termed in modern:* George Washington Parke and Mary Randolph Lee Custis, *Recollections and Private Memoirs of Washington* (Philadelphia: J.W. Bradley, 1861), 422.

137 *It was while preparing the Thursday or Congress dinner:* Ibid., 423.

138 *The Reverend Andrew Burnaby, who travelled:* Ibid., 166.

138 *Joshua Brookes, a young Englishman who visited Mount Vernon:* Joshua Brookes, "A Dinner at Mount Vernon," *New York Historical Society Quarterly* (1947), 72–85.

138 *Although similar foods were likely cooked in the presidential mansions:* "Hercules and Hemings: Presidents' Slave Chefs," Kitchen Sisters.

139 *After Jefferson left France, Washington named him:* "Rank by Population of the 100 Largest Urban Places, Listed Alphabetically by State: 1790–1990," U.S. Census Bureau, www

.census.gov/population/www/documentation/twps0027/tab01.txt; Hailman, *Thomas Jefferson on Wine*, 203.

139   *His brief time in New York marked the beginning of a rift:* Michael Farquhar, *A Treasury of Great American Scandals* (New York: Penguin Books, 2003), 43.

139   *But at least Jefferson still had his cook:* "The Nine Capitals of the United States," U.S. Senate, www.senate.gov/reference/reference_item/Nine_Capitals_of_the_United_States.htm; "Rank by Population of the 100 Largest Urban Places, Listed Alphabetically by State: 1790–1990," U.S. Census Bureau; Sharron E. Wilkins, "The President's Kitchen," *American Visions*, www.pbs.org; and Gordon-Reed, *The Hemingses of Monticello*, 460, 455.

140   *Jefferson himself was "noticeably Frenchified":* Gordon-Reed, *The Hemingses of Monticello*, 455–56; Hailman, *Thomas Jefferson on Wine*, 213.

140   *But he overdid it and was then criticized by Senator:* Hailman, *Thomas Jefferson on Wine*, 213–14.

140   *President Washington didn't take much issue:* Ibid., 207–8.

141   *In July 1791, Jefferson reverted again to his French ways:* Gordon-Reed, *The Hemingses of Monticello*, 468–69.

141   *Because of the French Revolution and the slave rebellion:* Hines, Marshall, and Weaver, *The Larder Invaded: Reflections on Three Centuries of Philadelphia Food and Drink*, 23.

141   *The title of the first English translation:* Priscilla Parkhurst Ferguson, *Accounting for Taste: The Triumph of French Cuisine* (Chicago: University of Chicago Press, 2004), 41.

142   *Biscuits Ordinaires:* Carolyn Smith Kiser, "Biscuits Ordinaires," 18thccuisine Blog, http://18thccuisine.blogspot.com.

143   *In 1789, a year after his article was published:* "Sugar Maple," Thomas Jefferson Encyclopedia, wiki.monticello.org.

143   *The Quakers, of course, were abolitionists:* Ibid., "Sugar Maple."

143   *In an astonishing letter to Benjamin Vaughn:* Ibid., "Sugar Maple."

144   *Jefferson began buying maple sugar refined:* Ibid., "Sugar Maple."

144   *Indeed, a rather naïve Jefferson was so sold:* Ibid., "Sugar Maple"; and "Maple History," Massachusetts Maple Producers Association, www.massmaple.org/history.html.

145   *In May 1791, he set off with James Madison:* "Sugar Maple," Thomas Jefferson Encyclopedia.

145   *Maple Sugar Sauce, by Jennie June:* Jane Cunningham Croly, *Jennie June's American Cookery Book: Containing Upwards of Twelve Hundred Choice and Carefully Tested Receipts…*(New York: American News, 1866), 168.

145   *Arthur Noble tried one other maple product:* "Sugar Maple," Thomas Jefferson Encyclopedia.

146   *At the age of fifty-one, Thomas Jefferson moved from:* Gabler, *The Wines and Travels of Thomas Jefferson*, 192; and Gordon-Reed, *The Hemingses of Monticello*, 509.

146   *He found that his farmlands, after a decade under the care:* Gabler, *The Wines and Travels of Thomas Jefferson*, 191; Gordon-Reed, *The Hemingses of Monticello*, 509; and Hailman, *Thomas Jefferson on Wine*, 240–42.

147   *In April 1796, Peter's training was complete:* Wilkins, "The President's Kitchen," *American Visions*; and Gordon-Reed, *The Hemingses of Monticello*, 528.

147   *Hemings's return to Philadelphia as a free man:* Wilkins, "The President's Kitchen," *American Visions*.

147   *Jefferson spoke with Hemings in Philadelphia:* Gordon-Reed, *The Hemingses of Monticello*, 528–29.

148   *Hemings couldn't make a go of things:* Jack McLaughlin, *Jefferson and Monticello: The Biography of a Builder* (New York: Macmillan, 1990), 222.

148   *Incredulous, Jefferson had a friend in Baltimore:* McLaughlin, *Jefferson and Monticello: The Biography of a Builder,* 222; and Gordon-Reed, *The Hemingses of Monticello,* 553.

148   *As the wine historian John Hailman commented:* Hailman, *Thomas Jefferson on Wine,* 254; and Gabler, *The Wines and Travels of Thomas Jefferson,* 297.

149   *Exactly one hundred years after Jefferson took office:* William Eleroy Curtis, *The True Thomas Jefferson* (Philadelphia: J.B. Lippincott, 1901), 319; and "Jefferson's Financial Diary," *Harper's Magazine Making of America Project,* vol. 70 (New York: *Harper's Magazine,* 1885), 540.

149   *Curtis is the first biographer to document Jefferson's:* Curtis, *The True Thomas Jefferson,* 318.

150   *He had wanted to hire James Hemings as the President's House chef:* Wilkins, "The President's Kitchen," *American Visions;* and Gordon-Reed, *The Hemingses of Monticello,* 545–46.

150   *Jefferson proceeded to host three dinners a week:* "Dining at the President's House," Thomas Jefferson Encyclopedia, wiki.monticello.org.

150   *At President's House dinners, Jefferson always:* Margaret Bayard Smith and Gaillard Hunt, *The First Forty Years of Washington Society: Portrayed by the Family Letters of Mrs. Samuel Harrison Smith* (New York: Scribner, 1906), 69.

151   *Some guests reported that, in addition to dumbwaiters:* "Dining with Congress," Thomas Jefferson Encyclopedia; Gabler, *The Wines and Travels of Thomas Jefferson,* 199; and Hailman, *Thomas Jefferson on Wine,* 294.

151   *A longtime tradition that Jefferson banned was toasting:* "Dinner Etiquette," Thomas Jefferson Encyclopedia, wiki.monticello.org.

151   *Yet even without toasting, the alcohol flowed freely:* Gabler, *The Wines and Travels of Thomas Jefferson,* 199; and Hailman, *Thomas Jefferson on Wine,* 256.

151   *In his meticulous manner, Jefferson kept a tabulation:* Merry Ellen Scofield, "The Fatigues of His Table: The Politics of Presidential Dining During the Jefferson Administration," *Journal of the Early Republic* (2006), 449–52, 459, 469.

152   *Women were occasional guests and usually:* Ibid., 456, 461–63.

152   *Not much is known about Jefferson's chef:* Gabler, *The Wines and Travels of Thomas Jefferson,* 198–99; Hailman, *Thomas Jefferson on Wine,* 289; and Lucia Stanton, "Nourishing the Congress," in Damon Fowler, ed., *Dining at Monticello* (Charlottesville: Thomas Jefferson Foundation, 2005), 16.

153   *a huge wheel of cheese:* "Chesire Mammoth Cheese," Wikipedia, www.wikipedia.org.

153   *This "mammoth cheese":* Ibid.

154   *Two months after the mammoth cheese was delivered:* Richard Zacks, *The Pirate Coast: Thomas Jefferson, the First Marines, and the Secret Mission of 1805* (New York: Hyperion, 2005), 41; and "Chesire Mammoth Cheese," Wikipedia, www.wikipedia.org.

154   *When Mammoth Cheese shall be no more:* Moses Guest, *Poems on Several Occasions* (Cincinnati: Looker & Reynolds, 1824), 34.

155   *During his eight years in office, Jefferson purchased:* Gabler, *The Wines and Travels of Thomas Jefferson,* 200; and Curtis, *The True Thomas Jefferson,* 318.

155   *In the spring of 1808, Jefferson:* Scofield, "The Fatigues of His Table: The Politics of Presidential Dining During the Jefferson Administration," *Journal of the Early Republic,* 457; and Brodie, *Thomas Jefferson: An Intimate History,* 364.

155   *The private navy of Massachusetts, given permission:* Samuel Eliot Morison, *The Maritime History of Massachusetts* (Boston: Houghton Mifflin, 1921), 30.

156   *As maritime historian Samuel Morison observed:* Ibid., 30–31.

156   *Soon after the popular introduction of the spice:* Dave DeWitt and Nancy Gerlach, *The Spicy Food Lover's Bible* (New York: Stewart, Tabori & Chang, 2005), 101–3.

156   *There were two principle factors:* Ibid., 100.

156–57   *The origins of the American pepper trade began:* Ibid., 101.

158   *One pepper shipment aboard Crowninshield's flagship:* David L. Ferguson, *Cleopatra's Barge: The Crowninshield Story* (Boston: Little, Brown, 1976), 26; and DeWitt and Gerlach, *The Spicy Food Lover's Bible*, 101.

158   *The import duties at Salem at one time had paid:* DeWitt and Gerlach, *The Spicy Food Lover's Bible*, 101.

158   *A major problem was cheating:* Ibid., 102.

158   *By the end of 1807:* James Duncan Phillips, *Salem in the Seventeenth Century* (Boston and New York: Houghton Mifflin Company, 1933), 467–68.

159   *Is it possible that Jefferson did not realize the financial impact:* Brodie, *Thomas Jefferson: An Intimate History*, 418; and Phillips, *Salem in the Seventeenth Century*, 496.

159   *The Federalists in Congress led the revolt:* Brodie, *Thomas Jefferson: An Intimate History*, 418; and Phillips, *Salem in the Seventeenth Century*, 476–78.

160   *Salem's pepper trade with Sumatra revived:* DeWitt and Gerlach, *The Spicy Food Lover's Bible*, 103.

160   *One of the results of the Salem black pepper trade:* Ibid., 103.

160   *The popularity of black pepper in America probably began:* Jane Carson, *Colonial Virginia Cookery* (Williamsburg, VA: Colonial Williamsburg Foundation, 1985), xv.

161   *To Make Pepper-Cakes:* Glasse, *The Art of Cookery, Made Plain and Easy*, 274.

163   *He was ordering seeds for his new garden:* Edwin Morris Betts and James Adam Bear Jr., eds., *The Family Letters of Thomas Jefferson* (Charlottesville: University Press of Virginia, 1966), 315; and Barbara McEwan, *Thomas Jefferson: Farmer* (Jefferson, NC: McFarland, 1991), xii.

163   *Jefferson's slaves shared his eagerness to return:* McLaughlin, *Jefferson and Monticello: The Biography of a Builder*, 239–40.

163–64   *Martha Jefferson recalled in a letter the reaction:* Ibid., 239–40.

164   *Jefferson often threw parties and celebrations:* McWilliams, *A Revolution in Eating: How the Quest for Food Shaped America*, 118.

164   *The actual slave celebration probably included:* Ed Crews, "Juba and Djembe: Music Helps Interpret Slavery," *Colonial Williamsburg, Winter 2002–03*, www.history.org/foundation/journal/winter02-03/music.cfm.

165   *Other dishes they made included stewed collard greens:* Jessica B. Harris, *The Welcome Table: African-American Heritage Cooking* (New York: Simon and Schuster, 1995), 13.

165   *Jefferson supplied his slaves:* "Slaves," Thomas Jefferson Encyclopedia, www.wiki.monticello.org.

165   *Vegetables were extremely important to the:* Peter J. Hatch, "African-American Gardens at Monticello," *Twinleaf Journal* (January 2001), www.twinleaf.org, 1–4.

165   *Peter Hatch, the director of gardens and grounds:* Ibid., 1–4.

166   *Beginning in 1809, the first year:* Peter J. Hatch, "Thomas Jefferson's Favorite Vegetables," *Twinleaf Journal* (January 2000), www.twinleaf.org.

167 *Mary Randolph's "To Scollop Tomatoes":* Randolph, *The Virginia Housewife; or, Methodical Cook,* 101.

167 *An archaeological study of the dry well:* McWilliams, *A Revolution in Eating: Hoe the Quest for Food Shaped America,* 118–19.

168 *Jefferson formed his culinary preferences:* Thomas Jefferson Encyclopedia, www.wiki.monticello .org.

168 *On his return to America, many of his recipes:* Fowler, *Dining at Monticello,* 16–17, 51, 53; and Daniel Webster, *The Works of Daniel Webster* (Boston: Little, Brown, 1853), 371.

168 *Thomas Jefferson and his family:* Thomas Jefferson Encyclopedia, www.wiki.monticello.org.

168 *Peter Hemings moved on to other duties:* Gordon-Reed, *The Hemings of Monticello,* 570.

169 *Several guests recorded accounts of breakfast:* Smith, *The First Forty Years of Washington Society: Portrayed by the Family Letters of Mrs. Samuel Harrison Smith,* 69; and Webster, *The Works of Daniel Webster,* 371.

169 *Near the end of his life, in 1824:* Bee Wilson, "Gulp Fiction," *New Statesman* (1999), 48; and "Coffee," Thomas Jefferson Encyclopedia, www.wiki.monticello.org.

169 *The beans were roasted:* "Coffee," Thomas Jefferson Encyclopedia, www.wiki.monticello.org.

170 *The coffee urn:* "Coffee Urn," Thomas Jefferson Encycloedia, www.wiki.monticello.org.

170 *Desserts served at Monticello included trifle:* Fowler, *Dining at Monticello,* 152–86; and Beth L. Cheuk, "Jefferson and Ice Cream," in Damon Lee Fowler, ed., *Dining at Monticello* (Charlottesville: Thomas Jefferson Foundation, 2005), 172.

171 *Financial difficulties forced Jefferson to shift from:* Gabler, *The Wines and Travels of Thomas Jefferson,* 212; and Hailman, *Thomas Jefferson on Wine,* 321.

171 *Family would be there: Martha Randolph; her husband:* Alan Pell Crawford, *Twilight at Monticello: The Final Years of Thomas Jefferson* (New York: Random House, 2008), 64.

171 *The burden of maintaining Monticello's gracious level:* Katherine G. Revell, "The Order and Economy of the House," (1995), wiki.monticello.org.

172 *He wrote to George Washington in 1794:* Hailman, *Thomas Jefferson on Wine,* 240; and McEwan, *Thomas Jefferson: Farmer,* xi.

172 *After Jefferson's retirement:* "A Day in the Life," Thomas Jefferson Encyclopedia, www.wiki. monticello.org; and Cheuk, "Jefferson and Ice Cream," in Damon Lee Fowler, ed., *Dining at Monticello,* 34.

173 *because previous attempts had not been very productive:* McEwan, *Thomas Jefferson: Farmer,* 16.

173 *He wrote to Washington about his method of rotation:* Ibid., 25, 26.

173 *He wrote in a letter to his daughter Martha:* Ibid., 33; and "The Vegetable Garden," Thomas Jefferson Encyclopedia, www.wiki.monticello.org.

174 *He noted as early as 1781 in his:* McEwan, *Thomas Jefferson: Farmer,* 46; and Brodie, *Thomas Jefferson: An Intimate History,* 280.

174 *He experimented with more than a dozen different varieties:* McEwan, *Thomas Jefferson: Farmer,* 58, 59, 61, 52.

174 *Ice was plentiful in Monticello:* McEwan, *Thomas Jefferson: Farmer,* 120; and "Ice House," Thomas Jefferson Encyclopedia, www.wiki.monticello.org.

175 *He kept on working to improve the design and in 1794:* McEwan, *Thomas Jefferson: Farmer,* 86–89, 93; and Brodie, *Thomas Jefferson: An Intimate History,* 230.

175 *His thousand-foot-long kitchen-garden terrace:* Peter J. Hatch, "Thomas Jefferson's Favorite

Vegetables," in Damon Lee Fowler, ed., *Dining at Monticello* (Charlottesville: Thomas Jefferson Foundation, 2005), 55, 63.

175–76   *Many writers have attempted to determine:* Hatch, "Thomas Jefferson's Favorite Vegetables," *Twinleaf Journal;* Staib, *The City Tavern Cookbook,* 207; McEwan, *Thomas Jefferson: Farmer,* 155; and Hatch, "Thomas Jefferson's Favorite Vegetables," in Damon Lee Fowler, ed., *Dining at Monticello,* 62.

176   *Although Jefferson loved vegetables:* Peter J. Hatch, *The Fruits and Fruit Trees of Monticello* (Charlottesville: University Press of Virginia, 1998), 81; and "Peaches" Thomas Jefferson Encyclopedia, www.wiki.monticello.org.

176   *Two Favorite Monticello Peach Recipes:* Randolph, *The Virginia Housewife; or, Methodical Cook,* 156.

177   *In 1796, Jefferson had his best farm harvest:* McEwan, *Thomas Jefferson: Farmer,* 31.

178   *He wrote as early as 1776:* Hailman, *Thomas Jefferson on Wine,* 329.

178   *Jefferson also made cider from the Taliaferro variety:* Ibid., 330–31; and Hatch, *The Fruits and Fruit Trees of Monticello,* 65.

179–80   *How Dr. Chase Made Cider in 1876:* Alvin Wood Chase, *Dr. Chase's Recipes* (Ann Arbor, MI: R.A. Beal, 1876), 65–66.

180   *All people in all classes, from planter to slave:* Hatch, *The Fruits and Fruit Trees of Monticello,* 64.

180   *commented on the changing habits of apple consumption:* Ibid., 64; and Hailman, *Thomas Jefferson on Wine,* 329.

180   *there was a dramatic disappearance of cider as a favored drink:* David Williams, "The Mysterious Demise of Hard Cider," George Mason University, http://mason.gmu.edu/~drwillia/cider.html.

181   *beer was always as popular:* "Beer," Thomas Jefferson Encyclopedia, www.wiki.monticello.org.

181   *Jefferson heard than an English brewer:* Ann Lucas, "The Philosophy of Making Beer," (April 1995), wiki.monticello.org.

182   *The process began with malting the germinating:* Ibid., Lucas.

182   *He insisted on better corks than his daughter:* Ibid., Lucas; and Hailman, *Thomas Jefferson on Wine,* 331.

182   *Beer historian Stanley Baron commented on:* Stanley Baron, *Brewed in America: A History of Beer and Ale in the United States* (Boston: Little, Brown, 1962), 148.

183   *He had two vineyards at Monticello:* Thomas Pinney, *A History of Wine in America* (Berkeley: University of California Press, 1989), 129; and "Vineyard," Thomas Jefferson Encyclopedia, www.wiki.monticello.org.

183   *Probably dreaming of his second retirement:* McEwan, *Thomas Jefferson: Farmer,* 13, 1.

184   *All of these farmer friends suffered similar:* Ibid., 16–17, 23.

185   *By 1819, Jefferson had stopped growing:* Ibid., 58, 62–63, 162.

185   *Jefferson much preferred gardening to farming:* Peter Ling, "Thomas Jefferson and the Environment," *History Today* (2004), 48.

185   *In 1810, more olive stones arrived from a friend:* McEwan, *Thomas Jefferson: Farmer,* 70–71.

186   *He received seeds and attempted to grow it in 1808:* Ibid., 71–72; and Ling, "Thomas Jefferson and the Environment," *History Today,* 50.

186   *Some historians have taken Jefferson to task for planting:* McEwan, *Thomas Jefferson: Farmer,* 187; and Ling, "Thomas Jefferson and the Environment," *History Today,* 52.

187   *Jefferson liked his lamb:* "Jefferson Library," Thomas Jefferson Encyclopedia, www.wiki.monticello.org.

187 *Monticello's kitchen:* "Kitchen," Mount Vernon Explorer, www.mountvernon.org.

187 *When he heard about stew holes:* Priscilla J. Brewer, *From Fireplace to Cookstove: Technology and the Domestic Ideal in America* (Syracuse, NY: Syracuse University Press, 2000), 45; Staib, *The City Tavern Cookbook*, 125; and Justin Sarafin, "Like Clockwork: French Influence in Monticello's Kitchen" in Fowler, *Dining at Monticello*, 26.

188 *When he was president:* "Edith Fossett," Thomas Jefferson Encyclopedia, www.wiki.monticello .org.

188 *He bases the claim on Jefferson's concern with soil:* Claude R. Wickard, "Thomas Jefferson: Founder of Modern American Agriculture," *Agriculture History* (1945), 179–80.

189 *But he wasn't the founder of profitable agriculture:* Hailman, *Thomas Jefferson on Wine*, 371; and Joseph J. Ellis, *American Sphinx: The Character of Thomas Jefferson* (New York: Vintage Books, 1998), 165.

189 *Damon Lee Fowler, editor of:* Fowler, *Dining at Monticello*, 1, 9.

189 *It is significant that Jefferson's very last letter:* Hailman, *Thomas Jefferson on Wine*, 370.

191 *The rum ration was a daily tradition aboard:* Curtis, *The True Thomas Jefferson*, 260–61; Coulombe, *Rum: The Epic Story of the Drink That Conquered the World*, 126; and Barty-King and Massel, *Rum Yesterday and Today*, 42–43.

193 *Related to eggnog but considered a ladies' drink:* D. Syer Cuming, "Syllabub and Syllabub Vessels," *Journal of the British Archaeological Association* (1891), 212–13; and Mary Donovan, *The Thirteen Colonies Cookbook,* (Santa Barbara, CA: Praerger Publishers, 1975), 17.

194 *Fish House Punch:* "'Shocking' History of Fish House Punch," Great Party Recipes, www .greatpartyrecipes.com/history-of-fish-house-punch.html.

195 *"Sangaree" is a variation on sangria:* Donovan, *The Thirteen Colonies Cookbook*, 175.

195 *So named because it supposedly warmed up the imbiber:* Mrs. N.K.M. Lee, *The Cook's Own Book: Being a Complete Culinary Encyclopedia…With Numerous Original Receipts and a Complete System of Confectionary* (Boston: Munroe and Francis, 1832), 76; and Donovan, *The Thirteen Colonies Cookbook*, 96.

197 *Food etymologists believe that the word:* Donovan, *The Thirteen Colonies Cookbook*, 196.

198 *Food historian James E. McWilliams wrote:* McWilliams, *A Revolution in Eating: How the Quest for Food Shaped America*, 231.

198–99 *Codfish Cakes Appetizer:* E. Neill and James B. Herndon, *What Shall I Eat? The Housewife's Manual* (New York: Home Life Publishing, 1892), 33.

299 *published in Boston in 1842, who wrote:* Lee, *The Cook's Own Book: Being a Complete Culinary Encyclopedia…With Numerous Original Receipts and a Complete System of Confectionary*, 52; and Louise Tate King and Jean Stewart Wexler, *The Martha's Vineyard Cookbook* (New York: Harper & Row, 1971), 4–5.

200 *The prototype recipe for all Thanksgiving turkeys:* Simmons, *The First American Cookbook: A Facsimile of "American Cookery," 1796*, 18; Staib, *The City Tavern Cookbook*, 160; Smith, *The Oxford Encyclopedia of Food and Drink in America*, 538.

202 *Boston baked beans use pork and a sauce:* Ken Abala, *Beans: A History* (Oxford, UK: Berg Publishers, 2007), 164; Mrs. A.L. Webster, *The Improved Housewife* (Boston: Phillips, Sampson, 1855), 147; and Donovan, *The Thirteen Colonies Cookbook*, 30.

203–4 *Boston Brown Bread:* Donovan, *The Thirteen Colonies Cookbook*, 52.

205 *John Adams' wife, Abigail, wrote in 1798:* Ibid., 35; Hatch, *The Fruits and Fruit Trees of Monticello*, 170.

206   *Much of the food from the middle colonies:* Donovan, *The Thirteen Colonies Cookbook*, 97.

206   *Lewis Carroll in his 1897 book:* Lewis Carroll, *Alice in Wonderland* (Boston: Barta Press, 1897), 50; and Hines, Marshall, and Weaver, *The Larder Invaded: Reflections on Three Centuries of Philadelphia Food and Drink*, 21.

207–8   *Crab Imperial:* Google Books, various sources.

209–10   *Roasted Leg of Lamb with Potatoes:* Simmons, *The First American Cookbook: A Facsimile of "American Cookery," 1796*, 18; and Staib, *The City Tavern Cookbook*, 154.

211–12   *Applejack Apple Pie from Dried Apples:* Donovan, *The Thirteen Colonies Cookbook*, 113.

212   *According to Monticello.org:* "Pumpkins," wiki.monticello.org; Peter J. Hatch, "McMahon's Texas Bird Pepper: A Pretty Little Plant," *Twinleaf Journal* (January 1996), www.twin-leaf.org; and Marie Kimball, *Thomas Jefferson's Cook Book* (Greenville, MS: Lillie Ross Productions, 2004), 37.

214   *Both Washington and Jefferson had smokehouses:* "Country Ham," Wikipedia, www.wikipedia.org; Aidells, *Bruce Aidells's Complete Book of Pork*, 184–88; and Fowler, *Dining at Monticello*, 127.

215   *African-American cooking expert Jessica Harris wrote:* Harris, *The Welcome Table: African-American Heritage Cooking*, 110.

217   *President's House, Étienne Lemaire, for his recipe:* Fowler, *Dining at Monticello*, 136; and Hatch, "Thomas Jefferson's Favorite Vegetables," in Damon Lee Fowler, ed., *Dining at Monticello*, 61.

218   *A cobbler is a deep-dish fruit pie:* Webster, *The Improved Housewife*, 216; Smith, *The Oxford Encyclopedia of Food and Drink in America*, 273; and Google Books, various sources.

220   *The original version was published in 1990:* Kristie Lynn and Robert W. Pelton, *The Early American Cookbook* (Deerfield Beach, FL: Liberty Publishing, 1990), 30.

221   *Both of these recipes survive in Jefferson's own hand:* Fowler, *Dining at Monticello*, 114, 149; and Randolph, *The Virginia Housewife; or, Methodical Cook*, 98.

223   *After he returned from Europe:* Randolph, *The Virginia Housewife; or, Methodical Cook*, 84.

225   *The first macaroons originated in Italy:* "Macaroons," Wikipedia, www.wikipedia.org; and Fowler, *Dining at Monticello*, 155, 159, 174.

228   *Pecan orchards were first planted near:* Danny Fox, "Pecans: A Growing Tradition," www.foodeditorials.com; and Harris, *The Welcome Table: African-American Heritage Cooking*, 41–42.

229   *Peanuts originated in South America and migrated to:* Harris, *The Welcome Table: African-American Heritage Cooking*, 24.

229   *Because African Americans did the cooking on Southern:* Andrew F. Smith, *Peanuts: The Illustrious History of a Goober Pea* (Urbana: University of Illinois Press, 2002), 12, 14, 60.

229   *In 1897, Booker T. Washington, founder of:* "George Washington Carver," Wikipedia, www.wikipedia.org; Smith, *Peanuts: The Illustrious History of a Goober Pea*, 58–59; and George Washington Carver, *How to Grow the Peanut: And 105 Ways of Preparing It for Human Consumption* (Tuskegee, AL: Tuskegee Normal and Industrial Institute Experiment Station, 1921).

231   *African slaves who were brought to America considered:* Smith, *The Oxford Companion to American Food and Drink*, 239; and Harris, *The Welcome Table: African-American Heritage Cooking*, 161–62, 183–89.

233   *Okra is a variety of edible hibiscus native:* Philip Miller, *The Gardeners Dictionary*, vol. 2 (London: Printed for author, 1754); John Low, *The New and Complete American Encyclopedia*, vol. 4 (New York: Self-published, 1808), 368; "Okra, or 'Gumbo', from Africa," *Plant Answers*, http://aggie-horticulture.tamu.edu/plantanswers/publications/vegetabletravelers/okra.html; and Harris, *The Welcome Table: African-American Heritage Cooking*, 113.

235   *The first Louisiana pralines were pink or white:* Harris, *The Welcome Table: African-American Heritage Cooking*, 218; and Susan Tucker and S. Frederick Starr, *New Orleans Cuisine: Fourteen Signature Dishes and Their Histories* (Oxford: University Press of Mississippi, 2009), 190.

Index

About Dave DeWitt

I wrote a column called "People are Punny" for my high school newspaper before moving on to the University of Virginia and graduate school at the University of Richmond, specializing in literature and writing. It was all multimedia after that, and I wrote for newspapers and magazines while writing, producing, voicing, and acting in radio and TV commercials and my own TV show. Then I became a magazine editor with the launch of my project *Chile Pepper* magazine (still being published twenty-three years later but not by me!) and simultaneously a trade/consumer show producer by launching the National Fiery Foods & Barbecue Show, now in its twenty-thrid year. All of this led to forty-one books published since 1979. First I specialized in chile peppers, fiery foods, and international spicy cooking. Lately, I've focused on food history. *Da Vinci's Kitchen: A Secret History of Italian Food* has been published in twelve countries. *Founding Foodies* has been the most fascinating—and challenging—food history project I've worked on so far.